פרקי אבות

TRACTATE AVOTH

ETHICS OF THE FATHERS

(Being the Ninth Tractate of the Fourth Order Nezikin)

TEXT • INTRODUCTION • TRANSLATION • NOTES

BY

PHILIP BLACKMAN, F. C. S.

MS. of this Tractate revised by

RABBI ISAAC WALLER, B.A.

INCLUDING THE FOLLOWING ADDITIONAL MATERIAL:

SUPPLEMENT ON TARYAG MITZVOTH

(THE 613 COMMANDMENTS)

BY PHILIP BLACKMAN, F.C.S.

"THE IMPORTANCE OF THE MISHNAH THROUGHOUT THE AGES"

BY RABBI K. KAHANA KAGAN, M.A., M. LITT.

BIOGRAPHIES

BY REV. J. HALPERN, M.A.

Judaica Press, LTD.

Gateshead • 1985

ISBN: 0–910818–15–0

MANUFACTURED IN THE UNITED STATES OF AMERICA

PREFACE.

The MISHNAH—key to the correct interpretation of and second in importance to the TORAH—is for a variety of reasons a closed book to the great majority of Jews. There are numbers of Translations in various languages but none of them hitherto is very helpful to a simple, proper, and popular understanding of the Mishnah. An attempt is here made to give such intelligent aid with the hope that the reader possessing even only a minimum knowledge of Hebrew will find himself sufficiently interested to follow it up either privately or through the medium of the "Study Circle", which may lead even to some insight into the Gemara.

The Hebrew text has been carefully collated and important and interesting variations are shown. The "pointing" or vocalisation has been carried out with the utmost care. The original textual orthographic Hebrew terms have been retained. After serious deliberation the conclusion was arrived at that it is inadvisable and undesirable to alter the orthography of the Mishnaic Text on vowelisation—such a course is suitable rather for a single detached Tractate but not for the Mishnayoth as a whole. Nevertheless, where occcasionally textual construction seemingly rendered it necessary, such variant forms are presented in the Notes. For similar reasons, wherever terms in Scriptural quotations given in the Mishnah depart orthographically from the Massoretic Text, they have been left intact but the discrepancies have been indicated in the Notes.

The Translation has been made as closely literal to the Text as possible, at the expense perhaps of some elegance of style and niceties of diction which cannot be completely attained in the more important close and accurate renderings; and to avoid confusion the necessary interpolations to make the sense clear (with very few exceptions, indicated in square brackets) have been relegated to the Notes.

The Notes have been compiled with the aid of the well-known Hebrew Commentaries *Rashi, Bertinoro, Tosefoth Yom-Tov, Tiferet Yisrael* and *Hilchetha Gevartha*, and also valuable matter from other commentaries has been made use of. There are more than fifty recognised authoritative Hebrew commentaries on the whole Mishnah and parts of it, with much overlapping and many points of agreement as well as of variance, and it is quite obvious that it would be absolutely impossible to construct even an adequate digest of and to extract convincing conclusions from such an enormous mass of material within the moderate compass of this volume; hence only such matter has been used which makes the meaning of the Text lucid, and all disputative subjects— involved, inconclusive, and hopeless or mutually destructive arguments and irreconcilable views and opinions, which are only suitable for the expert, have been assiduously avoided.

The GENERAL INTRODUCTION, after very serious consideration, has been condensed into a very small compass—in fact, a mere summary or synopsis of the most essential facts, outlining the history, scope and contents of the Mishnah and giving various subjects in skeleton form. The author came to the conclusion that to treat this subject adequately would require a volume to itself and this would have added unfairly to the bulk of the work, and further, this has already been dealt with very fully in many excellent works.

My thanks are also due to Rev. J. Halpern, M.A. for the compilation of the BIOGRAPHIES.

Many other novel features have been added, notably an essay by the distinguished Rabbi K. Kahana 'On the Importance of the Mishnah throughout the Ages' to whom I wish to extend my gratitude for having lent his pen for the purpose.

PHILIP BLACKMAN.

CONTENTS

GENERAL INTRODUCTION

THE TALMUD—תַּלְמוּד

A description of the *Mishnah*—though in itself naturally the older portion of the *Talmud*—is better dealt with by a characterization of the *Talmud* as a whole of which the *Mishnah* forms a part. So much has been written on the subject that it is unnecessary here to give anything more than a clear and succinct summary of the essential details.

The appellation *Talmud* (תַּלְמוּד) means literally '*study*', and it embodies the mental labours, opinions and teachings of the ancient Jewish scholars in expounding and developing the religious and civil laws of the Bible during a period of some eight centuries (from 300 B.C.E. to 500 C.E.).

The **Talmud** includes two distinct elements, **Halachah** (הֲלָכָה), '*law*', and **Agadah** (אֲגָדָא), '*narrative*' (containing history, stories, fables, legends, prayers, meditations, reflexions, religious discourses, exegetical remarks, allegory, ethical, moral and metaphysical teachings and maxims, theosophical and philosophical discussions, and scientific observations of anatomical, anthropological, ethnographical, physiological, medical, physical, astronomical and mathematical character).

It is to be noted however that the name *Talmud* originally referred to the גְּמָרָא (*Gemara*) alone and it was only in later times that the name came to be applied to both the מִשְׁנָה (*Mishnah*) and the גְּמָרָא combined.

The *Mishnah* and the *Gemara* bear to each other the relation of *Text* and *Commentary* respectively.

THE MISHNAH—מִשְׁנָה

Authorities differ as regards the etymology and meaning of the word מִשְׁנָה (*Mishnah*). According to the view of some it is related to the word שְׁנַיִם, '*two*', and is meant to express the idea that it ranks in importance *second to the Bible*. Others connect it with the verb שָׁנָה, '*teach*', '*teach orally*', '*repeat*', '*learn by heart*', and according to this derivation the word *Mishnah* would indicate that its teachings were transmitted orally through the generations, in contradistinction to the '*written Law*' of the תּוֹרָה, *Pentateuch*, which is designated מִקְרָא (*Mikra*), '*which is read.*'

The *Mishnah* was first brought into order and arranged in six

11

principal divisions by Hillel (President of the Sanhedrin* in the time of Herod); this system was further improved upon by R. Akiba and subsequently by R. Meir. Finally R. Jehudah Hanasi (the President of the Sanhedrin who flourished towards the end of the second century C.E.) completed the work. It bears the simple name *Mishnah*, and we owe our order and system of the *Mishnah* to R. Jehudah Hanasi. But it is uncertain whether R. Jehudah Hanasi was actually the first to commit it to writing.

The language of the *Mishnah* is *New Hebrew* (לְשׁוֹן חֲכָמִים or לִשְׁנָא דְרַבָּנָן) as developed during the period of the Second Temple and therefore, though not in essential details, differs somewhat from *Biblical Hebrew*, because the Aramaic dialects had by then supplanted Hebrew as the language of everyday common life and the ancient classical Hebrew was employed and cultivated by the חֲכָמִים ('*Sages*') for legal and liturgical purposes only. The *Mishnah* contains many new terms and phrases, and new grammatical constructions and syntactical forms to supply the demand for new objects and ideas and for legal dialectics. Use was made of Biblical words and roots to create new words, and where these were inadequate for the huge demand, recourse was naturally had to the dominating languages (Aramaic mainly, but also some Latin, Greek and Persian). As the *Mishnah* was at first transmitted orally and had thus to be committed to memory, it is therefore not surprising that such a vast volume of material is very brief and concise in style—so much so indeed that the *Mishnah Text* would be quite impossible to be correctly interpreted and understood without the aid of the גְּמָרָא ('*Gemara Commentary*').

The *Mishnah* is divided into six sections, סְדָרִים (*Sedarim*, '*Orders*'), and the whole *Talmud* is thus designated by the term שַׁ״ס, an abbreviation of שִׁשָּׁה סְדָרִים ('*Six Orders*'). These six sections are:

1. זְרָעִים *Zeraim*, '*Seeds*' (deals with the ritual laws of the cultivation of the soil, prefaced by a part treating of the Liturgy).

2. מוֹעֵד *Moed*, '*Festival*', '*Season*' (deals with the ritual laws of the Sabbath, Festivals and Fasts).

3. נָשִׁים *Nashim*, '*Women*' (deals with the ritual laws of family life, marriage and divorce).

4. נְזִיקִין *Nezikin*, '*Damages*' (deals with civil and criminal law; the Government).

5. קָדָשִׁים *Kadashim*, '*Sacred things*' (laws on the clean and the unclean) (deals with Temple services and sacrifices).

* Also *Sandhedrim* and less frequently *Synhedrium*.

12

6.   טָהֳרוֹת   *Taharoth,* '*Purity*' (deals with ritual laws of cleanness and defilement).

Each סֵדֶר, *Seder,* '*Order*', is divided into מַסְכְתוֹת, '*Treatises*', '*Tractates*', each מַסֶּכֶת of which is further subdivided into פְּרָקִים, '*Chapters*', and every פֶּרֶק, '*Chapter*', consists of *Paragraphs* (each of which is called a *Mishnah,* מִשְׁנָה, or *Halachah,* הֲלָכָה, in the *Babylonian Talmud* and *Halachah,* הֲלָכָה, in the *Palestinian Talmud*).

The authorities quoted in the *Mishnah* belong to three different periods, *viz.,* סוֹפְרִים, '*Scribes*', זוּגוֹת, '*Pairs*', and תַּנָּאִים, '*Teachers*'. The סוֹפְרִים, also called אַנְשֵׁי *כְּנֶסֶת הַגְּדוֹלָה, 'Men of the Great Synod*' (or *Assembly*) succeeded Ezra for about 200 years; the זוּגוֹת (from Jose ben Joeser till Hillel) stood in pairs at the head of the Sanhedrin, one as נְשִׂיא, *Nasi,* '*President*,' and the other as אַב בֵּית דִּין, '*Head of the Beth-Din*', '*Vice-President*,' and flourished to the time of Herod; the תַּנָּאִים began with the disciples of Hillel and Shammai (10 B.C.E. to 220 C.E.), and the titles רַבִּי, '*My Teacher*,' for ordained Teachers and רַבָּן, '*Our Teacher*,' for the President of the Sanhedrin came into use.

The term תַּנָּא, '*Teacher*' of the *Oral Law,* is first mentioned in the *Gemara,* and a '*Teacher*' or '*Expounder*' of the *Mishnah* after R. Judah Hanasi is termed אֲמוֹרָא, *Amora.* (A Palestinian *Amora* had also the title רַבִּי, but the Babylonian was called רַב or מַר).

THE GEMARA—גְּמָרָא

The term גְּמָרָא is derived from the verb גְּמַר, '*complete,*' '*supplement,*' '*settle,*' '*decide,*' '*teach.*'

There are two compilations of the *Gemara,* the תַּלְמוּד בַּבְלִי, '**Babylonian Talmud**', and the תַּלְמוּד יְרוּשַׁלְמִי, **Palestinian** (or **Jerusalem**) **Talmud,** differing from each other in language and content, but the *Mishnah Text* in both is the same with but occasional slight variations. The former was compiled in Babylon (in the Academies of Nehardea, Sura and Pumbeditha) and the latter in the Palestinian Academies (Tiberias, Sepphoris and Caesarea). The Babylonian Talmud is fuller, couched in less difficult style and is more thorough in its discussions and details, and has therefore been accepted as authoritative to such an extent that the study of the Palestinian Talmud has been almost entirely neglected except by very few eminent scholars.

*Grammatically more correct כְּנֶסֶת.

13

THE מַסֶּכְתּוֹת, TRACTATES (or TREATISES),

OF THE TALMUD

* No גְּמָרָא in the Babylonian Talmud.
§ No גְּמָרָא in the Palestinian Talmud.
§§ Not treated at all in the Palestinian Talmud.

I. סֵדֶר זְרָעִים, Order Seeds

1.   בְּרָכוֹת   **Benedictions, Prayers** (Liturgical rules).
2. *   פֵּאָה   **Corner** (corners and gleanings of fields; forgotten sheaves; olives and grapes left for poor) [*Leviticus* **19**, 9, 10; *Deuteronomy* **24**, 19, 21].
3. *   דְּמַאי   **Doubtfully Tithed** (produce bought from those suspected of not having tithed it).
4. *   כִּלְאָיִם   **Mixtures** (prohibited mixtures in animals, plants, garments) [*Leviticus* **19**, 19; *Deuteronomy* **22**, 9, 11].
5. *   שְׁבִיעִית   **Sabbatical Year** [*Exodus* **23**, 11; *Leviticus* **25**, 2 to 7, 20 to 22; *Deuteronomy* **15**, 1 to 11].
6. *   תְּרוּמוֹת   **Heave Offerings** [*Numbers* **18**, 8, 12, 24, 26; *Deuteronomy* **18**, 4].
7. *   מַעַשְׂרוֹת   **Tithes** [*Leviticus* **21**, 3 to 33; *Numbers* **18**, 21 to 26].
8. *   מַעֲשֵׂר שֵׁנִי *   **Second Tithe** [*Leviticus* **27**, 30; *Deuteronomy* **14**, 22 to 29, **26**, 12].
9. *   חַלָּה   **Dough** (portion for priests) [*Numbers* **15**, 18 to 21].
10. *   עָרְלָה   **Uncircumcised** (fruits of trees during first four years after planting) [*Leviticus* **19**, 23, 24, 25].
11. *   בִּכּוּרִים   **First Fruits** (to be brought to the Temple; hermaphrodites) [*Exodus* **23**, 19; *Deuteronomy* **26**, 1 to 11].

II. סֵדֶר מוֹעֵד, Order Festivals

1.   שַׁבָּת   **Sabbath** (labours prohibited on Sabbath).
2.   עֵרוּבִין   **Combinations** (extension of Sabbath boundaries).
3.   פְּסָחִים   **Passover** (Passover laws; Paschal lamb).
4. *   שְׁקָלִים   **Shekels** (half-shekel Temple tax) [*Exodus* **30**, 12 to 16].
5.   יוֹמָא   **The Day** (Day of Atonement laws) [*Leviticus* **16**, 3 to 34; *Numbers* **29**, 7 to 11).
6.   סוּכָּה   **Tabernacle** (Feast of Tabernacles laws) [*Leviticus* **23**, 34, 35, 36, 42].
7.   בֵּיצָה   **Egg**, or יוֹם טוֹב, **Holyday** (labours prohibited on Festivals), [*Exodus* **12**, 16; *Leviticus* **23**, 7, 3, 21, 25, 35, 36].

14

8. רֹאשׁ הַשָּׁנָה **New Year** (New Year laws) [*Leviticus* **23**, 24; *Numbers* **29**,1].

9. תַּעֲנִית **Fast** (public fasts).

10. מְגִילָה **Scroll** (reading of *Book of Esther* on Purim).

11. מוֹעֵד קָטָן **Minor Festival** (חֹל הַמּוֹעֵד, *'Intervening Days'* of Passover and Feast of Tabernacles).

12. חֲגִיגָה **Festival Offering** (private offerings on Passover, Feast of Weeks and Feast of Tabernacles) [*Exodus* **23**, 14; *Deuteronomy* **16**, 16, 17].

III.   סֵדֶר נָשִׁים, Order Women

1. יְבָמוֹת **Sisters-in-Law** (Levirate Marriage) [*Leviticus* **18**, 18; *Deuteronomy* **25**, 5 to 10].

2. כְּתוּבוֹת **Marriage Deeds** (dower, marriage settlements).

3. נְדָרִים **Vows** [*Numbers* **30**, 3 to 16].

4. נָזִיר **Nazarite** [*Numbers* **6**, 2 to 21].

5. סוֹטָה **Wife suspected of adultery** [*Numbers* **5**, 11 to 31].

6. גִּיטִּין **Divorces** [*Deuteronomy* **24**, 1 to 5].

7. קִדּוּשִׁין **Betrothals.**

IV.   סֵדֶר נְזִיקִין, Order Damages

1. בָּבָא קַמָּא **First Gate** (damages, injuries) [*Exodus* **21**, 28 to 37, **22**, 1 to 6].

2. בָּבָא מְצִיעָא **Middle Gate** (found property; trust; buying, selling; lending, hiring, renting) [*Deuteronomy* **22**, 1 to 4; *Exodus* **22**,6 to 14; *Leviticus* **25**,14; *Exodus* **22**,24, 25, 26; *Leviticus* **25**, 35, 36, 37].

3. בָּבָא בַּתְרָא **Last Gate** (real estate; commerce; hereditary succession) [*Numbers* **27**, 7 to 11].

4. סַנְהֶדְרִין **Courts** (courts; capital crime punishment).

5. מַכּוֹת **Stripes** (false witnesses; cities of refuge; crimes punishable by stripes) [*Deuteronomy* **19**,16 to 19; *Numbers* **35**, 10 to 32; *Deuteronomy* **19**, 1 to 13].

6. שְׁבוּעוֹת **Oaths** [*Leviticus* **5**, 4, 5, 21, 22; *Exodus* **22**, 6 to 10].

7. § עֵדְיוֹת **Testimonies**

8. עֲבוֹדָה זָרָה **Idolatry**

9. §§ אָבוֹת **(Ethics of the) Fathers**

10. הוֹרָיוֹת **Decisions** (erroneous decisions and their effects) [*Leviticus* **4** and **5**].

15

The *Babylonian Talmud* appends to this Order these seven Tractates of later or extra-canonical origin.

a. אָבוֹת דְּרַבִּי נָתָן   **(Ethics of the) Fathers by R. Nathan** (Extension of אָבוֹת, **Ethics of the Fathers**).

b. סוֹפְרִים   **Scribes** (writing of the Scrolls of the *Pentateuch* and the *Book of Esther;* Masoretic grammatical rules; liturgical rules).

c. אֵבֶל רַבָּתִי   **Mourning,** or שְׂמָחוֹת, **Joys** (burial; mourning).

d. כַּלָּה   **Bride** (chastity).

e. דֶּרֶךְ אֶרֶץ רַבָּא   **Conduct (Major Treatise)** (prohibited marriages; religious, ethical, social teachings).

f. דֶּרֶךְ אֶרֶץ זוּטָא   **Conduct (Minor Treatise)** (ethical and social teachings).

g. פֶּרֶק הַשָּׁלוֹם   **Chapter on Peace.**

V.   סֵדֶר קָדָשִׁים, Order of Sacred Things

1. §§   זְבָחִים   **Sacrifices** [*Leviticus* 1 to 4].
2. §§   מְנָחוֹת   **Meal-Offerings** (meal and drink offerings) [*Leviticus* 2].
3. §§   חוּלִין   **Profane Things** (slaughtering; dietary laws).
4. §§   בְּכוֹרוֹת   **Firstborn** (of man and animals) [*Exodus* 8 12, 13; 13, 2, 12; *Numbers* 18, 15, 16, 17, 18; *Deuteronomy* 15, 19, 20].
5. §§   עֲרָכִין   **Evaluations** (appraisement for redemption) [*Leviticus* 27, 2 to 27].
6. §§   תְּמוּרָה   **Exchange** (exchange of sanctified things) [*Leviticus* 27, 10 to 27].
7. §§   כְּרִיתוֹת   **Excisions** (sins punishable by excision; their expiation).
8. §§   מְעִילָה   **Trespass, Sacrilege** [*Leviticus* 5, 15, 16].
9. §§   תָּמִיד   **Daily Sacrifice** [*Exodus* 29, 38 to 42; *Numbers* 28, 2 to 8].
10. * §§   מִדּוֹת   **Measurements** (measurements and descriptions of Temple and Courts; service of priestly guards).
11. * §§   קִנִּים   **Birds' Nests** (sacrifices of fowls; offerings of the poor) [*Leviticus*, 1, 14; 57; 12, 8; 15, 14, 29; *Numbers* 6.9].

VI. סֵדֶר טָהֳרוֹת, Order Purifications

1. * §§   כֵּלִים   **Vessels** (ritual uncleanness of garments, utensils) [*Leviticus* **11**, 33, 34, 35].

2. * §§   אָהֳלוֹת   **Tents** (ritual uncleanness caused by dead body to houses and tents) [*Numbers* **19**, 14, 15, 16, 22].

3. * §§   נְגָעִים   **Leprosy** [*Leviticus* **13** and **14**].

4. * §§   פָּרָה   **Heifer** [*Numbers* **19**, 1 to 22].

5. * §§   טַהֳרוֹת   **Purifications** (lesser degrees of uncleanness lasting until sunset) [*Leviticus* **11**, 24 to 28].

6. * §§   מִקְוָאוֹת   **Reservoirs** (ritual wells and reservoirs).

7.   נִדָּה   **Menstruant** [*Leviticus* **15**, 19 to 31, **12**, 2 to 8].

8. * §§   מַכְשִׁירִין   **Preparations** (liquids that render seeds and fruits unclean) [*Leviticus* **11**, 34, 38].

9. * §§   זָבִים   **Sufferers with Gonorrhoea** [*Leviticus* **15**, 2 to 18].

10. * §§   טְבוּל יוֹם   **Immersed at day-time** (and cleanness acquired at sunset.)

11. * §§   יָדַיִם   **Hands** (uncleanness of hands, their purification).

12. * §§   עוּקְצִין   **Fruit Stalks** (and their shells regarding conveying of uncleanness).

KINDRED WORKS TO THE MISHNAH

1. תּוֹסֶפְתָּא   **Tosephta,** *'Appendix', 'Supplement'.* It belongs to the 5th or 6th century C.E. It contains many הֲלָכוֹת, *Halachahs,* maxims and decisions (and throws much light on the *Mishnahs*) which are frequently quoted in the גְּמָרָא, *Gemara.*

2. מְכִילְתָּא   **Mechilta,** *'Measure'.* It consists of a collection of legal and homiletical interpretations (on the *Book of Exodus*) which are occasionally quoted in the *Talmud.*

3. סִפְרָא   **Siphra,** *'The Book',* or תּוֹרַת כֹּהֲנִים, **'Law of Priests',** or סִפְרָא דְּבֵי רַב, **The Siphra of the School of Rab,** comprises traditional interpretations (of the *Book of Leviticus*) which are extensively quoted in the *Talmud.*

4. סִפְרֵי   **Siphre,** *'The Books',* or סִפְרֵי דְבֵי רַב, **The Books of the School of Rab,** comprises traditional interpretations (of the *Book of Numbers* and the *Book of Deuteronomy*) which are quoted in the *Talmud.*

5. בָּרַיְתָא   **Baraitha,** or מַתְנִיתָא בָּרַיְתָא, **Extraneous Mishnah,** are the fragmentary remnants of lost collections of passages similar in character to those in the *Mishnah* but not having the same authoritative value, and are extensively quoted in the גְּמָרָא, *Gemara.*

17

THE *MISHNAH* AT A GLANCE

מִשְׁנָה

זְרָעִים
בְּרָכוֹת, פֵּאָה, דְּמַאי, כִּלְאַיִם, שְׁבִיעִית, תְּרוּמוֹת, מַעֲשְׂרוֹת, מַעֲשֵׂר שֵׁנִי, חַלָּה, עָרְלָה, בִּכּוּרִים

מוֹעֵד
שַׁבָּת, עֵרוּבִין, פְּסָחִים, שְׁקָלִים, יוֹמָא, סוּכָּה, בֵּיצָה, רֹאשׁ הַשָּׁנָה, תַּעֲנִית, מְגִילָה, מוֹעֵד קָטָן, חֲגִינָה

נָשִׁים
יְבָמוֹת, כְּתוּבוֹת, נְדָרִים, נָזִיר, סוֹטָה, גִּיטִין, קִדּוּשִׁין

נְזִיקִין
בָּבָא קַמָּא, בָּבָא מְצִיעָא, בָּבָא בַּתְרָא, סַנְהֶדְרִין, מַכּוֹת, שְׁבוּעוֹת, עֵדְיוֹת, עֲבוֹדָה זָרָה, אָבוֹת, הוֹרָיוֹת

קָדָשִׁים
זְבָחִים, מְנָחוֹת, חוּלִין, בְּכוֹרוֹת, עֲרַכִין, תְּמוּרָה, כְּרִיתוֹת, מְעִילָה, תָּמִיד, מִדּוֹת, קִנִּים

טָהֲרוֹת
כֵּלִים, אָהֳלוֹת, נְגָעִים, פָּרָה, טָהֲרוֹת, מִקְוָאוֹת, נִדָּה, מַכְשִׁירִין, זָבִים, טְבוּל יוֹם, יָדַיִם, עוּקְצִין

AUTHORITIES OF THE MISHNAH

The authorities named in the *Mishnah* (and *Baraitha*) belong to three periods, *viz.*,

1. סוֹפְרִים, **Scribes,**
2. זוּגוֹת, **Pairs,** and
3. תַּנָּאִים, **Teachers** (which is further subdivided into *Six Generations*).

Notes—1. The term תַּנָּא, *Teacher,* is used in the גְּמָרָא. 2. In the מִשְׁנָה the expounders are termed generally רַבִּי, and collectively חֲכָמִים, *Sages.* 3. The authorities of the סוֹפְרִים and זוּגוֹת periods are often referred to as זְקֵנִים הָרִאשׁוֹנִים, *Former Elders.* 4. After רַבִּי יְהוּדָה הַנָּשִׂיא the *Teachers* were termed אֲמוֹרָא, a Palestinian אֲמוֹרָא being designated רַבִּי and a Babylonian אֲמוֹרָא having the title of רַב or מַר.

1. סוֹפְרִים, Scribes

(1) חגי׳ (2) זכריה׳ (3) מלאכי׳ (4) זרובבל׳ (5) מרדכי בלשן׳ (6) עזרא׳ (7) יהושע בן יהוצדק׳ (8) שריה׳ (9) רעליה׳ (10) רחום׳ (11) בענה׳ (12) נחמיה בן חכליה׳ (13) שמעון הצדיק׳ (14) אנטיגנוס איש סוכו׃

2. זוּגוֹת, Pairs

(15) יוסי בן יועזר (16) and יוסי בן יוחנן׳ (17) יהושע בן פרחיה (18) and נתאי הארבלי׳ (19) יהודה בן טבאי (20) and שמעון בן שטח׳ (21) שמעיה (22) and אבטליון׳ (23) הלל ושמאי;

and to this period also belong:

(24) יוחנן כהן גדול׳ (25) בבא בן בוטי׳ (26) בן הא הא׳ (27) חוני המעגל׃

3. תַּנָּאִים, Teachers

(*First Generation, 10—80 C.E.*)

(28) עקביא בן מהללאל׳ (29) בני בתירא׳ (30) שמעון בן הלל׳ (31) רבן גמליאל הזקן׳ (32) רבי חנינא סגן הכהנים׳ (33) אדמון׳ (34) חנן׳ (35) נחום המדי׳ (36) רבן שמעון בן גמליאל׳ (37) רבי יוחנן בן זכאי׳ (38) בן בוכרי׳ (39) דוסתאי איש כפר יתמה׳ (40) אליעזר בן דולעאי׳ (41) חניא בן חזקיה בן גוריון׳ (42) יוחנן בן ההורני׳ (43) יועזר איש הבירה׳ (44) אבא יוסי חלי קופרי׳ (45) מנחם בן סגאי׳ (46) נחום הלבלר׳ (47) נחוניה בן גודגדא׃

(*Second Generation, 80—120 C.E.*)

(48) רבן גמליאל דיבנה׳ (49) שמעון הפקולי׳ (50) שמואל הקטן׳ (51) רבי צדוק׳ (52) פפיס׳ (53) רבי דוסא בן הרקינס׳ (54) רבי אליעזר בן יעקב׳ (55) רבי אליעזר בן הרקנוס׳ (56) רבי יהושע בן חנניא׳ (57) רבי יוסי הכהן׳ (58) רבי שמעון בן נתנאל׳ (59) רבי אלעזר בן ערך׳ (60) רבי אלעזר בן עזריה׳ (61) רבי יהודה בן בתירא׳

(65) נחום בן הקנה׳ (64) רבי נחוניה בן גודגדא׳ (63) רבי יוחנן בן גודגדא׳ (62) רבי אליעזר בן צדוק׳
איש גמזו׳ (66) רבי נחוניה בן אלינתן איש כפר הבבלי׳ (67) רבי זכריה בן הקצב׳
(68) רבי זכריה בן אבקולוס׳ (69) רבי שמעון בן הסגן׳ (70) שמעון אחי עזריה׳ (71) רבי
יוחנן בן בג בג׳ (72) רבי יוסי בן גילאי׳ (73) עקילס (אונקלס הגר)׳ (74) רבי אליעזר בן
דגלאי׳ (75) רבי חנינא בן דוסא׳ (76) הורקנוס בכפר עיטם׳ (77) רבי יוסי בן חוני׳
(78) רבי יהושע בן הורקנוס׳ (79) אבא יוסי בן חנן׳ (80) רבי יוסי בן דורמסקית׳
(81) יקים איש הדר׳

(Third Generation, 120—140 C.E.)

(82) רבי טרפון׳ (83) רבי ישמעאל׳ (84) רבי עקיבא (בן יוסף)׳ (85) רבי יוחנן בן נורי׳
(86) רבי יוסי הגלילי׳ (87) רבי אלעזר המודעי׳ (88) רבי חנינא בן אנטיגנוס׳ (89) רבי
שמעון בן נס׳ (90) רבי יהודה בן בבא׳ (91) רבי חנינא בן גמליאל׳ (92) רבי מתיא בן
חרש׳ (93) רבי יוחנן בן ברוקא׳ (94) רבי שמעון שזורי׳ (95) רבי אלעי׳ (96) רבי חלפתא׳
(97) רבי חנינא בן תרדיון׳ (98) רבי אלעזר בן פרטא׳ (99) רבי ישבב׳ (100) רבי
חוצפית (מתורגמן)׳ (101) רבי אליעזר בן מתיא׳ (102) רבי יהושע בן מתיא׳ (103) רבי
אליעזר בן יהודה איש ברתותא׳ (104) רבי אליעזר חסמא׳ (105) (שמעון) בן עזאי׳
(106) (שמעון) בן זומא׳ (107) רבי חנינא בן חכינאי׳ (108) שמעון התימני׳ (109) חנן
המצרי׳ (110) מונבז׳ (111) שמעון השקמוני׳ (112) רבי חדקא׳ (113) נחמיא איש בית
דלי׳ (114) רבי יהודה בן נחמיא׳ (115) רבי יהודה בן גדיש׳ (116) אבא חנן׳ (117) חנניא
בן אחי רבי יהושע׳ (118) שמעון בן טרפון׳ (119) שמעון העמסוני׳ (120) אבטולמוס׳
(121) אלעזר בן חסמא׳ (122) אלישע בן אבריה׳ (123) אלעי׳ (124) יוחנן בן יהושע׳
(125) יוחנן בן מתתיהו׳ (126) יוסי בן קיסמא׳ (127) יהודה הכהן׳ (128) לויטס איש יבנה׳
(129) שמעון בן עקשיה׳

(Fourth Generation, 140—165 C.E.)

(130) רבי מאיר (נהוראי)׳ (131) רבי יהודה (בן אלעי)׳ (132) רבי יוסי (בן חלפתא)׳
(133) רבי שמעון בן יוחי(or יוחאי)׳ (134) רבי אלעזר בן שמוע׳ (135) רבי יוחנן הסנדלר׳
(136) רבי אלעזר (or אליעזר) בן יעקב׳ (137) רבי נחמיה׳ (138) אבא שאול׳ (139) רבי
יהושע בן קרחא׳ (140) רבי אלעזר בן צדוק׳ (141) רבן שמעון בן גמליאל׳ (142) רבי
יאשיה׳ (143) רבי יונתן׳ [(142) and (143)תנא דבי רבי ישמעאל]׳ (144) אלעזר בן יוסי
הגלילי׳ (145) חלפתא בן דוסא׳ (146) חנינא איש אונו׳ (147) יוסי בן החוטף אפרתי׳

(Fifth Generation, 165—200 C.E.)

(148) רבי ישמעאל בנו של רבי יוחנן בן ברוקא׳ (149) רבי חנניא בן עקביא (or עקיבא)׳
(150) אבא אלעזר בן דולעי׳ (151) רבי אלעזר בן סילא (or סיאבי)׳ (152) רבי אלעזר
בנו של רבי יוסי הגלילי׳ (153) רבי חנניא בן עקשיא׳ (154) רבי יהושע בן קבוסאי (or
כפוסאי)׳ (155) רבי נתן (הבבלי)׳ (156) רבי יהודה הנשיא׳ (157) סומכוס׳ (158) רבי
יוסי בן יהודה׳ (159) רבי שמעון בן יהודה׳ (160) רבי אליעזר בן יהודה׳ (161) רבי
מנחם׳ (162) רבי אלעזר בן שמעון׳ (163) רבי שמעון בן אלעזר׳ (164) רבי יוסי בן
המשולם׳ (165) רבי שמעון בן מנסיא׳ (166) רבי יהודה בן תימא׳ (167) רבי יעקב׳

(171) אבא (170) רבי יצחק׳ (169) אבא אלעזר בן גמלא׳ (168) רבי אליעזר הקפר׳
גוריון׳ (172) דוסתאי בן ינאי׳ (173) ישמעאל בן יוסי בן חלפתא׳ (174) ידוע הבבלי׳
(175) יוסי איש כפר הבבלי׳ (176) נהוראי׳ (177) פנחס בן יאיר׳ (178) שמעון בן חלפתא
(179) ינאי׳ (180) יהושע בן לוי׳

(Sixth Generation, 200—240 C.E.)

[These are mentioned only in the תוספתא and ברייתא]

(181) רבי יהודה פלימו׳ (182) איסי בן יהודה׳ (183) רבי אלעזר בן יוסי׳ (184) רבי
ישמעאל בר יוסי׳ (185) יהודה בן לקיש׳ (186) רבי חייא׳ (187) רבי אחא׳ (188) רב
אבא (אריכא) הוא רב

INDEX TO THE FOREGOING

23

The *Mishnah* is almost pure *Hebrew*, the very few exceptions being some short *Chaldee* or *Aramaic* passages (כְּתוּבוֹת 47,8,9,10,11,12, סוֹטָה 915, גִּיטִין 93, אָבוֹת 84, עֵדוּיוֹת 102, בָּבָא בַּתְרָא 93, בָּבָא מְצִיעָא 113, 26, 522,23) and a few scattered words from the same sources, and a small number of words from the *Greek* and *Latin*.* Incidentally, the גְּמָרָא contains an enormous number of words, phrases and paragraphs from all these three sources.*

The following Table shows the relationship of *Hebrew* in the system of the *Semitic* languages and of the place of **Mishnaic Hebrew** in the parent tongue.

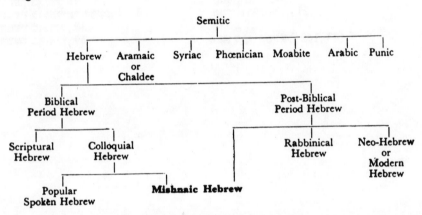

Some consider that **Mishnaic Hebrew** was mainly an artificial medium constructed by the Sages and based on the *Classical Hebrew* of the *Scriptures* influenced by the accidence and syntax of the *Chaldean* or *Aramæan* language, the common vernacular of the vast majority of the people who knew extremely little of the *Hebrew* tongue, especially in Post-Biblical times, up to the era of the rise of Rabbinic literature.

* The *Gemara* contains some 4000 words of Greek and Latin origin and many words of Arabic, Persian and Syriac origin.

"THE IMPORTANCE
OF THE MISHNAH
THROUGHOUT THE AGES"

BY

RABBI K. KAHANA KAGAN, M.A., M. LITT

Judaica Press, LTD.

Gateshead • 1985

INTRODUCTION

By Rabbi K. KAHANA, M.Litt.(Cantab.)

THE MISHNAH

It is taken for granted that the readers of this essay are cognisant of the fact that the Mishnah together with the Talmud (Babylonian and Palestinian) constitute the Oral Law, the Mishnah being the basis of the Talmud.

The relationship between the Written Law and the Oral Law

The relationship between the Written Law and the Unwritten Law has engaged the minds of many scholars. Some are of the opinion that the Oral Law is a separate branch of Jewish Law and that there are two Laws, one being the Written Law and the other the Unwritten Law. Judging from various expressions in the Talmud[1] it might indeed appear that there is some basis for this view. When, however, we study post-Talmudical literature written by such interpreters and expounders as Rav Saadiah Gaon, Maimonides and, in fact, by most of their contemporaries, we find that they persist in maintaining that there is only one Law and that the Written Law and Oral Law constitute a unity.

By the method of comparative study various writers have arrived at different conclusions. Philo submits that the Oral Law is a new development in Jewish jurisprudence. He is of the opinion that it is built upon the philosophy of the law of nature in much the same way as the Greek notion of law was built on nature. Eminent modern writers, influenced by the separation into two channels of both the Roman and the English systems of law, were to some extent led to apply this analogy to Pentateuchal and Rabbinical law. Thus Dr. Boaz Cohen, in referring to the development of the *ius honorarium* which resulted in the establishment of a dual system of law in Rome, states:—[2]

' This duality in the system of laws has its remarkable counterpart in Jewish jurisprudence. Ever since Tannaitic times we find the contrast between Biblical law and Rabbinical law.'

Philo was not correct in his assertion that the Oral Law is built upon the philosophy of the law of nature. For whilst the Greek law of nature is purely speculative, the Jewish Oral Law is eminently practical. Nor did the Greeks succeed in formulating a completely practical system of law.

Neither is there any comparison between the two channels of the Roman and English systems and the Jewish system. For there is no analogy between the new developments of prætorian law and the law of equity and the *derabbanan* of Jewish law.

Notes at the end of the Introduction

The defects of the civil law of Rome and the common law of England were due to their unadaptability. The prætors and chancellors developed new rules and these, on most occasions, were in entire contradiction to the existing laws. They would frequently give or withhold relief not based on rules at all but according to the effect produced on their own individual sense of right and wrong and by the merits of the particular case before them. The Rabbinical law of the Jewish system, however, was not a new development. Every rule had its origin in the Torah. The function of the Rabbinical law was to expound and explain the meaning of the Written Law.

The prætorian law of the Romans was based on ideas other than those of the civil law. Writers on Roman law indicate[3] that in every department of the law an antithesis arose between the law in the strict and proper sense and law made by officials and that it was miraculous that two contradictory systems could exist side by side. There is no less but an even sharper contrast in this relationship between equity and the old common law.[4]

In the Jewish system the Oral Law was promulgated with the purpose of strengthening the Pentateuchal Law. In so far as Rabbinical law is concerned it is acknowledged that everything in it which would seem to be contradictory to the Pentateuch is capable of being reconciled thereto.[5] The Tannaim of the Mishnah were the builders of the Halachah in the sense that they made it their task to discover the real meaning hidden in the sacred texts of the Pentateuch. In this they were entirely successful.

The idea that the unity of Jewish law is an absolute one is clearly stated by Maimonides in his Introduction to his Codes. Maimonides points out that Rabbinical law in no place regards itself as in any way distinct from or parallel to the Pentateuch. He says that the Oral Law contains the explanation of and the key to the exposition and development of Jewish law.[6] Thus there is not the slightest indication of any dualism in the Jewish system nor is the Rabbinical law in the nature of an amendment or intervention.

The Nature of the Oral Law

Whilst there is no dualism in Jewish law, we do in fact find two separate departments. These divisions, however, are complementary in nature. To understand this it must be noted that it is generally accepted that there is exceptionally great difficulty in presenting metaphysical notions.[7] In England, for instance, there is a distrust of abstract philosophy. It has been pointed out that the English genius has always had a strong aversion for and distrust of theory and principle.[8] This is also said of the United States.[9] It is a fact that the Americans and the English do not concern themselves with legal theoretical concepts as with matters of practical experience.[10]

Such apathy to theoretical concepts and metaphysical notions can only arise in relation to man-made principles, for these are merely speculative. The Written Law of the Torah is the origin of abstract high ideas and concepts. Being convinced that the Written Law is divine and expresses God's voice in every word and letter the Tannaim searched for the meaning of the words of the Torah and applied them to life. In the Mishnah and Talmud the

Notes at the end of the Introduction

Rabbis explain the meaning and define the terminologies of the Torah. For example—the Torah tells us of the idea of love ; the Talmud teaches us how to apply this love in actual reality. Again, on the subject of damages, only four headings were found in the Torah ; the Tannaim extracted from these headings the common ideas and principles of the law of damages which they extended to whatever type of damage could be classed under the four principal headings dealt with in the Scripture.

Again, the institution of the dietary laws, including shechitah (the ritual slaughtering of animals) and the laws concerning the prohibitions of working on the Sabbath, as well as other numerous institutions, are briefly set out in the Torah. In the Written Law only single words and sentences are uttered. These can only serve as headings for the concepts and principles underlying them. It is the Mishnah and the Talmud which gives life and meaning to the terminologies and principles of the Torah,[11] and because of this the antagonisms which generally arise in other systems of law between the letter and the spirit of the law are obviated.

To take the matter further, since the Written Law gives only headings and principles, disputes could arise as to the exact interpretation of these. But the Oral Law gives cases too. And it is because of these cases and their detailed description that the exact meaning and scope of the principles become so clear that no dispute can arise. Moreover, in the Jewish system, more than in any other system, great importance was attached to the teaching and expounding of the Law and it was felt that through oral instructions a better understanding of the Law could be arrived at than by written instruction.

Maimonides in his 'Guide of the Perplexed,' on referring to the prohibition of communicating the Oral Law in writing states :—[12]

' With reference to the Law, this rule was very opportune ; for while it remained in force it averted the evils which happened subsequently, viz., great diversity of opinion, doubts as to the meaning of written words, slips of the pen, dissensions among the people, formation of new sects, and confused notions about practical subjects. The traditional teaching was in fact, according to the words of the Law, entrusted to the Great Tribunal.' (Friedlander's Translation.)

The Historical Value

In addition to the concepts, rules and regulations and their analysis which are embodied in the Mishnah, these writings are of great value for the history of our people. It must be emphasised that, although we may be able to learn many facts concerning our past from other sources, in order to make the story of our people intelligible we must turn to the Talmud and in this connection a study of the Mishnah is particularly important. Indeed, it is impossible to understand and evaluate Jewish history without the Mishnah and the Talmud. The Mishnah really gives us a picture of that momentous epoch in our history, from before the common era to 220 c.e. and unfolds before our eyes the entire history of our people for many generations prior to the classical age of the Mishnah. The national, social, spiritual and economic life of the Jew is vividly portrayed.

Notes at the end of the Introduction

For instance, the first division which contains the laws of charity, the dues of the Priests and Levites and also the contributions which the Diaspora sent to the Temple illustrates the sociology of the people. Much light is thrown upon the agricultural life of the time. It also shows us the working of a welfare state idea, the relationship of world Jewry to one another and their love for the Temple and their homeland. In the second division, which contains the laws of the Sabbath and Festivals, the manner in which these events were observed is revealed and the temperament and mentality of the people is shown. The beauty of the scene of the pilgrimage to the Temple for the Festivals and the underlying ideas, including love and brotherhood, are clearly depicted.

In the third part of the Mishnah which relates to personal status and the fourth part which deals with damages and civil law in general, though these are essentially compiled for the promulgation of the laws, the moral characteristics of our people can clearly be observed. In the Jewish system there are rules and regulations which could not have been based on purely analytical legal concepts. These rules are based on equitable principles.[13] Commentators explain the reason for this as follows. It is written in the Torah, 'And thou shalt do that which is right and good.' In addition to the words, 'That which is right,' it is also stated, 'And good.' From this it is deduced that it is not sufficient for the people to act only in accordance with the strict letter of the law (*i.e.*, to limit themselves to keeping within their rights in the narrow legalistic sense of the words).[14] The Torah desires that the people should treat one another in a kind and equitable manner and, therefore, deal in a much wider sense than that of pure legality.

The last two parts of the Mishnah deal with holiness and purity and here, again, in addition to the laws of the two subjects the standards of holiness and purity characteristic of the Jewish people are exemplified.

The Personalities of the Mishnah

Through a study of the Mishnah in general and the thoughts and ideas of the Tannaim we can arrive at the character and personality of each Tanna. The best-known characters of the Mishnah are Rabbi Akiba, Rabbi Meir and Rabbi Judah the Prince. The reason for this is that these three Tannaim were in a very great measure responsible for the creation and development of our Mishnah. It was on Rabbi Meir's Mishnah, which was developed from Rabbi Akiba's, that Rabbi Judah the Prince built the present Mishnah. There are also other reasons for this special interest in these three Rabbis. Each of them was a unique and outstanding personality and the quality of their work as embodied in the Mishnah gives a clear picture of their uniqueness, their way of thinking, their characteristics and of their saintly and virtuous lives in general. A study of the Mishnah reveals the greatness and saintliness of the many Tannaim whose work is embodied in this magnificent compilation.

The Importance of the Mishnah in the Past

The Mishnah, together with the Talmud which is based on it, was the vital force for the civil and religious activity of the nation. Dr. Agus has

Notes at the end of the Introduction

30

pointed out[15] that during the Talmudic and Gaonic periods there were three distinct sources of authority in Jewish life. Two of them were (a) books, (b) living traditions. The Pentateuch, the Mishnah, certain collections of Baraitot, and later on the Talmud were invested with authority and served as guides to life. For living traditions, Talmudic law was an outgrowth of Jewish life. The customs and ceremonies, legal principles and standards of justice, embodied in the Talmud, originated and reached a high degree of development among the people; they were a product of the moral and religious ideas and attitudes of the Jewish people. These religious and legal principles, collectively called Halachah, were developed and expounded by the later generations and were handed down as a living tradition from father to son and from judges and leaders of one generation to those of the next generation.

The religious leaders, who lived after the compilation of the Talmud, were zealously concerned with the Mishnah no less than with the Torah. An example of this is Rav Saadiah's refutation of Karaite doctrines. We know that[16] Rav Saadiah persisted in fighting Karaism with literary weapons and throughout his chequered life he continued to combat his opponents with unrelenting vigour, so that he became the most hated opponent of the Karaite sect down to the present time. One of Rav Saadiah's main reasons for refuting the Karaites was their non-acceptance of the Mishnah.[17] Indeed, that the Karaites remained but a very small sect while the Jewish people survived as a nation is generally attributed to the fact of the Jewish people accepting the Mishnah.

Throughout the ages the Torah, the Mishnah and the Talmud which is based on it reigned supreme as the only guide to life.

The teachings of the Tannaim and the Amoraim were essential to the understanding of the Law and this was accepted by the community. Not only was Talmudic law accepted during the classical period, when central authorities still existed,[18] and in the Gaonate epoch, with its central authority, but even in the Middle Ages when there were no such forceful authorities to support the law, the Mishnah, the Talmud and its interpretations were nevertheless the dominating factors in the life of the people.

The Significance of the Mishnah in the Present and the Future

As the ultimate source of the Halachah the Mishnah is of great importance to-day. The Codes and Responsa are all based upon its contents and teachings; its maxims and principles are not outmoded. They can be applied to the problems of modern times and are in harmony with the true Jewish spirit of development.

The binding force of the Halachah applies in Israel and in the Diaspora, but there is naturally more occasion for its application in the Holy Land. With the establishment of the State of Israel, it is essential that the law should mould itself on its Jewish character. For only thus can the future of the Jewish State be assured. This can only be if the State's laws are based upon the true sources and principles; and for this the study of the Mishnah is vital.

Notes at the end of the Introduction

The Mishnah in Education

That education plays an important part in Jewish life is well known. In addition to the fact that every Jew has to know what the Torah contains and how to understand its meaning in order to be able to fulfil its commandments, it is a special duty to study the Torah for its own sake— ' And ye shall meditate therein by day and by night.' Throughout the ages this commandment was extensively obeyed, and though the study of the Torah was of paramount importance, the Mishnah came to be the very mainspring of learning.[19] From the third to the sixth centuries of the present era the great Yeshivoth of Rabbi Jochanan in Palestine and of Sura and Pumpeditha in Babylon concentrated on the Mishnah and built the Talmudic literature on the basis of the Mishnah. This study has continued in Jewry uninterrupted to our own day. Mishnah and Talmud became the basic subjects for Jewish education. Special groups, called Hevra Mishnayoth and Hevra Shass, were formed, and these could be found in every town and village. Even in our own day the study of the Mishnah and Talmud has a large following, as witnessed by the " Shiurim " which foster its study.

The commandment, ' And ye shall teach them diligently to your children,' makes it incumbent on a Jew not only to study the Torah himself, but to see that his children and grandchildren are taught and made familiar with the teachings of the Torah. Whilst this duty falls primarily upon the father, children other than a man's own are included in the commandment. Maimonides states that when the Torah speaks of educating one's children it emphasises a priority, but that in truth the command applies also to children[20] other than one's own. Generally for teaching the Unwritten Law it is permissible to take payment but not so for the Mishnah.[21] Though the *mitzvah* of teaching other people's children Mishnah is to be performed without receiving remuneration, nevertheless a father is under a duty to have his children taught Mishnah even if the circumstances are such that he must pay for it.[22]

The importance attached to spreading the knowledge of Mishnah and Gemara, combined with the duty of teaching other men's children, led eventually to the formation and development of the great Yeshivoth in Europe and, nowadays, also in Israel.

Based on the expression *veshinantom*, ' Ye Shall teach them diligently to your children,' the Mishnah was taught to many pupils and its teaching learned and relearned intensively until its words were known by heart; moreover, an intensive study of every word and every variation of phrase revealed the profound depths[23] of the subject of the Torah. Thus in the course of time the study of Mishnah led to elevation and exaltation of the Torah and of Israel.

---

1 See Tractate Shabbat, p. 31a. When Shammai was asked how many Torahs were given to the Jews his answer was two, one Written and one Unwritten. The same expression is also found in Tractate Yoma, p. 28b. See also Rosh Hashana, p. 19a, Taanith, p. 17a.

See also Gittin, p. 60b, where it says that it is prohibited to communicate the Written Law orally and that the Oral Law should not be communicated in writing. The distinction between the Pentateuchal Law and Rabbinical Law, in many aspects of practical application, may also suggest that there are two Laws.

See also Sifre Devarim, XXXIII, where Rabban Gamliel expresses the view that there are two Torahs, one Written and one Unwritten.

2 ' Peculium in Jewish and Roman Law,' (New York, 1951. Proceedings of the American Academy for Jewish Research, Vol. XX, p. 233).

See also Dr. Herzog, ' The Main Institutions of Jewish Law,' Vol. 1, p. 5, Note 1, where he says:—

'In a certain sense there are interesting resemblances as well as thought-provoking dissimilarities between equity in English law and the *derabbanan* in Jewish law.'

3 See Sohm's 'Institutes of Roman Law,' 3rd Edition, p. 81.

3,4 See Kahana Kagan, ' Three Great Systems of Jurisprudence,' (Stevens) p. 172.

5 See Harkavy, ' Fragments of Anti-Karaite Writings of Saadiah.' The Jewish Quarterly Review, Vol. 13, p. 658.
6 See also Maimonides' Introduction to his Commentary on the Mishnah.

7 See A. E. Taylor, ' Elements of Metaphysics,' p. 1.

8 Lord Macmillan, ' Two Ways of Thinking,' p. 11. See also Lord Justice Denning's foreword to Friedmann's ' Law and Social Change in Contemporary Britain ' (1951). Also Goodhart, 'English Contributions to the Philosophy of Law (Cardoza Lecture),' Oxford, 1949, p. 12, where it is stated:—

' This is true in a special sense of English legal philosophy, for English jurists have always been afraid of abstract ideas in the air. This does not mean that they disbelieve in reason, but it does mean that they hesitate to accept generalities which are unrelated to concrete facts.'

9 See Brooks Adams, ' Nature of Law,' in ' Methods and Aim of Legal Education,' Little Brown & Co., 1906 (Boston), p. 46.

10 See Brooks Adams, *ibid.*, also Lord Macmillan, ' Two Ways of Thinking,' pp. 12–13–14.

11 Rav Saadiah Gaon in discussing the Oral Law maintains that this was an explanation of the laws of the Pentateuch. His examples are the expositions regarding the work of the Tabernacle (Exodus xxv), the Chapter of Consecration (Leviticus viii-ix), the Numberings of Israel (Numbers 1), the Dedication of the Altar (Numbers vii). These institutions are explained in detail in the Pentateuch itself. Rav Saadiah says that it is obvious that a sufficient explanation must have accompanied the very many other ordinances in the Pentateuch; and as we do not possess such in writing, it was given by word of mouth. (See A. Harkavy, 'Fragments of Anti-Karaite writings of Saadiah,' The Jewish Quarterly Review, Vol. 13, p. 658.)

12 Vol. 1, Chapter LXXI. See also Kaufman's footnote to this. Also Maimonides' Introduction to his Code and to Mishnah Zeraim.

13 Hoshen Mishpat, 175, paras. 5 and 6.

14 *Ibid.* See Meirat Enaim on this.

15 Introduction to his book ' Rabbi Meir of Rothenburg,' p. XVI.

16 See Henry Malter, ' Saadia Gaon, His Life and Works ' (Philadelphia, 1921), p. 262. See also Samuel Poznanski, ' The Anti-Karaite writings of Saadiah Gaon,' The Jewish Quarterly Review, Vol. X, p. 239. He says that the work that had been neglected by the Gaonim of Babylon was taken up with great ardour by a young scholar of Egypt, namely Saadiah-al-Fajjuma, and that when a young man of 23 he stood up as an opponent of Anan, the founder of the sect of the Karaites, and a great portion of his chequered life was devoted to combating the Karaite doctrines. Poznanski also says that Saadiah's appointment as Gaon at Sura was owed, probably in part, to his activity in that direction (p. 240).

[17] See article by A. Harkavy, ' Fragments of Anti-Karaite writings of Saadia,' in the Imperial Public Library at St. Petersburg, The Jewish Quarterly Review, Vol. 13, p. 659. He quotes:—

'They reply to the questioner by returning the question. He asks, " Why do you contradict the Mishnah? " They reply, " Because we contradict the Mishnah." I mean to say, that he who simply turns the question put to him and makes an answer out of it, is the weakest (disputant); for it is just the same as if one were to reply to the question, "Why do you not accept the decision of the judge?" with the answer, " Because I do not accept the decision of the judge." '

As to the method of study of Rav Saadia and his way of refuting the Karaite doctrines, see Graetz's History, Part 3, S. P. Rabbinowitz's Edition (Warsaw, 1893), pp. 305, 307.

It was not merely from the philosophical and theoretical angle that Rav Saadia launched his campaign against the Karaites for not accepting the Mishnah.

It went further than this for, being convinced that the Mishnah is the very soul of the nation, he saw in the Karaite doctrines a danger to the very foundation of Judaism. A. S. Halkin points out that though the Samaritans were a large party in Rav Saadia's day, yet he does not mention them. The reason for this, Halkin says, is that Saadia's zealous campaign against sectarians did not extend to this group as they were not Jewish and did not present a threat to Jewish unity. (See article, ' The Relation of the Samaritans to Saadia Gaon,' in Saadia Anniversary Volume, New York, 1943, pp. 271-2.)

[18] In Palestine the authoritative power was the Patriarch and his court. Not only were the Patriarchs the greatest scholars of their generation but were also teachers and expounders of Halachah to the people. (See Tractate Sanhedrin, p. 5.)

In the Diaspora the power lay in the Exilarch (the head of the Diaspora). Those leaders also based their decisions on Halachah. (See Maimonides, Mishnah Bechoroth, Chapter 4. Also in his Code Sanhedrin, Chapter 4, Section 13.)

[19] The rule is that one ought to devote twice as much time to the study of the Oral Law than to the Written Law (see Tractate Kedushin, p. 30a, also Maimonides, Chap. 1, 11-12, Talmud Torah).

[20] Hilchoth Talmud Torah, Chapter 1.

[21] See Tractate Bechoroth, p. 29.

[22] *Ibid.*, also Shulchan Aruch, sec. 245

[23] See Tractate Kedushin, p. 30.

מַסֶּכֶת

אָבוֹת

TRACTATE

AVOTH

INTRODUCTION

אָבוֹת, **Avoth,§** or פִּרְקֵי אָבוֹת, **Pirke Avoth,§** is the ninth מַסֶּכֶת (*Tractate or Treatise*) of סֵדֶר נְזִיקִין (the *Fourth Order Nezikin*) of the מִשְׁנָה (*Mishnah*).

The term אָבוֹת 'Fathers', is the *plural* form of the Biblical substantive אָב, and פִּרְקֵי אָבוֹת means '*Chapters of the Fathers*'.

It contains a collection of ethical maxims or rules and principles of conduct and aphorisms or precise moral precepts and principles (ascribed to some sixty Sages who lived during the period 300 B.C.E. to 200 C.E.), all of which have their origin or parallel in Scripture.

The *Tractate* is aptly designated **The Ethics of the Fathers,** and also even more appropriately **Sayings of the Fathers,** in keeping with its contents that are so eminently ethical in character.

This *Tractate* is given only in the תַּלְמוּד בַּבְלִי, *Babylonian Talmud*, but without גְמָרָא.

There is a very voluminous extension—an homiletical exposition—of this *Tractate* under the title of אָבוֹת דְּרַ' נָתָן, **The Sayings of R. Nathan,** which is incorporated in the *Appendix* of the fourth volume of the *Babylonian Talmud*.

The entire *Tractate* (together with an extra, sixth, Chapter, a בְּרַיְתָא) is in comparatively simple attractive language, easily understood by the humblest Jewish reader, and is of such paramount practical interest and supremely moral importance that it has been incorporated in the *Liturgy* and is read on Sabbath afternoons during the summer months. The סְפָרְדִּים have not followed this custom though in Spain the *Tractate* used to be read on Sabbath mornings. Among the אַשְׁכְּנַזִים these Chapters used to be read—probably the oldest custom—by some on the six Sabbaths between פֶּסַח and שָׁבוּעוֹת, but the more general practice is to read these (one Chapter on each Sabbath*) on all the Sabbaths between פֶּסַח and רֹאשׁ הַשָּׁנָה.

The *Tractate* contains five Chapters, but in some *Mishnah* editions a sixth Chapter (which being a בְּרַיְתָא, *Extraneous Mishnah*, forms no part of the *Mishnah*) is added, and, as already mentioned, is also included in the סִדּוּר (*Daily Prayer Book*). The title of this sixth Chapter is פֶּרֶק קִנְיַן הַתּוֹרָה, *The Chapter of the Acquisition of the Law*, or קִנְיַן הַתּוֹרָה, *The Acquisition of the Law*, and it is also termed בְּרַיְתָא דְּרַ' מֵאִיר, *The Boraitha of R. Meir*.

37

Chapters 1–4 are largely ethical and metaphysical; Chapter 5 is predominantly *Haggadah* (folk-lore); and Chapter 6 contains homiletical exhortations and is characteristically similar to the preceding Chapters.

In the Prayer Book each Chapter is preceded, as a prologue, by a passage from סַנְהֶדְרִין 10[1], including a Scriptural quotation from *Isaiah 60, 21*, כָּל יִשְׂרָאֵל יֵשׁ לָהֶם חֵלֶק לָעוֹלָם הַבָּא, שֶׁנֶּאֱמַר וְעַמֵּךְ כֻּלָּם צַדִּיקִים לְעוֹלָם יִירְשׁוּ אָרֶץ, נֵצֶר מַטָּעַי מַעֲשֵׂה יָדַי לְהִתְפָּאָר, *All Israel have a portion in the world to come, as it is said, And thy people shall be all righteous, they shall inherit the land for ever, the branch of My planting, the work of My hands, that I be glorified*, and concludes, as an epilogue, with a sentence from מַכּוֹת 3[16] followed by a quotation from *Isaiah 42, 21* (as given at the end of Chapter 6).

Note. The text given in the Prayer Book varies considerably from the *Mishnayoth* text in the numbering of some of the *Mishnahs* and in some terms and phrases; these discrepancies are indicated in the **Notes.**

* Sometimes it is necessary to read two Chapters on one or two Sabbaths before רֹאשׁ הַשָּׁנָה for completion of the whole *Tractate*.

§ Some prefer the orthography **Aboth.**

מַסֶּכֶת

אָבוֹת

TRACTATE
AVOTH

| CHAPTER 1 | פֶּרֶק א |

Mishnah 1   מִשְׁנָה א

Moses received the Law[1] from Sinai and handed it down to Joshua, and Joshua to the elders,[2] and the elders to the prophets,[3] and the prophets handed it down to the men of the Great Assembly.[4] They said three things: Be deliberate in judgment,[5] raise up many disciples, and make a fence[6] round the Law.[7]

מֹשֶׁה קִבֵּל ¹תּוֹרָה מִסִּינַי, וּמְסָרָהּ לִיהוֹשֻׁעַ, וִיהוֹשֻׁעַ ²לִזְקֵנִים, וּזְקֵנִים ³לִנְבִיאִים, וּנְבִיאִים מְסָרוּהָ לְאַנְשֵׁי ⁴כְנֶסֶת הַגְּדוֹלָה. הֵם אָמְרוּ שְׁלֹשָׁה דְבָרִים, ⁵הֱווּ מְתוּנִים בַּדִּין, וְהַעֲמִידוּ תַלְמִידִים הַרְבֵּה, וַעֲשׂוּ ⁶סְיָג ⁷לַתּוֹרָה.

1 In this *Mishnah* the term תּוֹרָה refers to the *Oral Tradition* or *Oral Law* (תּוֹרָה שֶׁבְּעַל פֶּה); but it is also variously used for the *Pentateuch* (תּוֹרָה שֶׁבִּכְתָב, *The Written Law*) and the entire *Scriptures* (תּ'נַ'ך or תּוֹרָה נְבִיאִים וּכְתוּבִים, *Pentateuch, Prophets and Hagiographa*). **2** *Joshua* 24, 31. The 'elders' were the 'Judges' of whom Eli was the last.* לִזְקֵנִים would perhaps be preferable to לַזְּקֵנִים (but the difficulty arises with the *indefinite* form זְקֵנִים). **3** *Jeremiah* 7, 25. Samuel was the first and Haggai, Zechariah and Malachi were the last of these prophets. **4** Or *Great Synagogue*, a body of one hundred and twenty elders, judges, prophets, sages, teachers and scribes who returned from exile with Ezra whose spiritual regeneration of the people they continued by drawing up and enacting new rules and regulations and restrictions and laid the foundation of the *Liturgy*. כְּנֶסֶת is the popular reading, but כְּנֶסֶת (given in some Prayer Books) is grammatically the more correct form. **5** This was originally an injunction to judges to weigh facts and arguments and not pronounce hasty decisions. **6** סְיָג in the Prayer Book. **7** *i.e.*, to draw up cautionary regulations to act as a check against the committal of transgressions. Compare תְּמוּרָה 16¹, חֻלִּין 110a, יְבָמוֹת 20a. *See ADDENDA at the end of this Tractate.

39

Mishnah 2

Simon the Just[1] was one of the last survivors of the Great Assembly. He used to say, Upon three things is the world based:[2] upon the Law, upon [Divine] service,[3] and upon the practice of charity.[4]

ב מִשְׁנָה

יּשִׁמְעוֹן הַצַּדִּיק הָיָה מִשְׁיָרֵי כְנֶסֶת הַגְּדוֹלָה· הוּא הָיָה אוֹמֵר עַל שְׁלֹשָׁה דְבָרִים הָעוֹלָם יעוֹמֵד, עַל הַתּוֹרָה, וְעַל יהָעֲבוֹדָה, וְעַל יגְּמִילוּת חֲסָדִים·

1 Either Simon ben Onias I (High Priest 310-291 b.c.e.), or, more probably, his grandson Simon II (High Priest 219-199 b.c.e.). 2 Compare *Mishnah* 18 of this Chapter. 3 In its original sense, *Temple service.* 4 Corresponding to *religion, divine prayer,* and *humaneness.* גְּמִילוּת חֲסָדִים to all in need of help (not only to the habitual poor).

Mishnah 3

Antigonus of Socho[1] received [the tradition] from Simon the Just. He used to say, Be not like servants that minister[2] to the master on the condition of receiving a reward, but be[3] like servants that minister[2] to the master without the condition of receiving a reward;[4] and let the fear[5] of heaven be upon you.[6]
*In some texts עַל מְנָת שֶׁלֹא.

ג מִשְׁנָה

אַנְטִיגוֹנוֹס אִישׁ יסוֹכוֹ קִבֵּל מִשִׁמְעוֹן הַצַּדִּיק· הוּא הָיָה אוֹמֵר אַל תִּהְיוּ כַעֲבָדִים יהַמְשַׁמְּשִׁין אֶת־הָרַב עַל מְנָת לְקַבֵּל פְּרָס, אֶלָּא יהְיוּ כַעֲבָדִים יהַמְשַׁמְּשִׁין אֶת־הָרַב *שֶׁלֹּא עַל מְנָת לְקַבֵּל יפְּרָס; וִיהִי ימוֹרָא שָׁמַיִם יעֲלֵיכֶם·

1 Or *Soco.* In some texts, the Biblical Hebrew form שׂוֹכוֹ. There are two towns of this name, both in *Judah,* one seven miles N.E. of Gath and the other ten miles S.W. of Ziph. See *Joshua* 15, 35. (See *Mishnah* 11.) 2 הַמְשַׁמְּשִׁים in the Prayer Book. 3 הֱווּ in some texts. 4 *viz.,* God must be served from pure motives. 5 *i.e.,* awe and reverence. 6 Compare בְּרָכוֹת 5b.

Mishnah 4

Jose[1] ben[2] Joezer of Zeredah[3] and Jose ben Jochanan of Jerusalem[4] received [the tradition] from them.[5] Jose ben Joezer[6] said, Let thy house be a meeting-house for the wise[7] and[8] sit amidst the dust of their feet[9] and[8] drink in their words with thirst.

ד מִשְׁנָה

יּיוֹסֵי יבֶּן יוֹעֶזֶר אִישׁ יצְרֵידָה, וְיוֹסֵי בֶּן יוֹחָנָן אִישׁ יירוּשָׁלַיִם קִבְּלוּ ימֵהֶם· יוֹסֵי בֶּן יוֹעֶזֶר אוֹמֵר יְהִי בֵיתְךָ בֵית וַעַד ילַחֲכָמִים, יוֶהֱוֵי מִתְאַבֵּק בַּעֲפַר ירַגְלֵיהֶם, יוֶהֱוֵי שׁוֹתֶה בַצָּמָא אֶת־דִּבְרֵיהֶם·

40

1 These two belonged to the period of the זוגות, *Pairs* (see זְרֵעִים, INTRO-
DUCTION; פֵּאָה 2⁶; חֲגִיגָה 2²). **2** The term בֶּן in the translations of this *Tractate*
in the Prayer Book is given as *son*, but here *ben* is retained throughout in uniformity
with *ben* in all the other *Tractates*. **3** A city in *Manasseh* (*I Kings* **11**, 26;
II Chronicles **4**, 17; identical with צְרֵדָה, *Judges* **7**, 22; probably the same as צַרְתָן
near Beth-Shean and Succoth, *Joshua* 3, 16). **4** See חֲגִיגָה 20a. **5** In some
editions מִמַּו. This refers to the two preceding Sages (in *Mishnah* 3), or, less
probably, to the unnamed teachers in the period between Antigonus of Socho
and Jose ben Joezer. **6** In some editions אִישׁ צְרֵידָה is added here. **7** Compare
סַנְהֶדְרִין 100b, בְּרָכוֹת 7b. **8** וְהֶוֵה in some texts. **9** Disciples as a rule used to sit
on the floor or on a lower level before their teacher.

Mishnah 5

Jose ben Jochanan of Jerusalem
said,[1] Let thy house be open wide,[2]
and let the needy be members of
thy household;[3] and engage not
in much gossip with womankind.[4]
They said this of one's own wife;[5]
how much more* [does this apply]
to the wife of one's fellow! Hence[6]
the Sages have said, Whensoever[7] a
man engages in much gossip with
womankind he brings evil[8] upon
himself, (and) neglects the study of
the Law, and in the end will inherit
Gehenna.[9]

יוֹסֵי בֶּן יוֹחָנָן אִישׁ יְרוּשָׁלַיִם ¹אוֹמֵר
יְהִי בֵיתְךָ יִּפָּתוּחַ לָרְוָחָה, וְיִהְיוּ
עֲנִיִּים בְּנֵי בֵיתֶךָ, וְאַל תַּרְבֶּה שִׂיחָה
עִם ²הָאִשָּׁה. ³בְּאִשְׁתּוֹ אָמְרוּ, * קַל
וָחֹמֶר בְּאֵשֶׁת חֲבֵרוֹ. ⁴מִכָּאן אָמְרוּ
חֲכָמִים יָכָּל־זְמַן שֶׁאָדָם מַרְבֶּה
שִׂיחָה עִם הָאִשָּׁה גּוֹרֵם יָרָעָה לְעַצְמוֹ
וּבוֹטֵל מִדִּבְרֵי תוֹרָה וְסוֹפוֹ יוֹרֵשׁ
יִּגֵּיהִנָּם.

1 Literally *says*. **2** As a sign of cordiality, welcome and hospitality (compare
סֻוכָּה 92). **3** Hospitableness must be practised. **4** Protracted gossip leads to loose
talk and lewdness. **5** Trivial talk with even one's own wife may lead to trouble.§
6 מִכָּאן traditional reading. **7** In some texts כָּל־הַמַּרְבֶּה שִׂיחָה, *Whosoever engages
in much gossip.* **8** The risk of immorality. **9** Or *Gehinnom* (גֵּיהִנֹּם), a glen to the S.W.
of Jerusalem where Moloch was worshipped; it was used as a term for *purgatory, hell*
(as opposed to גַּן עֵדֶן) where the wicked suffered punishment in the hereafter.
*קַל וָחֹמֶר, an inference a minori ad majus (a conclusion from minor to major—and vice
versa). §See the ADDENDA at the end of this *Tractate*.

Mishnah 6

Joshua ben Perachiah and Nittai[1]
the Arbelite[2] received [the tradition]
from them.[3] Joshua ben Perachiah

יְהוֹשֻׁעַ בֶּן פְּרַחְיָה ¹וְנִתַּאי ²הָאַרְבֵּלִי
קִבְּלוּ מֵהֶם. ³יְהוֹשֻׁעַ בֶּן פְּרַחְיָה

said,[4] Procure thyself a teacher, (and) acquire unto thyself an associate,[5] and[6] judge all men in the scale of merit.[7]

יֹּאמֵר, עֲשֵׂה לְךָ רַב וּקְנֵה לְךָ חָבֵר, וֶהֱוֵי דָן אֶת־כָּל־הָאָדָם לְכַף זְכוּת.

1 In some texts וְנִתַּי. **2** These two were of the זוּגוֹת (see *Mishnah* 4 of this Chapter). אַרְבֵּל, *Arbel, Arbela*, north of Tiberias and near Zepphoris in Galilee. **3** *i.e.*, the preceding. **4** Literally *says.* **5** See *Appendix*, **Note 12.** **6** וֶהֱוֵה in some texts. **7** *i.e.*, charitably.

Mishnah 7

Nittai* the Arbelite said,[1] Keep thee far from an evil neighbour, (and) associate not thyself with the godless[2] and abandon not belief in retribution.[3]

נִתַּאי הָאַרְבֵּלִי אוֹמֵר הַרְחֵק מִשְּׁכֵן רָע, וְאַל תִּתְחַבֵּר לְרָשָׁע וְאַל תִּתְיָאֵשׁ מִן־הַפּוּרְעָנוּת.

1 See the preceding *Mishnah*, **Notes 1-4.** **2** Literally *wicked.* **3** *sc.*, when one sees the transgressors prosper the idea of Divine punishment must not be given up. Some render this *nevertheless yield not thyself to despair in view of retribution.* הַפֻּרְעָנוּת in some texts. *נִתַּי in some texts.

Mishnah 8

Judah ben Tabbai[1] and Simon ben Shetach[2] received [the tradition] from them.[3] Judah ben Tabbai said, Act not the part of the counsel,[4] (and) when the parties to a cause[5] stand before thee let them be in thine eyes as wicked,[6] but when they have departed from thy presence let them be regarded as innocent[7] so soon as they have acquiesced in the verdict.[8]

יְהוּדָה בֶּן טַבַּאי, יְשִׁמְעוֹן בֶּן שָׁטַח קִבְּלוּ מֵהֶם. יְהוּדָה בֶּן טַבַּאי אוֹמֵר אַל תַּעַשׂ עַצְמְךָ כְּעוֹרְכֵי הַדַּיָּנִין, וּכְשֶׁיִּהְיוּ בַּעֲלֵי דִינִים עוֹמְדִים לְפָנֶיךָ יִהְיוּ בְעֵינֶיךָ כִּרְשָׁעִים, וּכְשֶׁנִּפְטָרִים מִלְּפָנֶיךָ יִהְיוּ בְעֵינֶיךָ כְּזַכָּאִין כְּשֶׁקִּבְּלוּ עֲלֵיהֶם אֶת־הַדִּין.

1 טַבַּי in some texts. **2** They belonged to the זוּגוֹת (see *Mishnah* 4 of this Chapter). **3** *sc.*, the foregoing. **4** One must not attempt to influence the judges. הַדַּיָּנִים in some editions. **5** הַדִּין in some texts. **6** *i.e.*, as guilty. **7** כְּזַכָּאִים in some texts. **8** A defendant must not be suspected as a robber nor the sworn witness as a liar once a case is settled (see שַׁבָּת 97a, 127b).

Mishnah 9

מִשְׁנָה ט

Simon ben Shatach said, Be[1] most searching in the examination of (the) witnesses, and be[2] heedful of thy words,[3] lest therefrom they learn to utter falsehood.

שִׁמְעוֹן בֶּן שָׁטַח אוֹמֵר ¹הֱוֵי מַרְבֶּה לַחֲקוֹר אֶת־הָעֵדִים, ²הֱוֵי זָהִיר ³בִּדְבָרֶיךָ, שֶׁמָּא מִתּוֹכָם יִלְמְדוּ לְשַׁקֵּר.

1 In some texts, הֲוֵה. **2** וֶהֱוֵה in some texts. **3** Not to suggest to a witness by an injudicious remark to distort and falsify his evidence.

Mishnah 10

מִשְׁנָה י

Shemaiah and Abtalion[1] received [the tradition] from them.[2] Shemaiah said, Love labour,[3] (and) hate lordship[4] and seek not intimacy with the ruling powers.[5]

¹שְׁמַעְיָה וְאַבְטַלְיוֹן קִבְּלוּ מֵהֶם. שְׁמַעְיָה אוֹמֵר אֱהַב אֶת־הַמְּלָאכָה, וּשְׂנָא אֶת־הָרַבָּנוּת, וְאַל תִּתְוַדַּע ⁴לָרָשׁוּת.

1 They belonged to the זוּגוֹת (see *Mishnah* 4 of this Chapter). **2** *viz.*, the preceding. **3** Literally '*the* labour.' Manual labour was not to be despised—in fact it was laid down as a virtuous necessity for a man to train his son a handicraft (compare קִדּוּשִׁין 2¹). **4** Compare הוֹרָיוֹת 10a; רֹאשׁ הַשָּׁנָה 17a; יוֹמָא 6b. **5** When having business transactions or otherwise (compare עֵירוּבִין 41b; פְּסָחִים 113a).

Mishnah 11

מִשְׁנָה יא

Abtalion said, Ye sages, be cautious of your words,[1] lest ye incur the penalty of exile and be banished to a place of evil waters[2] [whereof] the disciples that come after you drink and die, and the Heavenly Name be profaned.[3]

אַבְטַלְיוֹן אוֹמֵר חֲכָמִים הִזָּהֲרוּ ¹בְּדִבְרֵיכֶם, שֶׁמָּא תָּחוּבוּ חוֹבַת גָּלוּת, וְתִגְלוּ לִמְקוֹם מַיִם הָרָעִים, וְיִשְׁתּוּ הַתַּלְמִידִים הַבָּאִים אַחֲרֵיכֶם וְיָמוּתוּ, וְנִמְצָא שֵׁם שָׁמַיִם מִתְחַלֵּל.

1 *viz.*, that their teaching should be most precise and unequivocal and leave no room for misrepresentation and heterodoxy. **2** Referring to Alexandria in Egypt where the Jews fostered Hellenistic Judaism and heresy. **3** In illustration the commentators refer to *Mishnah* 3 of this Chapter that the teaching of Antigonus of Socho was misrepresented by two of his disciples, Zadok (צָדוֹק) and Boëthus (בַּיְיתוֹס), who taught that there is no immortality of the soul and no reward in the hereafter and led to the foundation of the two anti-Pharisaic parties, the *Sadducees* (צְדוֹקִים) and *Boëthusians* (בַּיְיתוֹסִין).

43

Mishnah 12

Hillel and Shammai[1] received [the tradition] from them.[2] Hillel said, Be[3] thou of the disciples of Aaron, loving peace, and pursuing peace, loving [thy] fellow-creatures,[4] and drawing them nigh to the Law.[5]

מִשְׁנָה יב

יְהַלֵּל וְשַׁמַּאי קִבְּלוּ מֵהֶם. הַלֵּל אוֹמֵר יֶהֱוֵי מִתַּלְמִידָיו שֶׁל אַהֲרוֹן, אוֹהֵב שָׁלוֹם, וְרוֹדֵף שָׁלוֹם, אוֹהֵב אֶת־הַבְּרִיּוֹת, וּמְקָרְבָן יֹלַתּוֹרָה.

1 The last and most renowned of the זוגות (see *Mishnah* 4 of this Chapter).   **2** The foregoing (see יוֹמָא 32b, שַׁבָּת 31a).   **3** הֲוֵי in some texts.   **4** Irrespective of race or creed. Compare 1[15], 2[10], 4[1,3], 6[1].   **5** To an understanding of the existence of One God and the recognition and practice of His just moral laws.

Mishnah 13

He used to say, A[1] name made great is a name[2] destroyed;[3] (and) he that adds not to his [store of] knowledge decreases it;[4] (and) he who studies[5] not is deserving of death;[6] and one who makes wordly use of the crown [of the Law][7] shall waste away.[8]

מִשְׁנָה יג

הוּא הָיָה אוֹמֵר יֹנְגַד שְׁמָא, יֹאֲבַד יֹשְׁמֵיה; וְדְלָא מוֹסִיף יֹיָסִיף; וְדְלָא יָלֵיף יֹקְטָלָא יֹחַיָּיב; וּדְיִשְׁתַּמֵּשׁ יֹבְּתָגָא יֹחָלָף.

1 These sayings by Hillel are in *Aramaic* (compare 2[6], 5[22,23]).   **2** In some editions שְׁמָא.   **3** The ambitious seeker after fame is liable to lose his reputation.   **4** יָסַף in some texts.   **5** Some render it *teaches* (from the *Piel* form of יָלֵיף). יָלַף in some texts.   **6** Compare יוֹמָא 4[1], 38b.   **7** *i.e.*, makes use of his knowledge for self-advancement or for non-moral and non-spiritual advantage. In some editions וְדְאִשְׁתַּמֵּשׁ.   **8** *i.e.*, he will abandon his faith and his people from whom he will disappear as if wasted away.

Mishnah 14

He[1] was [also] wont to say, If I am not for myself, who will be for me?[2] And if I am for mine own self, what am I?[3] And if not now, when [then]?[4]

מִשְׁנָה יד

יֹהוּא הָיָה אוֹמֵר אִם אֵין אֲנִי לִי מִי יֹלִי? וּכְשֶׁאֲנִי לְעַצְמִי מָה יֹאֲנִי? וְאִם לֹא עַכְשָׁיו יֹאֵימָתַי?

1 *sc.*, Hillel.   **2** *i.e.*, one can only attain virtue through his own strivings.   **3** Selfishness and disregard of others are traits of inhumanity.   **4** Moral duties must be carried out as occasions arise and must not be postponed, lest the opportunities pass by.

Mishnah 15

מִשְׁנָה טו

Shammai said, Make thy [study of the] Law a fixed duty,[1] say little and do much,[2] and[3] receive every man with a cheerful countenance.[4]

שַׁמַּאי אוֹמֵר עֲשֵׂה תוֹרָתְךָ קֶבַע,[1] אֱמֹר מְעַט וַעֲשֵׂה הַרְבֵּה, וֶהֱוֵי[3,2] מְקַבֵּל אֶת־כָּל־הָאָדָם בְּסֵבֶר פָּנִים יָפוֹת·[4]

1 viz., at regular periods.   2 Compare נָזִיר 6b.   3 וֶהֱוֵי in some editions. 4 Showing friendliness in all transactions and on all occasions. Compare 1[12], 2[10], 3[12], 4[1, 3].

Mishnah 16

מִשְׁנָה טז

Rabban Gamaliel[1] said, Provide thyself a teacher,[2] (and) relieve thyself of doubt, and accustom not thyself to tithe by conjecture.[3]

רַבָּן גַּמְלִיאֵל אוֹמֵר עֲשֵׂה לְךָ רַב[1] וְהִסְתַּלֵּק מִן־הַסָּפֵק, וְאַל תַּרְבֶּה לְעַשֵּׂר יאוֹמָדוֹת·[3]

1 Gamaliel I, the grandson of Hillel (some take him to be the son of Hillel).   See שַׁבָּת 15a.   2 Compare Mishnah 6 of this Chapter.   Here the reference is to a scholar or judge who is urged to consult another authority before formulating any decisions on legal questions.   3 Compare תְּרוּמוֹת 46.   There must be no guesswork in apportioning the תְּרוּמוֹת and מַעַשְׂרוֹת (see Appendix, Note 1).

Mishnah 17

מִשְׁנָה יז

Simon his son[1] said, I was brought up all my life amongst the Sages and I have found naught so essentially good as silence,[2] (and) not the study [of the Law] is of fundamental import[3] but the practice [thereof],[4] and whosoever is profuse of words occasions sin.[5]

שִׁמְעוֹן בְּנוֹ אוֹמֵר כָּל־יָמַי גָּדַלְתִּי בֵּין הַחֲכָמִים וְלֹא מָצָאתִי לַגּוּף טוֹב אֶלָּא שְׁתִיקָה, וְלֹא הַמִּדְרָשׁ הוּא[3] הָעִיקָר אֶלָּא הַמַּעֲשֶׂה, וְכָל[4] הַמַּרְבֶּה דְבָרִים מֵבִיא חֵטְא·[5]

1 R. Simon the son of Rabban Gamaliel.   2 Compare Proverbs 17, 28; בָּבָא קַמָּא 117a; עֵירוּבִין 41; בָּבָא מְצִיעָא 41.   In some texts שְׁתִיקָה instead of אֶלָּא שְׁתִיקָה.   3 עִקָּר instead of הוּא הָעִיקָר in some texts.   4 Theory must be followed by practice; but correct practice cannot be achieved without the understanding of the underlying theoretical principles.   Compare 3[9], [17], 5[14]; כְּתוּבּוֹת 7a; יוֹמָא 6[1]. 5 Compare Proverbs 10, 19; גִּטִּין 31; חוּלִּין 63b.

Mishnah 18

Rabban Simon[1] ben Gamaliel said,
By three things is the world sustained:[2] by judgment, (and) by
truth,[3] and by peace, as it is said,[4]
*execute the judgment of truth and peace
in your gates.*

מִשְׁנָה יח

יּרַבָּן שִׁמְעוֹן בֶּן גַּמְלִיאֵל אוֹמֵר עַל
שְׁלֹשָׁה דְבָרִים הָעוֹלָם יֹעוֹמֵד, יֹעַל
הַדִּין, וְעַל הָאֱמֶת, וְעַל הַשָּׁלוֹם,
יֹשֶׁנֶּאֱמַר אֱמֶת וּמִשְׁפַּט שָׁלוֹם, שִׁפְטוּ
בְּשַׁעֲרֵיכֶם·

1 Son of Gamaliel II and father of Rabbi; some identify him with Simon in the
preceding *Mishnah*.   **2** Compare *Mishnah* 2 of this Chapter.   In some texts, קָיָם
instead of עוֹמֵד.   **3** The order in some texts is עַל הָאֱמֶת, וְעַל הַדִּין, *by truth, (and)
by judgment.*   **4** See *Zechariah* **8**, 16.

CHAPTER 2

Mishnah 1

Rabbi[1] said, Which[2] is the right
path that a man should choose[3] for
himself? Any that is an honour to
those that pursue it,[4] and brings
him honour from mankind.[5] (And)
be[6] heedful [in the performance of
a seemingly] light precept[7] as of a
grave one, for thou knowest not the
grant of the reward of each precept.
(And)[6] ponder the loss incurred
through [the non-fulfilment of] a
precept against its reward [secured
by the observance thereof], and the
gain [that ensues] from transgression[8]
against its loss [which is involved].
(And) contemplate[9] three things,[10]
and thou wilt not[11] come within the
power of transgression: know what
is above thee—an [all-] seeing eye,[12]
and an [all-] hearing ear,[12] and all
thy deeds recorded[13] in a book.[14]

פֶּרֶק ב

מִשְׁנָה א

יּרַבִּי אוֹמֵר יֹאֵיזֶהוּ דֶרֶךְ יְשָׁרָה
שֶׁיָּבוֹר לוֹ הָאָדָם? כָּל־שֶׁהִיא
תִפְאֶרֶת יְלְעוֹשֶׂיהָ וְתִפְאֶרֶת לוֹ מִן־
הָאָדָם· יֹוֶהֱוֵי זָהִיר יֹּבְמִצְוָה קַלָּה
כְּבַחֲמוּרָה, שֶׁאֵין אַתָּה יוֹדֵעַ מַתַּן
שְׂכָרָן שֶׁל מִצְוֹת· יֹוֶהֱוֵי מְחַשֵּׁב הֶפְסֵד
מִצְוָה כְּנֶגֶד שְׂכָרָה, וּשְׂכַר יֹּעֲבֵירָה
כְּנֶגֶד הֶפְסֵדָהּ· יֹוְהִסְתַּכֵּל יֹּבִשְׁלֹשָׁה
דְבָרִים יֹּוְאִי אַתָּה בָא לִידֵי יֹּעֲבֵירָה,
דַּע מַה־לְמַעְלָה מִמְּךָ, יֹּעַיִן רוֹאָה
יֹּוְאֹזֶן שׁוֹמַעַת, וְכָל־מַעֲשֶׂיךָ
יֹּבַסֵּפֶר יֹּנִכְתָּבִין·

1 Judah ha-Nasi (135-219 c.e.).   **2** וְאֵיזוֹ in some texts.   **3** Compare 3¹⁹.   **4** Some
prefer the form לְעוֹשָׂהּ and render it *to its Maker*, sc., meeting with the approbation

of the Almighty. **5** See 3¹³, 4¹⁷. **6** וְהָיָה in some texts. **7** Compare 4². **8** עֲבֵרָה in some editions. **9** הַסְתַּכֵּל in some editions. **10** Compare 3¹, חֲמִיָּה 2¹. **11** In some texts וְאֵין. **12** Referring to the Omniscient. **13** נִכְתָּבִים in some texts. **14** Compare 3²⁰; *Exodus* 32, 32; *Malachi* 3, 16; *Daniel* 7, 10; note the frequent forms בְּסֵפֶר גְּאוּלָה וִישׁוּעָה, בְּסֵפֶר הַחַיִּים, etc., in the *Liturgy*.

Mishnah 2 — מִשְׁנָה ב

Rabban Gamaliel the son of R. Judah¹ the Prince said, Excellent is the study of the Law in combination with some worldly pursuit,² for the exertion entailed by them both makes thoughts of sin to be forgotten. All study of the Law without toil must eventually prove futile³ and bring iniquity in its train.⁴ (And) let all that labour⁵ with [the interests of] the congregation labour⁶ with them from heavenly motives, for then the merit of their fathers supports them,⁷ and their righteousness endures for ever.⁸ 'And as for you', [will God then say,] 'I will bestow on you great reward,⁹ as if¹⁰ you had [yourselves] wrought [it all]'.

רַבָּן גַּמְלִיאֵל בְּנוֹ שֶׁל רַבִּי יְהוּדָה הַנָּשִׂיא אוֹמֵר, יָפֶה תַלְמוּד תּוֹרָה עִם דֶּרֶךְ אֶרֶץ, שֶׁיְּגִיעַת שְׁנֵיהֶם מַשְׁכַּחַת עָוֹן · וְכָל תּוֹרָה שֶׁאֵין עִמָּהּ מְלָאכָה, סוֹפָהּ יְבֵטֵלָה, יְוְגוֹרֶרֶת עָוֹן · וְכָל יִהְעֲמֵלִים עִם הַצִּבּוּר, יִהְיוּ יַעֲמֵלִים עִמָּהֶם לְשֵׁם שָׁמַיִם, שֶׁזְּכוּת אֲבוֹתָם יְמְסַיַּעְתָּן וְצִדְקָתָם עוֹמֶדֶת יָלָעַד · וְאַתֶּם מַעֲלֶה אֲנִי עֲלֵיכֶם שָׂכָר הַרְבֵּה יָכְּאִלּוּ עֲשִׂיתֶם ·

1 רַבִּי (see the foregoing *Mishnah*). Compare שַׁבָּת 32b, קִדּוּשִׁין 63a. **2** Some authorities render it *with good manners* (*meekness* and *morality*). **3** Study is of no avail without material support; compare 3¹⁷, אִם אֵין קֶמַח אֵין תּוֹרָה. **4** Poverty leads to sin. **5** הָעוֹסְקִים, *that occupy themselves*, in some texts. **6** In some texts, עוֹסְקִים. **7** In some texts, מְסַיַּעְתָּם. **8** Effort imbued with righteousness leads to permanent good result. **9** Some render this by the less definite and less direct: '*I will account you worthy of great recompense.*' **10** כְּאִלּוּ in some texts.

Mishnah 3 — מִשְׁנָה ג

Be on your guard¹ [in your relations] with the ruling power, for they bring no man near to them except for their own interests;² seeming to be friends such time as it is to their own advantage, they stand not with a man in the hour of his need.

יֶהֱווּ זְהִירִין בָּרְשׁוּת שֶׁאֵין מְקָרְבִין לוֹ לָאָדָם אֶלָּא יְלְצוֹרֶךְ עַצְמָן; נִרְאִין כְּאוֹהֲבִין בִּשְׁעַת הַנָאָתָן, וְאֵין עוֹמְדִין לוֹ לָאָדָם בִּשְׁעַת דָּחֳקוֹ ·

1 This admonition, applicable at all times, was particularly pertinent in the period of the Roman occupation and administration of the Holy Land. Or זְהִירִים in some texts (and similarly here מְקָרְבִים, עַצְמָם, נִרְאִים, כְּאוֹהֲבִים, הֲנָאָתָם, עוֹמְדִים). 2 In some texts לְצֹרֶךְ.

Mishnah 4   מִשְׁנָה ד

He[1] used to say, Do His will as though it were thy will[2] that He may carry out thy will as if it were His will.[3] Nullify thy will before His will[4] in order that He may annul the will of others[5] before thy will. Hillel[6] said, Separate not thyself from the community;[7] (and) trust not in thyself until the day of thy death;[8] (and) judge not thy fellow until thou art come into his position;[9] (and) utter not aught that can not be[10] [straightway] understood,[11] [on the assumption] that it will eventually be understood; and say not, 'When I have leisure I will study'—perchance thou wilt have no leisure.[12]

¹הוּא הָיָה אוֹמֵר, עֲשֵׂה רְצוֹנוֹ כִרְצוֹנֶךָ, כְּדֵי שֶׁיַּעֲשֶׂה רְצוֹנְךָ כִרְצוֹנוֹ· בַּטֵּל רְצוֹנְךָ ³מִפְּנֵי רְצוֹנוֹ, כְּדֵי שֶׁיְּבַטֵּל רָצוֹן ⁴אֲחֵרִים מִפְּנֵי רְצוֹנֶךָ ⁶הִלֵּל אוֹמֵר אַל תִּפְרֹשׁ מִן־הַצִּבּוּר; וְאַל תַּאֲמֵן בְּעַצְמְךָ עַד ⁸יוֹם מוֹתָךְ; וְאַל תָּדִין אֶת־חֲבֵרְךָ עַד שֶׁתַּגִּיעַ ⁹לִמְקוֹמוֹ; וְאַל תֹּאמַר דָּבָר ¹⁰שֶׁאִי אֶפְשָׁר ¹¹לִשְׁמוֹעַ שֶׁסּוֹפוֹ לְהִשָּׁמֵעַ; וְאַל תֹּאמַר לִכְשֶׁאֶפָּנֶה אֶשְׁנֶה, שֶׁמָּא ¹²לֹא תִפָּנֶה·

1 Rabban Gamaliel. 2 One should give ready and joyful obedience to God. 3 Compare בְּרָכוֹת 35b. 4 i.e., one should be heedful to observe strictly God's commandments. 5 viz., those who seek to act wrongly. 6 In the Prayer Book Mishnah 5 begins here. 7 viz., cutting oneself off from the community leads to the abandonment of the Jewish way of life. Compare בָּבָא מְצִיעָא 86b, תַּעֲנִית 11a. 8 i.e., the only safe way of life lies in the Law. Compare בְּרָכוֹת 29a; יוֹמָא 38b, גִּטִּין 68b; עֵירוּבִין 27a. 9 viz., one must not pass judgment without full knowledge of all the circumstances. 10 An alternative reading is שֶׁאֶפְשָׁר (sc., instead of אִי אֶפְשָׁר) which would suggest the rendering 'and disclose not [forthwith] aught that can be kept a close secret [and should not be revealed] on the plea that it must be ultimately divulged'. 11 i.e., there must be no room for doubt or uncertainty. 12 Compare 1⁴.

Mishnah 5   מִשְׁנָה ה

He[1] used to say, An empty-minded[2] man doth not fear sin, nor can an ignorant man be pious, nor can the

¹הוּא הָיָה אוֹמֵר אֵין ²בּוֹר יְרֵא חֵטְא וְלֹא עַם הָאָרֶץ חָסִיד, וְלֹא ³הַבַּיְשָׁן

diffident man[3]* learn,[4] nor can the hot-tempered man[5] teach, nor can one who occupies himself overmuch in business grow wise;[6] and in a place§ where there are no [competent] men strive to be an [authoritative] man.[7] * הַבַּיְשָׁן in some texts. § Perhaps וּבְמָקוֹם.

יִלְמֵד, וְלֹא יְהַקַּפְּדָן מְלַמֵּד, וְלֹא כָּל־הַמַּרְבֶּה בִסְחוֹרָה יְמַחְכִּים; וּבְמָקוֹם שֶׁאֵין אֲנָשִׁים, הִשְׁתַּדֵּל לִהְיוֹת יאִישׁ.

1 *Mishnah* 6 begins here in the Prayer Book. 'He' refers to Hillel. 2 Or *uneducated, uncultured, unmannered;* some prefer the meanings *brutish, ruffianly*. 3 Popular—faulty—reading, בּוּר. 4 Or *shamefaced, bashful*. He is too shy to ask for his difficulties to be made clear. 5 Or *impatient, impetuous, choleric, passionate*. The quick-tempered teacher will not be successful in his teaching for the pupils fear to ask him any questions. Compare פְּסָחִים 66b. 6 A man must find leisure to study the Law. Compare עֵירוּבִין 55a. 7 *i.e.,* one must perform necessary duties if there is none else more qualified to do so or to co-operate. Compare בְּרָכוֹת 28b.

Mishnah 6

מִשְׁנָה ו

Moreover,[1] he saw a skull[2] floating on the surface of the water [and] said to (it),[3] 'Because[4] thou hast drowned[5] [others], they have drowned thee, and, at the last, they who have drowned thee shall themselves be drowned.[6]

יאַף הוּא רָאָה יגּוּלְגֹּלֶת אַחַת שֶׁצָּפָה עַל פְּנֵי הַמָּיִם, אָמַר י(לָהּ) יעַל יּדְּאַטֵּפְתְּ אַטְּפוּךְ וְסוֹף מְטַיְּפַיִךְ יִיטוּפוּן.

1 *Mishnah* 7 commences here in the Prayer Book. 'He' refers to Hillel. 2 In some texts גֻּלְגֹּלֶת. 3 לָהּ is considered redundant by some. Hillel evidently knew the man and his character whose skull it was. 4 This last past is in *Aramaic* (compare 1[13], 5[22, 23]). 5 In some texts, דִּיאַטֵּיפְתְּ אֲטִיפוּךְ. 6 Compare בְּרָכוֹת 5b.

Mishnah 7

מִשְׁנָה ז

He[1] used to say, The more flesh, the more worms;[2] the more possessions, the more anxiety; the more wives,[3] the more witchery;[4] the more maidservants,[5] the more lasciviousness; the more menservants,[6] the more robbery;[7] the more [study of] the Law, the more life;[8] the more [academic] schooling, the more

יהוּא הָיָה אוֹמֵר מַרְבֶּה בָשָׂר מַרְבֶּה יּרִמָּה; מַרְבֶּה נְכָסִים, מַרְבֶּה דְאָגָה; מַרְבֶּה יּנָשִׁים, מַרְבֶּה יּכְשָׁפִים; מַרְבֶּה יּשְׁפָחוֹת, מַרְבֶּה זִמָּה; מַרְבֶּה יעֲבָדִים, מַרְבֶּה יּגָזֵל; מַרְבֶּה תוֹרָה, מַרְבֶּה יּחַיִּים; מַרְבֶּה יְשִׁיבָה, מַרְבֶּה

49

wisdom; the more counsel, the more
understanding;[9] the more charity,[10]
the more peace. He that has gained
a good name has acquired [a gain]
for himself; one who has acquired
for himself words of the Law has
gained for himself life in the world
to come.[11]

חָכְמָה; מַרְבֶּה עֵצָה, מַרְבֶּה יּתְבוּנָה;
מַרְבֶּה יּצְדָקָה, מַרְבֶּה שָׁלוֹם· קָנָה
שֵׁם טוֹב, קָנָה לְעַצְמוֹ; קָנָה לוֹ
דִּבְרֵי תוֹרָה, קָנָה לוֹ חַיֵּי יּהָעוֹלָם
הַבָּא‎

---

1 *Mishnah 8* begins here in the Prayer Book. 'He' refers to Hillel. **2** A denounce-
ment of gluttony. Compare שַׁבָּת 52a. **3** Compare בְּרָכוֹת 57a, נִדָּה 31b. **4** A
denunciation of polygamy. **5** They are given to lewdness. **6** They are frequently
dishonest. **7** Compare הוֹרָיוֹת 3b. Or גֵּל. **8** Compare *Proverbs* 3, 2, בְּרָכוֹת 63b,
סַנְהֶדְרִין 26b. **9** The גְּמָרָא gives תוֹרָה, *Law*. **10** Or righteousness. Compare
Isaiah 32, 17. **11** In the Hereafter. Or perhaps, 'fame lives on for ever'.

Mishnah 8

Rabban[1] Jochanan ben Zakkai received [the tradition] from Hillel and
Shammai.[2] He[3] used to say, If thou
hast learned much Law, ascribe[4] no
merit to thyself,[5] for thereunto wast
thou created.[6] Five[7] disciples had
Rabban Jochanan ben Zakkai, and
these are they: R. Eliezer ben
Hyrcanus, (and)[8] R. Joshua ben
Chananiah,[9] (and)[8] R. Jose the
Priest, (and)[8] R. Simon ben
Nathaniel and R. Elazar ben
Arach.[10] He[11] used thus to recount
their [respective] praise: R.[12] Eliezer
ben Hyrcanus is a cemented[13] cistern
that loses not a drop;[14] R.[12]
Joshua ben Chananiah—happy is
she that bare him;[15] R.[12] Jose[16]
is a pious man; R.[12] Simon ben
Nathaniel is a fearer of sin;[17] and
R.[12] Elazar ben Arach is a spring[18]
flowing with ever-sustained strength.
He[19] used to say, If all the Sages
of Israel were in one scale of a

מִשְׁנָה ח

יּרַבָּן יוֹחָנָן בֶּן זַכַּאי קִבֵּל מֵהִלֵּל
וְשַׁמַּאי· יּהוּא הָיָה אוֹמֵר אִם לָמַדְתָּ
תוֹרָה הַרְבֵּה, אַל יּתַּחֲזִיק טוֹבָה
יּלְעַצְמֶךָ, כִּי לְכָךְ יּנוֹצָרְתָּ· יּחֲמִשָּׁה
תַלְמִידִים הָיוּ לוֹ לְרַבָּן יוֹחָנָן בֶּן
זַכַּאי וְאֵלּוּ הֵן, רַבִּי אֱלִיעֶזֶר בֶּן
הוֹרְקָנוֹס, יּוְרַבִּי יְהוֹשֻׁעַ בֶּן יּחֲנַנְיָה,
יּוְרַבִּי יוֹסֵי הַכֹּהֵן, יּוְרַבִּי שִׁמְעוֹן בֶּן
נְתַנְאֵל, וְרַבִּי אֶלְעָזָר בֶּן יּעֲרָךְ·
יּהוּא הָיָה מוֹנֶה שְׁבְחָן, יּרַבִּי
אֱלִיעֶזֶר בֶּן הוֹרְקָנוֹס בּוֹר יּסִיד
שֶׁאֵינוֹ מְאַבֵּד יּטִפָּה; יּרַבִּי יְהוֹשֻׁעַ
אַשְׁרֵי יּיוֹלַדְתּוֹ; יּרַבִּי יּיוֹסֵי חָסִיד;
יּרַבִּי שִׁמְעוֹן בֶּן נְתַנְאֵל יּיְרֵא חֵטְא
יּוְרַבִּי אֶלְעָזָר בֶּן עֲרָךְ יּמַעְיָן
הַמִּתְגַּבֵּר· יּהוּא הָיָה אוֹמֵר אִם
יִהְיוּ כָּל־חַכְמֵי יִשְׂרָאֵל בְּכַף

50

balance, and Eliezer ben Hyrcanus in the other scale, he would outweigh them all. Abba Saul said in his name, If all the Sages of Israel were in one scale of a balance, and also R.[20] Eliezer ben Hyrcanus with them, and R.[20] Elazar ben Arach in the other scale, he would outweigh them all.[21]

מֹאזְנַיִם, וֶאֱלִיעֶזֶר בֶּן הוֹרְקְנוֹס בְּכַף שְׁנִיָּה מַכְרִיעַ אֶת־כֻּלָּם· אַבָּא שָׁאוּל אוֹמֵר מִשְּׁמוֹ, אִם יִהְיוּ כָל־חַכְמֵי יִשְׂרָאֵל בְּכַף מֹאזְנַיִם, ⁱⁱⁱ⁰וְרַבִּי אֱלִיעֶזֶר בֶּן הוֹרְקְנוֹס אַף עִמָּהֶם, ²⁰וְרַבִּי אֶלְעָזָר בֶּן עֲרָךְ בְּכַף שְׁנִיָּה, מַכְרִיעַ אֶת־ⁱⁱⁱ⁶כֻּלָּם·

1 *Mishnah* 9 commences here in the Prayer Book. 2 וּמִשַּׁמַּאי in some texts. 3 Compare סוּכָּה 28a. 4 הַחֲזֵק, given in some texts, is more correct grammatically. 5 *i.e.*, one must not exhibit boastful self-righteousness. 6 It is one's moral duty to acquire the righteous way of life through the study of the Law. 7 In the Prayer Book *Mishnah* 10 starts here. 8 וְ, *and*, is omitted in some texts. 9 Compare בְּרָכוֹת 27b, גִּיטִין 56a, תַּעֲנִית 7b, חוּלִין 59b. 10 He was רַבִּי נְהוֹרַאי; some say he was רַבִּי מֵאִיר (see שַׁבָּת 147a) and others say he was רַבִּי נְחֶמְיָה (עֵירוּבִין 13). 11 *Mishnah* 11 starts here in the Prayer Book. 12 רַבִּי is omitted in some texts. 13 According to some סוּד [*Kal Passive Participle*]. 14 He had a remarkably retentive memory. Compare סוּכָּה 28a, תַּעֲנִית 7a. 15 Compare יְבָמוֹת 5a. 16 Some texts have יוֹסֵי הַכֹּהֵן, Jose the Priest. See עֵדֻיּוֹת 8². Compare שַׁבָּת 19a. 17 Compare 2⁵. 18 כְּמַעְיָן, *as a spring*, in some texts. 19 In the Prayer Book *Mishnah* 12 commences here. 20 וְרַבִּי is omitted in some texts. 21 Compare הוֹרָיוֹת 14a.

Mishnah 9

He[1] said to them, Go forth and see which[2] is the right[3] way whereto a man should cleave. R. Eliezer said, A good eye;[4] R. Joshua said, A good companion; R. Jose said, A good neighbour; R. Simon said, One who foresees the [ultimate] consequences [of an action];[5] R. Elazar said, A good heart.[6] [Thereupon] he said to them, I commend the words of Elazar ben Arach rather than your words for in his words are your words included. He[7] said to them, Go forth and see which[2] is the evil road that a man should

מִשְׁנָה ט

¹אָמַר לָהֶם צְאוּ וּרְאוּ ²אֵיזוֹהִי ³דֶרֶךְ יְשָׁרָה שֶׁיִּדְבַּק בָּהּ הָאָדָם· רַבִּי אֱלִיעֶזֶר אוֹמֵר ⁴עַיִן טוֹבָה; רַבִּי יְהוֹשֻׁעַ אוֹמֵר חָבֵר טוֹב; רַבִּי יוֹסֵי אוֹמֵר שָׁכֵן טוֹב; רַבִּי שִׁמְעוֹן אוֹמֵר הָרוֹאֶה אֶת־הַנּוֹלָד; רַבִּי אֶלְעָזָר אוֹמֵר לֵב טוֹב· אָמַר לָהֶם רוֹאֶה אֲנִי אֶת־דִּבְרֵי אֶלְעָזָר בֶּן עֲרָךְ מִדִּבְרֵיכֶם, שֶׁבִּכְלַל דְּבָרָיו דִּבְרֵיכֶם· ⁷אָמַר לָהֶם צְאוּ וּרְאוּ

51

shun. R. Eliezer said, An evil eye;[8] R. Joshua said, An evil associate; R. Jose said, An evil neighbour; R. Simon said, One that borrows and does not repay—he that borrows from man is as one who borrows[9] from the Omnipresent, Blessed be He,[10] as it is said,[11] *The wicked borroweth, and payeth not again, but the righteous dealeth graciously and giveth;*[12] R. Elazar said, A wicked heart. [Whereupon] he said to them, I commend the words of Elazar ben Arach more than your words, for in his words are included your words.

יֶֽאֵיזֹוהִי דֶֽרֶךְ רָעָה שֶׁיִּתְרַחֵק מִמֶּֽנָּה הָאָדָם. רַבִּי אֱלִיעֶֽזֶר אוֹמֵר עַֽיִן רָעָה ; רַבִּי יְהוֹשֻֽׁעַ אוֹמֵר חָבֵר רָע ; רַבִּי יוֹסֵי אוֹמֵר שָׁכֵן רָע ; רַבִּי שִׁמְעוֹן אוֹמֵר הַלֹּוֶה וְאֵינוֹ מְשַׁלֵּם, אֶחָד הַלֹּוֶה מִן־הָאָדָם, יּכְּלֹוֶה מִן־ הַמָּקוֹם יּבָּרוּךְ הוּא, יּשֶׁנֶּאֱמַר לֹוֶה רָשָׁע וְלֹא יְשַׁלֵּם וְצַדִּיק חוֹנֵן יּוְנוֹתֵן ; רַבִּי אֶלְעָזָר אוֹמֵר לֵב רָע. אָמַר לָהֶם רוֹאֶה אֲנִי אֶת־דִּבְרֵי אֶלְעָזָר בֶּן־עֲרָךְ מִדִּבְרֵיכֶם, שֶׁבִּכְלַל דְּבָרָיו דִּבְרֵיכֶם.

---

1 Rabban Jochanan ben Zakkai. *Mishnah* 13 starts here in the Prayer Book. **2** In some texts, טוֹבָה *good*, in some texts. **3** *אֵיזוֹ הִיא דֶֽרֶךְ. **4** Kindly disposition, absence of envy, jealousy, greed, covetousness and ill-will. **5** And will avoid harmful action. **6** Unselfishness, absence of ill-will and hate. **7** *Mishnah* 14 commences here in the Prayer Book. **8** Jealousy, envy, covetousness, greed, ill-will. **9** Or the *definite* כְּלֹוֶה, *as 'the' one who borrows*—in agreement with the *definite* antecedent הַלֹּוֶה. **10** בָּרוּךְ הוּא is omitted in some texts. **11** Psalm 37, 21. **12** He repays acts of kindness (compare יְבָמוֹת 20a). *Or אֵיזוּ; see Volume II, Page 12.

Mishnah 10

They[1] each said three[2] things. R. Eliezer said, Let the honour of thy fellow-man[3] be as precious to thee as thine own; (and) be not easily moved to wrath;[4] (and) repent one day[5] before thy death; (and)[6] warm thyself by the fire of the Sages,[7] but[6] beware of their glowing coals, lest thou be burnt, for their bite is the bite of a fox, and their sting is the sting of a scorpion, and their hiss is the hiss of a serpent, and all their utterances are like coals of fire.[8]

מִשְׁנָה י

יהֵם אָמְרוּ שְׁלֹשָׁה יּשְׁלֹשָׁה דְבָרִים. רַבִּי אֱלִיעֶֽזֶר אוֹמֵר יְהִי כְבוֹד יּחֲבֵֽרְךָ חָבִיב עָלֶֽיךָ כְּשֶׁלָּךְ ; וְעַל תְּהִי נֽוֹחַ יּלִכְעוֹס ; וְשׁוּב יּיוֹם אֶחָד לִפְנֵי מִיתָתְךָ ; יּוֶהֱוֵי מִתְחַמֵּם כְּנֶֽגֶד אוּרָן שֶׁל יּחֲכָמִים, וֶהֱוֵי זָהִיר בְּגַחַלְתָּן שֶׁלֹּא תִכָּוֶה, שֶׁנְּשִׁיכָתָן, נְשִׁיכַת שׁוּעָל, וַעֲקִיצָתָן, עֲקִיצַת עַקְרָב, וּלְחִישָׁתָן, לְחִישַׁת שָׂרָף, וְכָל דִּבְרֵיהֶם יּכְגַחֲלֵי אֵשׁ.

52

1 Referring to the disciples of Rabban Jochanan ben Zakkai in the preceding *Mishnah*. Here begins *Mishnah* 15 in the Prayer Book. 2 The second שְׁלֹשָׁה is omitted in the גְּמָרָא and is not given in the Prayer Book. 3 Or תַּלְמִידְךָ, *thy disciple*, according to some. Any word or deed intended to injure one's good name or to uphold one to mockery and contempt is strongly condemned. Compare 1[12],[15], 4[1],[3]. 4 סַנְהֶדְרִין 7a. 5 And as no one knows which will be his last day he must always be on his guard against evil. 6 וֶהֱוֵה in the Prayer Book. 7 Compare בְּרָכוֹת 7b. One must imbibe the knowledge imparted by his teacher. 8 One must not endeavour to become too intimate with his teacher and try to impress him with his superior intelligence. The abuse and misapplication of the finest gifts will cause disadvantage instead of benefit.

Mishnah 11

מִשְׁנָה יא

R. Joshua[1] said, The evil eye,[2] (and) the evil inclination, and hatred of [one's] fellow-creatures[3] put[4] a man out of the world.[5]

רַבִּי יְהוֹשֻׁעַ אוֹמֵר יַעַן הָרַע וְיֵצֶר הָרַע יְשִׂנְאַת הַבְּרִיּוֹת מוֹצִיאִין אֶת־הָאָדָם מִן־הָעוֹלָם.

1 In the Prayer Book *Mishnah* 16 starts here. 2 See 2[10], **Note 8.** 3 Misanthropy. 4 מוֹצִיאִים in the Prayer Book. 5 Compare 2[2].

Mishnah 12

מִשְׁנָה יב

R. Jose[1] said, Let the property of thy fellow-man be as dear to thee as thine own; (and) qualify thyself[2] for the study of the Law, for [the knowledge of] it is not a heritage[3] of thine;[4] and let all thy deeds [be prompted] for the sake of Heaven.[5]

רַבִּי יוֹסֵי אוֹמֵר יְהִי מָמוֹן חֲבֵרְךָ חָבִיב עָלֶיךָ כְּשֶׁלָּךְ; יְהַתְקֵן עַצְמְךָ לִלְמוֹד תּוֹרָה שֶׁאֵינָהּ יְרוּשָׁה לָךְ; וְכָל־מַעֲשֶׂיךָ יִהְיוּ לְשֵׁם שָׁמָיִם.

1 In the Prayer Book *Mishnah* 17 starts here. 2 Or *fit thyself, prepare thyself.* 3 יְרֻשָּׁה in some texts. 4 Knowledge is an acquisition and not a bequeathal or heritance. 5 *i.e.*, one should be inspired by high moral motives (see בְּרָכוֹת 63a). A parallel expression is לִשְׁמָהּ (literally *for its name*), *for its own sake, selflessly, without ulterior selfish motives.*

Mishnah 13

מִשְׁנָה יג

R. Simon[1] said, Be[2] heedful to read the *Shema*[3] and [to recite] the *Amidah*;[4] and when thou prayest make not thy prayer a fixed mechanical task,[5] but [an appeal for] mercy

רַבִּי שִׁמְעוֹן אוֹמֵר הֱוֵי זָהִיר בִּקְרִיאַת שְׁמַע וּבַתְּפִלָּה; וּכְשֶׁאַתָּה מִתְפַּלֵּל, אַל תַּעַשׂ תְּפִלָּתְךָ קֶבַע,

53

and supplication before the Omni-present, Blessed be He,⁶ as it is said,⁷ *For Thou, O God, art gracious and full of compassion, slow to anger and abounding in lovingkindness, and repented Him of the evil,* and be not wicked in thine own estimation.⁸

אֶלָּא רַחֲמִים וְתַחֲנוּנִים לִפְנֵי הַמָּקוֹם בָּרוּךְ הוּא, ⁷שֶׁנֶּאֱמַר כִּי־אַתָּה אֵל חַנּוּן וְרַחוּם אֶרֶךְ אַפַּיִם וְרַב־חֶסֶד וְנִחָם עַל הָרָעָה, וְאַל תְּהִי רָשָׁע בִּפְנֵי ⁸עַצְמֶךָ.

1 In the Prayer Book *Mishnah* 18 begins here. **2** הֱוֵי in some texts. **3** *Deuteronomy* 6, 4-9, 11, 13-21; *Numbers* 15, 37-41. **4** The שְׁמֹנֶה עֶשְׂרֵה, *Eighteen Benedictions,* on week-days and the corresponding עֲמִידוֹת on special occasions (Sabbaths, Holydays, New Moons). See בָּבָא קַמָּא 30a. **5** Perfunctoriness in the recital of prescribed prayers is severely deprecated. Mechanical praying is particularly and inevitably the result of lack of the understanding of the Hebrew. **6** בָּרוּךְ הוּא is omitted in the Prayer Book. **7** See *Joel* 2, 13. But Scripture has כִּי חַנּוּן and not as here כִּי אַתָּה אֵל חַנּוּן, and the Prayer Book gives כִּי חַנּוּן וְרַחוּם הוּא. **8** An individual must not lose his self-respect and so abandon hope for God's forgiveness and mercy through repentance.

Mishnah 14

מִשְׁנָה יד

R. Elazar said, Be¹ assiduous in the study of the Law;² (and know³) what answer to give to the sceptic;⁴ and know before Whom thou toilest, and faithful⁵ is thy Employer, Who will requite thee the reward of thy labour.⁶

רַבִּי אֶלְעָזָר אוֹמֵר ¹הֱוֵי שָׁקוּד לִלְמוֹד ²תּוֹרָה; ³(וְדַע) מַה־ שֶׁתָּשִׁיב ⁴לָאֶפִּיקוֹרוֹס; וְדַע לִפְנֵי מִי אַתָּה עָמֵל, ⁵וְנֶאֱמָן הוּא בַּעַל מְלַאכְתְּךָ שֶׁיְשַׁלֶּם־לְךָ שְׂכַר ⁶פְּעֻלָּתֶךָ.

1 הֱוֵה in some texts. **2** One must learn with eagerness and enthusiasm for the successful acquisition of the knowledge and practice of correct morality. **3** וְדַע is omitted in the גְּמָרָא. **4** Literally *Epicurean.* Or *heretic, unbeliever.* **5** וּמִי, *and Who,* instead of וְנֶאֱמָן in some texts. Compare 2¹⁶. **6** See בְּרָכוֹת 35b. In some texts, פְּעֻלָּתְךָ. *Some vocalise this לָאֶפִּיקוֹרוֹס.

Mishnah 15

מִשְׁנָה טו

R. Tarfon¹ said, The day is short,² and the task is great,³ and the labourers are sluggish,⁴ and the recompense is ample, and the Master of the house⁵ is urgent.²

¹רַבִּי טַרְפוֹן אוֹמֵר הַיּוֹם ²קָצֵר וְהַמְּלָאכָה ³מְרוּבָּה. וְהַפּוֹעֲלִים ⁴עֲצֵלִים וְהַשָּׂכָר הַרְבֵּה וּבַעַל הַבַּיִת ⁵דּוֹחֵק.

54

1 Here commences *Mishnah* 20 in the Prayer Book. **2** Compare 1¹⁴, *And if not now, when [then]* ? **3** מְרֻבָּה in some texts. **4** Compare 3¹⁴. **5** The Creator of the universe.

Mishnah 16

He[1] also used to say, It is not thy obligation to complete the task, nevertheless thou art not at liberty to desist therefrom;[2] if thou hast studied much in the Law much reward shall be given thee,[3] for[4] faithful is thy Employer who shall requite thee the reward of thy labour; and know that the bestowal of reward[5] upon the righteous will be in the time to come.[6]

מִשְׁנָה טז

¹הוּא הָיָה אוֹמֵר לֹא עָלֶיךָ הַמְּלָאכָה לִגְמוֹר, וְלֹא אַתָּה בֶן חוֹרִין ²לִיבָּטֵל מִמֶּנָּה; אִם לָמַדְתָּ תּוֹרָה הַרְבֵּה נוֹתְנִים לְךָ שָׂכָר הַרְבֵּה, ³וְנֶאֱמָן הוּא בַּעַל מְלַאכְתְּךָ שֶׁיְּשַׁלֵּם לְךָ שְׂכַר פְּעוּלָתֶךָ; וְדַע ⁴מַתַּן שְׂכָרָן שֶׁל צַדִּיקִים ⁵לֶעָתִיד לָבֹא.

1 *viz.*, R. Tarfon. *Mishnah* 21 begins here in the Prayer Book. **2** לְהִבָּטֵל in some texts. The premonition that one may not be able to finish a good work must not be a deterrent to continue with it—one must not be disheartened and discouraged by seemingly insurmountable difficulties from attempting a worthy task. Compare בְּרָכוֹת 16a. **3** In this life and in the world to come. **4** Compare 2¹⁴. In some texts, פָּעֳלָתֶךָ. **5** שֶׁמַּתַּן שְׂכָרָם in some texts. **6** לָבוֹא in some texts.

CHAPTER 3

Mishnah 1

Akabia ben Mahalalel said,[1] Reflect upon three things and thou wilt not come within the power of transgression:[2] know whence thou art come, and whither thou art going, and before Whom thou wilt in future render[5] account and reckoning.[3] 'Whence thou art come'—from a fetid drop; 'and whither thou art going'—to a place of dust,[4] worms and maggots; 'and before Whom thou wilt in future render account[5] and reckoning'—before the Supreme King of kings,[6] the Holy One, Blessed be He.

פֶּרֶק ג

מִשְׁנָה א

¹עֲקַבְיָא בֶּן מַהֲלַלְאֵל ¹אוֹמֵר הִסְתַּכֵּל בִּשְׁלשָׁה דְבָרִים וְאֵין אַתָּה בָא לִידֵי ²עֲבֵירָה, דַּע מֵאַיִן בָּאתָ וּלְאָן אַתָּה הוֹלֵךְ וְלִפְנֵי מִי אַתָּה עָתִיד ⁵לִיתֵּן דִּין וְחֶשְׁבּוֹן· מֵאַיִן בָּאתָ מִטִּפָּה סְרוּחָה; וּלְאָן אַתָּה הוֹלֵךְ לִמְקוֹם ⁴עָפָר רִמָּה וְתוֹלֵעָה; וְלִפְנֵי מִי אַתָּה עָתִיד ⁵לִיתֵּן דִּין וְחֶשְׁבּוֹן לִפְנֵי ⁶מֶלֶךְ מַלְכֵי הַמְּלָכִים הַקָּדוֹשׁ בָּרוּךְ הוּא·

1 Compare 2[1].   2 עֲבֵרָה in some texts.   3 Compare בָּבָא בַּתְרָא 8a.   4 See
Genesis 3, 19.   5 In some texts, לְתֵן?   6 Literally *before the King of kings of kings.*

Mishnah 2

R. Chanina, the chief of the priests,[1]
said, Pray[2] for the welfare of the
ruling power, since but for the fear
thereof men would engulf one another
alive.[3] R. Chanania[4] ben Teradion
said, If two sit together[5] and inter-
change no words of the Law, they
are a meeting of the scornful,[6] as it
is said,[7] *Nor sitteth* [the godly man]
in the seat of the scoffers; but if two
sit together[8] and words of the Law
[pass] between them, the Divine
Presence abides between them, as
it is said,[9] *then they that feared the
Eternal spake one with the other; and
the Eternal hearkened and heard, and a
book of remembrance was written before
Him, for them that feared the Eternal,
and that thought upon[10] His Name.*
[But] the Scripture teaches this in
respect to *two* only; when [can it
be inferred] that if even[11] one person
sits and occupies himself with the
Law, the Holy One, blessed be He,
appoints to him a reward?[12] Because
it is said,[13] *Let him sit alone and keep
silence*[14] because He hath laid it[15]
upon him.

מִשְׁנָה ב

רַבִּי חֲנִינָא [1]סְגַן הַכֹּהֲנִים אוֹמֵר
[2]הֱוֵי מִתְפַּלֵּל בִּשְׁלוֹמָהּ שֶׁל מַלְכוּת
שֶׁאַלְמָלֵא מוֹרָאָהּ, אִישׁ אֶת־רֵעֵהוּ
חַיִּים בְּלָעוֹ· רַבִּי[4]חֲנַנְיָא בֶּן תְּרַדְיוֹן
אוֹמֵר שְׁנַיִם [5]שֶׁיּוֹשְׁבִין וְאֵין בֵּינֵיהֶן
דִּבְרֵי תוֹרָה הֲרֵי זֶה מוֹשַׁב [6]לֵצִים,
[7]שֶׁנֶּאֱמַר וּבְמוֹשַׁב לֵצִים לֹא יָשָׁב;
אֲבָל שְׁנַיִם [8]שֶׁיּוֹשְׁבִין וְיֵשׁ בֵּינֵיהֶם
דִּבְרֵי תוֹרָה שְׁכִינָה שְׁרוּיָּה בֵינֵיהֶם,
[9]שֶׁנֶּאֱמַר אָז נִדְבְּרוּ יִרְאֵי ה' אִישׁ אֶל־
רֵעֵהוּ וַיַּקְשֵׁב ה' וַיִּשְׁמַע וַיִּכָּתֵב סֵפֶר
זִכָּרוֹן לְפָנָיו לְיִרְאֵי ה' [10]וּלְחוֹשְׁבֵי
שְׁמוֹ· אֵין לִי אֶלָּא שְׁנַיִם, מִנַּיִן
[11]שֶׁאֲפִילוּ אֶחָד שֶׁיּוֹשֵׁב וְעוֹסֵק
בַּתּוֹרָה, שֶׁהַקָּדוֹשׁ בָּרוּךְ הוּא קוֹבֵעַ
לוֹ [12]שָׂכָר? [13]שֶׁנֶּאֱמַר יֵשֵׁב בָּדָד
[14]וְיִדֹּם כִּי [15]נָטַל עָלָיו·

1 Or *deputy High-Priest, vice-High-Priest, prefect of the priests, adjutant High-Priest.*
Compare יוֹמָא 7[1], סוֹטָה 7[7, 8].   2 הֲוֵה in some editions.   3 *i.e.,* chaos and anarchy
would ensue.   4 In the Prayer Book *Mishnah* 3 begins here. Compare 5[10].   5 In
some texts, שֶׁיּוֹשְׁבִים וְאֵין בֵּינֵיהֶם in some texts.   6 From which the Divine Presence
is absent (see סוֹטָה 42a).   7 *Psalm* 1, 1.   8 In some texts, שֶׁיּוֹשְׁבִים.   9 *Malachi* 3, 16.
10 Scripture has וּלְחוֹשְׁבֵי.   11 אֲפִילוּ in some texts.   12 By allowing His Divine
Presence rest upon him (compare בְּרָכוֹת 3b, רֹאשׁ הַשָּׁנָה 26b, תַּעֲנִית 20b).
13 *Lamentations* 3, 28.   14 וְיִדֹּם in the Scripture.   15 The reward.

Mishnah 3

R. Simon[1] said, If three have eaten at one table and have not spoken there words of the Law,[2] it is as if[3] they had eaten of sacrifices of the dead,[4] as it is said,[5] *For all [their] tables are full of vomit and filthiness;*[6] *the Omnipresent is not* [in their thoughts]. But if three have eaten at one table and have spoken over it matters concerning the Law, it is as though[3] they had eaten from the table of the Omnipresent, blessed be He, as it is said,[7] *and he said unto me, ' This is the table*[8] *that is before the Eternal'*.

מִשְׁנָה ג

ׁרַבִּי שִׁמְעוֹן אוֹמֵר שְׁלֹשָׁה שֶׁאָכְלוּ
עַל שֻׁלְחָן אֶחָד, וְלֹא אָמְרוּ עָלָיו
דִּבְרֵי תוֹרָה יְכְאִילוּ אָכְלוּ מִזִּבְחֵי
מֵתִים, ׁשֶׁנֶּאֱמַר כִּי כָּל־שֻׁלְחָנוֹת
מָלְאוּ קִיא יצוֹאָה בְּלִי מָקוֹם· אֲבָל
שְׁלֹשָׁה שֶׁאָכְלוּ עַל שֻׁלְחָן אֶחָד וְאָמְרוּ
עָלָיו דִּבְרֵי תוֹרָה יְכְאִילוּ אָכְלוּ
מִשֻּׁלְחָנוֹ שֶׁל מָקוֹם ׁבָּרוּךְ הוּא
ׁשֶׁנֶּאֱמַר וַיְדַבֵּר אֵלַי זֶה יהַשֻּׁלְחָן
אֲשֶׁר לִפְנֵי ה'·

1 *Mishnah* 4 begins here in the Prayer Book. 2 Reference to the recital of *Grace after meals*. Some say it means that people should refrain from discussion at a meal for fear of accident (see תַּעֲנִית 5b) but not neglect religious talk *after* the meal; yet others take it literally, *sc.*, conversation during a meal should at least not entirely be banal but should partake of a religious and moral character. 3 כְּאִלּוּ in some texts. 4 *Psalm* 106, 28. *i.e.*, idols. 5 *Isaiah* 28, 8. 6 The Scriptural orthography is צֹאָה. R. Simon was hinting at the revolting practices of the Roman ruling classes in the use of emetics or other means to empty their stomachs in order to enjoy further gluttony. 7 *Ezekiel* 41, 22. 8 Referring to the *Altar*. Prayer and seriousness at a table sanctify it as though it is an Altar. *בָּרוּךְ הוּא* is omitted in some texts.

Mishnah 4

R. Chanina[1] ben Chachinai said, He that keeps awake in the night,[2] or goes on his way alone,[3] and directs[4] his heart to vain thoughts, such a one is guilty against himself.[5]

מִשְׁנָה ד

ׁרַבִּי חֲנִינָא בֶּן חֲכִינַאי אוֹמֵר הַנֵּעוֹר
ׁבַּלַּיְלָה וְהַמְהַלֵּךְ בַּדֶּרֶךְ יְחִידִי
ׁוְהַמְפַנֶּה לִבּוֹ לְבַטָּלָה הֲרֵי זֶה
מִתְחַיֵּיב ׁבְּנַפְשׁוֹ·

1 In the Prayer Book *Mishnah* 5 begins here. 2 *Psalm* 63, 6ff.—sleepless hours should be spent in religious meditation. 3 And is not on guard against frivolous thoughts. 4 וּמְפַנֶּה in some editions. 5 *viz.*, *he imperils his own soul* or *he forfeits his own life* or *he sins against himself*.

Mishnah 5

R. Nechunia[1] ben Hakanah said, Whosoever accepts* the yoke[2,3] of the Law from him shall be removed the yoke[2,4] of the kingdom and the yoke[2] of mundane care,[5] but he that casts off from him the yoke[2] of the Law upon him shall be laid the yoke[2] of the kingdom and the yoke[2] of worldly care.

מִשְׁנָה ה

יְרַבִּי נְחוּנְיָה בֶּן הַקָנָה אוֹמֵר כָּל־
הַמְּקַבֵּל עָלָיו ²ִ·¹עוֹל תּוֹרָה,
מַעֲבִירִין מִמֶּנּוּ ²·¹עוֹל מַלְכוּת וְעוֹל
¹דֶּרֶךְ אֶרֶץ, וְכָל הַפּוֹרֵק מִמֶּנּוּ ²עוֹל
תּוֹרָה נוֹתְנִין עָלָיו ²עוֹל מַלְכוּת
וְעוֹל דֶּרֶךְ אֶרֶץ.

1 Mishnah 6 starts here in the Prayer Book.   2 [וְעוֹל] עַל in some texts.   3 Of service and guidance.   4 The burdens, oppressions and sufferings imposed by the ruling powers.   5 The troubles and anxieties to earn one's livelihood and communal obligations.   *Literally 'accepts upon himself.'

Mishnah 6

R. Chalafta[1] of Kfar-Chanania[2] said, If ten men sit together[3] and occupy themselves with the Law, the Divine Presence abides among them, as it is said,[4] God standeth in the congregation[5] of God. And whence [can it be concluded that it applies equally] even to five?[6] Because it is said,[7] And he hath founded His band[8] upon the earth. And whence [can it be inferred that it also applies] even to three? Because it is said,[9] In the midst of the judges[10] He judgeth. And whence [can it be deduced that it applies too] even of two?[11] Because it is said,[12] Then they that feared the Eternal spake one with another; and the Eternal hearkened, and heard, etc.* And whence [can it be shown that the same applies] even of one? Because it is said,[13] In every place where I cause My Name to be mentioned I will come[14] unto thee[15] and I will bless thee.

מִשְׁנָה ו

יְרַבִּי חֲלַפְתָּא אִישׁ ²כְּפַר חֲנַנְיָא
אוֹמֵר עֲשָׂרָה ³ֶשֶׁיּוֹשְׁבִין וְעוֹסְקִין
בַּתּוֹרָה שְׁכִינָה שְׁרוּיָה בֵּינֵיהֶם
⁴ֶשֶׁנֶּאֱמַר אֱלֹהִים נִצָּב ⁵בַּעֲדַת אֵל·
וּמִנַּיִן אֲפִילוּ ⁶חֲמִשָּׁה, ⁷ֶשֶׁנֶּאֱמַר
⁸וַאֲגוּדָתוֹ עַל אֶרֶץ יְסָדָהּ· וּמִנַּיִן
אֲפִילוּ שְׁלֹשָׁה, ⁹ֶשֶׁנֶּאֱמַר בְּקֶרֶב
¹⁰אֱלֹהִים יִשְׁפּוֹט· וּמִנַּיִן אֲפִילוּ
¹¹שְׁנַיִם, ¹²ֶשֶׁנֶּאֱמַר אָז נִדְבְּרוּ יִרְאֵי
ה׳ אִישׁ אֶל־רֵעֵהוּ וַיַּקְשֵׁב ה׳ וַיִּשְׁמַע
*וְגוֹ׳· וּמִנַּיִן אֲפִילוּ אֶחָד, ¹³ֶשֶׁנֶּאֱמַר
בְּכָל הַמָּקוֹם אֲשֶׁר אַזְכִּיר אֶת־שְׁמִי
¹⁴אָבֹא ¹⁵אֵלֶיךָ וּבֵרַכְתִּיךָ·

1 רַבִּי חֲלַפְתָּא בֶּן דּוֹסָא אִישׁ כְּפַר חֲנַנְיָא in some editions.   2 A place in Galilee.
3 In some texts שֶׁיּוֹשְׁבִים וְעוֹסְקִים.   4 Psalm 82, 1.   5 עֵדָה (Numbers 14, 27) refers

58

to *ten* (סַנְהֶדְרִין 16; מְגִילָה 23b). **6** See סַנְהֶדְרִין 13. **7** *Amos* **9**, 6. **8** Or *bundle* grasped by the 'five' fingers of one's hand. Scripture has וַאֲגֻדָּתוֹ. **9** *Psalm* **82**, 1. **10** According to Jewish law *three* is the minimum number of judges to form a tribunal, nevertheless one judge may adjudicate in a suit involving property. יִשְׁפֹּט is the Scriptural orthography. **11** See כְּתוּבּוֹת 22a. **12** *Malachi* **3**, 16. **13** *Exodus* **20**, 21. **14** The Scripture orthography is אָבוֹא. **15** *thee* can indicate only 'one' person. [וְנֹמֵר וְגוֹ'] is omitted in the Prayer Book.

Mishnah 7

R. Eliezer[1] of Bertotha[2] said, Render unto Him what is His, for thou and what thou hast are His, as David has said,[3] *For all things come of Thee, and of Thine own have we given to Thee.* R. Simon[4] said, If one were walking by the way and is studying,[5] and interrupts his study and says, 'How fine is this tree!' or,[6] 'How fine is this newly ploughed field!' [then] Scripture regards him as if[7] he were guilty against his own soul.[8]

מִשְׁנָה ז

רַבִּי אֱלִיעֶזֶר אִישׁ בַּרְתּוֹתָא אוֹמֵר תֶּן לוֹ מִשֶּׁלּוֹ, שָׁאַתָּה וְשֶׁלָּךְ שֶׁלּוֹ, וְכֵן בְּדָוִד הוּא אוֹמֵר כִּי מִמְּךָ הַכֹּל וּמִיָּדְךָ נָתַנּוּ לָךְ. רַבִּי שִׁמְעוֹן אוֹמֵר הַמְהַלֵּךְ בַּדֶּרֶךְ וְשׁוֹנֶה, וּמַפְסִיק מִמִּשְׁנָתוֹ, וְאוֹמֵר מַה־נָּאֶה אִילָן זֶה! וּמַה־נָּאֶה נִיר זֶה! מַעֲלֶה עָלָיו הַכָּתוּב כְּאִילוּ מִתְחַיֵּיב בְּנַפְשׁוֹ.

1 *Mishnah* 8 commences here in the Prayer Book. אֶלְעָזָר, *Elazar*, in some texts. **2** In upper Galilee (see עָרְלָה 14). Perhaps identical with בְּרוֹתָה between Damascus and Hamath (*Ezekiel* **47**, 16, *II Samuel* **8**, 8) or with the Syrian port Beyrut. **3** *I Chronicles* **29**, 14. **4** Simon ben Jochai. The Prayer Book reads R. *Jacob* (רַבִּי יַעֲקֹב), *i.e.*, the father of R. Eliezer; see 4¹¹, ¹⁶). Here commences *Mishnah* 9 in the Prayer Book. **5** Compare 3⁵; תַּעֲנִית 10b. **6** מַה־ in the Prayer Book. **7** כְּאִלּוּ in the Prayer Book. **8** The study of the Law is of the greatest importance and not to be lightly broken off to admire even the beauties of nature (compare 1¹).

Mishnah 8

R. Dostai[1] ben* Jannai said in the name[2] of R. Meir, Whosoever forgets one word of his study, him Scripture accounts as though[3] he had forfeited his life,[4] for it is said,[5] *Only take heed to thyself, and keep[6] thy soul diligently, lest thou forget the things which thine eyes have seen.* One

מִשְׁנָה ח

רַבִּי דּוֹסְתַּאי בְּרַבִּי יַנַּאי מִשּׁוּם רַבִּי מֵאִיר אוֹמֵר כָּל־הַשּׁוֹכֵחַ דָּבָר אֶחָד מִמִּשְׁנָתוֹ, מַעֲלֶה עָלָיו הַכָּתוּב כְּאִילוּ מִתְחַיֵּיב בְּנַפְשׁוֹ, שֶׁנֶּאֱמַר רַק הִשָּׁמֶר לְךָ וּשְׁמוֹר נַפְשְׁךָ מְאֹד

might suppose this to apply even if⁷ one's study were too difficult for him. To avoid such a conclusion,⁸ it is said,⁵ *And lest they depart from thy heart all the days of thy life*; thus one is not guilty against his soul unless he deliberately⁹ removes them [—those lessons—] from his heart.

פֶּן־תִּשְׁכַּח אֶת־הַדְּבָרִים אֲשֶׁר רָאוּ
עֵינֶיךָ. יָכוֹל יַאֲפִילוּ תָּקְפָה עָלָיו
מִשְׁנָתוֹ, יִתַּלְמוּד לוֹמַר יוּפֶן־יָסוּרוּ
מִלְּבָבְךָ כֹּל יְמֵי חַיֶּיךָ; הָא אֵינוֹ
מִתְחַיֵּיב בְּנַפְשׁוֹ, עַד יְשֵׁשֵׁב וִיסִירֵם
מִלִּבּוֹ. *See ADDENDA, Page 552.

1 Here commences *Mishnah* 10 in the Prayer Book. 2 רַבִּי יַיֵּי מְשֵׁם in the Prayer Book. 3 כְּאִלּוּ in some texts. 4 Probably an admonition to the Sages and their disciples not to be culpable of remissness in the study of the Law. 5 *Deuteronomy* 4, 9. 6 Scripture gives וּשְׁמֹר. 7 וַאֲפִילוּ in some texts. 8 Not all have powerful retentive memories. But assiduous, persistent study will prevail over unintentional forgetfulness. 9 Literally *unless he sits and.*

Mishnah 9   מִשְׁנָה ט

R. Chanina¹ ben Dosa said, He in whom the fear of sin predominates over his wisdom,² his wisdom endures,³ but he whose wisdom predominates over his fear of sin, his wisdom does not endure. He⁴ used to say, He whose deeds exceed⁵ his wisdom, his wisdom endures, but he whose wisdom exceeds his deeds, his wisdom does not endure.⁶

יַרַבִּי חֲנִינָא בֶּן דּוֹסָא אוֹמֵר כֹּל
שֶׁיִּרְאַת חֶטְאוֹ קוֹדֶמֶת יִלְחָכְמָתוֹ
חָכְמָתוֹ יִמְתַקַיֶּימֶת, וְכֹל שֶׁחָכְמָתוֹ
קוֹדֶמֶת לְיִרְאַת חֶטְאוֹ אֵין חָכְמָתוֹ
מִתְקַיֶּימֶת. יהוּא הָיָה אוֹמֵר כֹּל
שֶׁמַּעֲשָׂיו יִמְרוּבִּין מֵחָכְמָתוֹ, חָכְמָתוֹ
מִתְקַיֶּימֶת, וְכֹל שֶׁחָכְמָתוֹ מְרוּבָּה
מִמַּעֲשָׂיו אֵין חָכְמָתוֹ יִמְתַקַיֶּימֶת.

1 See בְּרָכוֹת 5⁵, סוֹטָה 9¹⁵. *Mishnah* 11 in the Prayer Book begins here. 2 Or *the acquisition of knowledge.* 3 And guards him against error (סוֹטָה 3a). 4 *Mishnah* 12 begins here in the Prayer Book. 5 In the Prayer Book מְרֻבִּים. 6 Compare 1¹⁷, 3¹⁷, 6⁵, וְלֹא הַמִּדְרָשׁ הוּא הָעִקָּר אֶלָּא הַמַּעֲשֶׂה.

Mishnah 10   מִשְׁנָה י

He¹ used to say, He in whom² the spirit of mankind takes delight, in him the Spirit of the Omnipresent finds pleasure, but he in whom the spirit of his fellow-creatures finds no pleasure, in him the Spirit of the Omnipresent takes no delight. R.

יהוּא הָיָה אוֹמֵר כֹּל שֶׁרוּחַ הַבְּרִיּוֹת
נוֹחָה יְהֵימֶנּוּ, רוּחַ הַמָּקוֹם נוֹחָה
הֵימֶנּוּ, וְכֹל שֶׁאֵין רוּחַ הַבְּרִיּוֹת נוֹחָה
הֵימֶנּוּ, אֵין רוּחַ הַמָּקוֹם נוֹחָה הֵימֶנּוּ.
רַבִּי יְדוֹסָא בֶּן יְהַרְכִּינַס אוֹמֵר שֵׁינָה

Dosa[3] ben Harkinas[4] said, Morning sleep, (and) midday wine,[5] (and) children's talk,[6] and sitting in the houses of assembly of the ignorant[7] drive[8] a man from the world.

שֶׁל שַׁחֲרִית, יַיִן שֶׁל צָהֳרַיִם, וְשִׂיחַת הַיְלָדִים, וִישִׁיבַת בָּתֵּי כְנֵסִיּוֹת שֶׁל עַמֵּי הָאָרֶץ, מוֹצִיאִין אֶת־הָאָדָם מִן־הָעוֹלָם.

1 sc., R. Chanina ben Dosa. In the Prayer Book Mishnah 13 starts here. 2 Or הֵימֶנּוּ. 3 Mishnah 14 begins here in the Prayer Book. 4 See עֵדוּיוֹת 32ᵃ. 5 Compare בָּבָא בַּתְרָא 38b. 6 Compare פְּסָחִים 117a, סוּכָּה 21b. 7 See Appendix, Note 12. 8 מוֹצִיאִים in the Prayer Book.

Mishnah 11

מִשְׁנָה יא

R. Elazar[1] of Modim[2] said, If one profane sacred things,[3] and despise the Holydays, and put his fellow-man to shame publicly, and make void the covenant[4] of Abraham our father, peace be unto him,[5] and cause the Law to bear a meaning other than in accordance with traditional law,[6] then even though knowledge of the Law and good deeds are his, he has no share in the world to come.[7]

רַבִּי אֶלְעָזָר הַמּוֹדָעִי אוֹמֵר הַמְחַלֵּל אֶת־הַקֳּדָשִׁים, וְהַמְבַזֶּה אֶת־הַמּוֹעֲדוֹת, וְהַמַּלְבִּין פְּנֵי חֲבֵרוֹ בָּרַבִּים, וְהַמֵּפֵר בְּרִיתוֹ שֶׁל אַבְרָהָם אָבִינוּ עָלָיו הַשָּׁלוֹם, וְהַמְגַלֶּה פָנִים בַּתּוֹרָה שֶׁלֹּא כַהֲלָכָה, אַף עַל פִּי שֶׁיֵּשׁ בְּיָדוֹ תּוֹרָה וּמַעֲשִׂים טוֹבִים, אֵין לוֹ חֵלֶק לָעוֹלָם הַבָּא.

1 Here starts Mishnah 15 in the Prayer Book. 2 הַמּוּדָעִי is the vowelization preferred by some. Literally the Modaimite. Or Modin, Madaim, Modain (מוֹדָעִין, מוֹדְעִים), in Judaea about ten miles north-west of Beth Horon, the native place of the Hasmonean family. See שַׁבָּת 55b, פְּסָחִים 92, בָּבָא בַּתְרָא 10b. 3 Or הַקֳּדָשִׁים. Especially holy sacrifices (זְבָחִים 51-8). 4 i.e., they either use means to conceal their circumcised state or repudiate circumcision altogether (as used to be practised by Hellenists). 5 An expression similar to 'may he rest in peace', 'may his name be remembered for good.' This phrase is omitted in some texts. 6 i.e., disclose interpretations in the Law other than the right ones. Compare מְגִלָּה 49. 7 Such a one forfeits the right to be considered a member of the Jewish faith.

Mishnaah 12

מִשְׁנָה יב

R. Ishmael[1] said, Be[2] prompt [to serve] a superior,[3] (and) affable towards youth,[4] and receive all men with cheerfulness.[5]

רַבִּי יִשְׁמָעֵאל אוֹמֵר הֱוֵי קַל לְרֹאשׁ, וְנֹחַ לְתִשְׁחֹרֶת, וֶהֱוֵי מְקַבֵּל אֶת־כָּל־הָאָדָם בְּשִׂמְחָה.

1 *Mishnah* 16 commences here in the Prayer Book.   2 וֶהֱוֵה, הֱוֵה in some texts.
3 *i.e.*, give swift obedience to authority, be submissive to your senior.   4 Some
prefer the rendering *be amenable under forced service*.   5 Compare 1¹⁵.

Mishnah 13

מִשְׁנָה יג

R. Akiba[1] said, Jesting and levity
habituate[2] [a man] to lewdness.[3]
[The] *Tradition*[4] is a fence* to the
Law; *tithes*[5] are a fence* to riches;[6]
vows[7] are a fence* to abstinence; a
fence* to wisdom[6] is silence.

* סָיָג in some texts.

¹רַבִּי עֲקִיבָא אוֹמֵר שְׂחוֹק וְקַלּוּת
רֹאשׁ, ²מַרְגִּילִין ³לְעֶרְוָה· ⁴מָסֹרֶת,
*סְיָג לַתּוֹרָה; ⁵מַעַשְׂרוֹת, *סְיָג
⁶לְעֹשֶׁר; ⁷נְדָרִים, *סְיָג לִפְרִישׁוּת;
*סְיָג ⁶לְחָכְמָה שְׁתִיקָה·

1 In the Prayer Book *Mishnah* 17 commences here.   2 In some texts, מַרְגִּילִים
אֶת־הָאָדָם.   3 Jesting and levity between the sexes accustom them to immorality.
But restrained joy and joyfulness are not deprecated.   4 מָסֹרֶת, the non-vowelized
traditional text of the Scripture (in contradistinction to the מִקְרָא, the vocalised
traditional Scriptural text).   5 The giving of *tithes* does not impoverish a man; and
they lead him to acquire charitable habits.   6 Some prefer the pointing לַחָכְמָה,
לָעֹשֶׁר.   7 But see נְדָרִים, INTRODUCTION.   They do help in self-restraint.

Mishnah 14

מִשְׁנָה יד

He[1] used to say, Beloved [of God] is
man[2] for he was created in the
image [of God]; [but] greater still
was the love [shown him] in that it
was made known to him that he
was created in the image of God,
as it is said,[3] *For in the image of God
made He man*.   Beloved[4] [of God]
are Israel, for they were called
children of the Omnipresent; but
by a special[5] love was it made known
to them that they were called
children of the Omnipresent, as it
is said,[6] *Ye are children unto the Eternal
your God*.   Beloved[4] [of God] are
Israel, for to them was given[7] the
desirable instrument;[8] [but] still
greater[5] was the love since it was
made known to them that to them
was given[7] the desirable instrument[8]

¹הוּא הָיָה אוֹמֵר חָבִיב ²אָדָם שֶׁנִּבְרָא
בְּצֶלֶם; חִבָּה יְתֵרָה נוֹדַעַת לוֹ
שֶׁנִּבְרָא בְּצֶלֶם, ³שֶׁנֶּאֱמַר בְּצֶלֶם
אֱלֹהִים עָשָׂה אֶת־הָאָדָם· ⁴חֲבִיבִין
יִשְׂרָאֵל, שֶׁנִּקְרְאוּ בָנִים לַמָּקוֹם; חִבָּה
⁵יְתֵירָה נוֹדַעַת לָהֶם שֶׁנִּקְרְאוּ בָנִים
לַמָּקוֹם, ⁶שֶׁנֶּאֱמַר בָּנִים אַתֶּם לַה׳
אֱלֹהֵיכֶם· ⁴חֲבִיבִין יִשְׂרָאֵל שֶׁנִּתַּן
לָהֶם כְּלִי ⁸חֶמְדָּה; חִבָּה ⁵יְתֵירָה
נוֹדַעַת לָהֶם ⁷שֶׁנִּתַּן לָהֶם כְּלִי⁸חֶמְדָּה
שֶׁבּוֹ נִבְרָא הָעוֹלָם, ⁶שֶׁנֶּאֱמַר כִּי
לֶקַח טוֹב נָתַתִּי לָכֶם תּוֹרָתִי אַל־
¹⁰תַּעֲזֹבוּ·

wherewith the universe was created, as it is said,[9] *For I give you good doctrine; forsake ye*[10] *not my Law.*

1 *viz.,* R. Akiba. In the Prayer Book *Mishnah* 18 begin here. **2** Irrespective of
race, colour or creed. **3** *Genesis* **9,** 6. **4** חֲבִיבִים in some texts. **5** In some texts,
יְתֵרָה. **6** *Deuteronomy* **14,** 1. **7** שֶׁנִּתַּן in some texts. **8** Referring to God's Law
whose moral truths are valid eternally. Compare the § שְׁלֹשָׁה עָשָׂר עִקָּרִים* *Article* 9§
in the Prayer Book (* *The Thirteen Principles* [*of the Faith*] formulated by Maimonides).
9 *Proverbs* **4,** 2. **10** Scripture gives תַּעֲזֹבוּ. §Also repeated in the hymn יִגְדַּל אֱלֹהִים
חַי (line 9) in the Daily Prayer Book.

Mishnah 15

All[1] is foreseen [by God], yet freedom of choice is granted; and by
grace[2] is the universe[3] judged, yet
all[4] is according to the amount[5] of
the work.[6]

מִשְׁנָה טו

[1]הַכֹּל צָפוּי, וְהָרְשׁוּת נְתוּנָה; [2]וּבְטוֹב
[3]הָעוֹלָם נָדוֹן, [4]וְהַכֹּל לְפִי [5]רוֹב
[6]הַמַּעֲשֶׂה.

1 Here begins *Mishnah* 19 in the Prayer Book. **2** Literally *goodness.* **3** Compare
Psalm **145,** 9. **4** *i.e.,* reward and punishment. **5** רֹב in some texts. **6** *i.e.,* the
prevalence of good or bad deeds. An alternative reading according to some:
אֲבָל לֹא לְפִי רֹב הַמַּעֲשֶׂה, 'but not according to the amount of work', *viz.,* the 'grace'
is greater in proportion to the amount of the virtues or evils.

Mishnah 16

He[1] used to say, All is given on
pledge,[2] and a net is spread[3] over
all the living; the shop is open,
(and) the dealer gives credit, (and)
the ledger lies open, (and) the hand
writes, and whosoever desires to
borrow may come and borrow, but
the collectors regularly go their
round every day and exact payment[4]
from man with his consent or without his consent,[5] since they have
that whereon they can rely [in their
demand],[6] and the judgment is a
judgment of truth; and all is
prepared[7] for the feast.[8]

מִשְׁנָה טז

[1]הוּא הָיָה אוֹמֵר, הַכֹּל נָתוּן [2]בְּעֵרָבוֹן,
וּמְצוּדָה [3]פְרוּסָה עַל כָּל־הַחַיִּים;
הֶחָנוּת פְּתוּחָה, וְהַחֶנְוָנִי מַקִּיף,
וְהַפִּנְקָס פָּתוּחַ, וְהַיָּד כּוֹתֶבֶת, וְכָל
הָרוֹצֶה לִלְווֹת יָבֹא וְיִלְוֶה, וְהַגַּבָּאִים
מַחֲזִירִים תָּדִיר בְּכָל יוֹם, [4]וְנִפְרָעִין
מִן־הָאָדָם מִדַּעְתּוֹ וְשֶׁלֹּא [5]מִדַּעְתּוֹ,
וְיֵשׁ לָהֶם עַל מַה־[6]שֶּׁיִּסְמֹכוּ, וְהַדִּין
דִּין אֱמֶת; וְהַכֹּל [7]מְתֻקָּן [8]לִסְעוּדָה.

63

1 *sc.*, R. Akiba. *Mishnah* 20 begins here in the Prayer Book. 2 A picturesque series of sayings stressing that man is reponsible and accountable for all his deeds. 3 In some editions פְּרוּשָׁה. 4 תְּמְרָעִים in some texts. 5 Referring to reward and punishment. 6 *i.e.*, the judgments are just and the penalties are just. 7 מְתָקָן in some texts. 8 A symbolical reference to the world to come.

Mishnah 17   מִשְׁנָה יז.

R.[1] Elazar ben Azariah said, If there be no [study of the] Law there is no good conduct, if there be no good conduct there is no [study of the] Law; if there be no wisdom there is no fear [of the Almighty], if there be no fear [of the Almighty] there is no wisdom; if[2] there be no understanding there is no knowledge, if there be no knowledge there is no understanding; if there be no meal there is no [study of the] Law,[3] if there be no [study of the] Law there is no meal.[4] He[5] used to say, He[6] whose wisdom excels his deeds, to what is he like?[7] To a tree[8] whose branches are many[9] but whose roots are few,[9] and the wind comes and uproots it and overturns it (upon its face), as it is said,[10] *For he shall be like a tamarisk in the desert, and shall not see when good cometh,[11] but shall inhabit the parched places in the wilderness, a salt land and not inhabited.* But he[6] whose works exceed[9] his wisdom, to what is he like? To a tree[8] whose branches are few[9], but whose roots are many,[9] so that even though all the winds in the world come and blow against it, it can not be stirred[12] from its place, as it is said,[13] *For he shall be as a tree planted by the waters, and that spreadeth out its roots by the river, and shall not*

יַרַבִּי אֶלְעָזָר בֶּן עֲזַרְיָה אוֹמֵר אִם
אֵין תּוֹרָה אֵין דֶּרֶךְ אֶרֶץ, אִם אֵין
דֶּרֶךְ אֶרֶץ אֵין תּוֹרָה; אִם אֵין
חָכְמָה אֵין יִרְאָה, אִם אֵין יִרְאָה אֵין
חָכְמָה; יאִם אֵין בִּינָה אֵין דָּעַת,
אִם אֵין דַּעַת אֵין בִּינָה; אִם אֵין
קֶמַח אֵין יתּוֹרָה, אִם אֵין תּוֹרָה אֵין
יקֶמַח יהוּא הָיָה אוֹמֵר יכֹּל שֶׁחָכְמָתוֹ
מְרוּבָּה מִמַּעֲשָׂיו, לְמָה הוּא ידוֹמֶה?
יּלְאִילָן שֶׁעֲנָפָיו יִמְרוּבִּין, וְשָׁרָשָׁיו
ימוּעָטִין, וְהָרוּחַ בָּאָה וְעוֹקַרְתּוֹ
וְהוֹפַכְתּוֹ עַל פָּנָיו, יּשֶׁנֶּאֱמַר וְהָיָה
כְּעַרְעָר בָּעֲרָבָה וְלֹא יִרְאֶה כִּי־
ייבָא טוֹב וְשָׁכַן חֲרֵרִים בַּמִּדְבָּר
אֶרֶץ מְלֵחָה וְלֹא תֵשֵׁב. אֲבָל יכֹּל
שֶׁמַּעֲשָׂיו יִמְרוּבִּין מֵחָכְמָתוֹ לְמָה
הוּא דוֹמֶה? ילְאִילָן שֶׁעֲנָפָיו
ימוּעָטִין, וְשָׁרָשָׁיו יִמְרוּבִּין, שֶׁאֲפִילוּ
כָּל־הָרוּחוֹת שֶׁבָּעוֹלָם בָּאוֹת
וְנוֹשְׁבוֹת בּוֹ, אֵין ייּמְזִיזִין אוֹתוֹ
מִמְּקוֹמוֹ, יּשֶׁנֶּאֱמַר וְהָיָה כְּעֵץ שָׁתוּל
עַל־מַיִם וְעַל־יוּבַל יְשַׁלַּח שָׁרָשָׁיו

64

see[14] *when heat*[15] *cometh, but its foliage shall be green; and shall not be anxious in the year of drought,*[16] *neither shall cease from yielding fruit.*

וְלֹא ¹⁴יִרְאֶה כִּי־יָבֹא ¹⁵חֹם וְהָיָה
עָלֵיהוּ רַעֲנָן וּבִשְׁנַת ¹⁶בַּצֹּרֶת לֹא
יִדְאָג וְלֹא יָמִישׁ מֵעֲשׂוֹת פֶּרִי.

1 *Mishnah* 21 commences here in the Prayer Book. 2 The Prayer Book has אִם *אֵין דֵּעַת אֵין בִּינָה אִם אֵין בִּינָה אֵין דֵּעַת 3 Compare 2²; מְנָחוֹת 103b. 4 Contrast 4⁸. He who neglects the study of the Law because of his wealth will in the end disregard the study in poverty (compare סוֹטָה 20a, יוֹמָא 7¹). 5 *Mishnah* 22 in the Prayer Book commences here. 6 Literally *Everyone.* 7 Compare 1¹⁷, 3⁹, 5¹⁴, 6⁵. 8 The vowelization could be the *definite* form לָאִילָן *to 'the' tree.* 9 מַרְבִּים, מַעֲטִים, in the Prayer Book. 10 *Jeremiah* 17, 6. 11 יָבוֹא in the Scripture. 12 In the Prayer Book, מְזִיזִים. 13 *Jeremiah* 17, 8. 14 The Scripture gives יִרְאֶ as the כְּתִיב and יִרְאֶה as the קְרִי [in foot-note]. 15 חֹם is in the Scriptural text. 16 The Scripture gives בַּצֹּרֶת. **If there be no knowledge there is no understanding, if there be no understanding there is no knowledge.*

Mishnah 18

R.[1] Eliezer ben[2] Chisma said, [The law concerning] *bird-offerings*[3] and the *onset of menstruation*[4] are essential traditional ordinances, but the calculations of the seasons[5] and geometry are but the after-courses[6] of wisdom.

מִשְׁנָה יח

¹רַבִּי אֱלִיעֶזֶר ²בֶּן חִסְמָא אוֹמֵר,
²קִנִּין, ³וּפִתְחֵי נִדָּה, הֵן הֵן
גּוּפֵי הֲלָכוֹת, ⁵תְּקוּפוֹת וְגֵמַטְרִיָאוֹת
⁶פַּרְפְּרָאוֹת לַחָכְמָה.

1 *Mishnah* 23 starts here in the Prayer Book. In some editions, רַבִּי אֶלְעָזָר, *R. Elazar.* 2 Some consider בֶּן redundant. 3 *Leviticus* 12, 13, 15. קֵן in the Prayer Book. 4 *Leviticus* 15, 19ff. 5 The *equinoxes* (the two opposite points at which the sun's centre crosses the celestial equator, and day and night are everywhere of equal length; also the times of crossing, *viz.*, about March 21—*vernal equinox*—and September 22-23—*autumnal equinox*; the term is also used for the *equinoctial points* (where the celestial equator and the elliptic intersect) and the *solstices* (the points and times in the elliptic when the sun is at its greatest declination or farthest from the equator, north or south, *viz.*, the point of the sign Cancer) usually on June 21-22 —the *summer solstice*—and December 22—*the winter solstice*—the first point of the sign Capricorn. Some render this *astronomy.* 6 Compare בְּרָכוֹת 6⁵, שַׁבָּת 23². In some texts פַּרְפָּרִיוֹת. Scientific studies are not as important as the knowledge of the Law.

65

CHAPTER 4

Mishnah 1

Ben Zoma[1] said, Who is wise? He that learns from all men, as it is said,[2] *From all my teachers have I acquired understanding.*[3] Who[4] is mighty? One who subdues his passions,[5] as it is said,[6] *He that is slow to anger is better than the mighty, and he that ruleth*[7] *over his spirit than he that taketh*[8] *a city.* Who is rich? He who rejoiceth in his portion,[9] as it is said,[10] *When thou eatest the labour of thine hands, happy shalt thou be, and it shall be well with thee.* 'Happy[11] shalt thou be'—in this world, '*and it shall be well with* thee'—in the world to come. Who is honoured?[12] One that honours [his] fellow-men, as it is said,[13] *For them that honour Me will I honour, and they that despise Me*[14] *shall be lightly esteemed.*

פֶּרֶק ד

מִשְׁנָה א

[1]בֶּן זוֹמָא אוֹמֵר אֵיזֶהוּ חָכָם? הַלּוֹמֵד מִכָּל אָדָם, [2]שֶׁנֶּאֱמַר [3]מִכָּל מְלַמְּדַי הִשְׂכַּלְתִּי. [4]אֵיזֶהוּ גִבּוֹר? [5]הַכּוֹבֵשׁ אֶת־יִצְרוֹ, [6]שֶׁנֶּאֱמַר טוֹב אֶרֶךְ אַפַּיִם מִגִּבּוֹר [7]וּמוֹשֵׁל בְּרוּחוֹ [8]מִלּוֹכֵד עִיר. אֵיזֶהוּ עָשִׁיר? [9]הַשָּׂמֵחַ בְּחֶלְקוֹ, [10]שֶׁנֶּאֱמַר יְגִיעַ כַּפֶּיךָ כִּי תֹאכֵל אַשְׁרֶיךָ וְטוֹב לָךְ, [11]אַשְׁרֶיךָ בָּעוֹלָם הַזֶּה וְטוֹב לָךְ לְעוֹלָם הַבָּא. אֵיזֶהוּ [12]מְכוּבָּד? הַמְכַבֵּד אֶת־הַבְּרִיּוֹת, [13]שֶׁנֶּאֱמַר כִּי מְכַבְּדַי אֲכַבֵּד [14]וּבוֹזַי יֵקָלוּ.

---

1 Compare סוֹטָה 9[15].   2 Psalm 119, 99.   3 Some render this *I have more understanding than all my teachers.*   4 אֵיזוֹהִי in some editions.   5 *i.e.*, evil inclination.   6 Proverbs 16, 32.   7 וּמֹשֵׁל is the orthography in Scripture.   8 מִלְּכַד is the Scriptural orthography.   9 Psalm 128, 2. This is repeated in 6[4].   10 *i.e.*, one who is contented with his lot and makes the best of things.   11 These two phrases are repeated in 6[4].   12 מְכֻבָּד in some texts.   13 I Samuel 2, 30.   14 The Scripture has וּבֹזַי.

Mishnah 2

Ben Azzai[1] said, Run[2] to [the fulfilment of even] a slight precept as [thou wouldst to fulfil] a grave one,[3] and flee from transgression,[4] for one good deed draws another good deed [in its wake],[5] and one transgression draws another transgression [in its train];[6] for[7] the recompense of a good deed is a good deed, and the reward of a transgression is a transgression.

מִשְׁנָה ב

בֶּן [1]עַזַּאי אוֹמֵר [2]הֱוֵי רָץ לְמִצְוָה קַלָּה [3]כִּבַחֲמוּרָה, וּבוֹרֵחַ מִן־[4]הָעֲבֵירָה, שֶׁמִּצְוָה [5]גּוֹרֶרֶת מִצְוָה וַעֲבֵירָה [6]גּוֹרֶרֶת עֲבֵירָה; [7]שֶׁשְּׂכַר מִצְוָה, מִצְוָה, וּשְׂכַר עֲבֵירָה, עֲבֵירָה.

66

1 עֲצֵי in some editions.   2 In some editions, הֱוֵי רָץ.   3 Some consider כְּבַחֲמִירָה
as *a grave one*, redundant.   Compare 2[1].   4 עֲבֵרָה ,וַעֲבֵרָה ,הָעֲבֵרָה in the Prayer
Book.   5 *i.e.*, one can practise and cultivate good moral habits.   6 The committal
of evil actions can become a fearful habit—it may indeed be heritable* and be
passed on as an inheritance (see סוּכָּה 52a).   7 This is a variation of the foregoing.
*Or *hereditable;* conversely, *it may be hereditary.*

Mishnah 3

He[1] used to say, Despise not any
man,[2] and discard not any thing,[3]
for there is not a man who has not
his hour and there exists not a thing
which has not its place.[4]

מִשְׁנָה ג

הוּא הָיָה אוֹמֵר אַל תְּהִי בָז לְכָל
אָדָם וְאַל תְּהִי מַפְלִיג לְכָל דָּבָר,
שֶׁאֵין לְךָ אָדָם שֶׁאֵין לוֹ שָׁעָה, וְאֵין
לְךָ דָּבָר שֶׁאֵין לוֹ מָקוֹם.

1 בֶּן עַזַּאי.   2 Compare 1[12, 15], 2[10], 4[1].   3 One should be on his guard against
saying that anything is unlikely or will not happen or is not possible.   4 The
Creator has ordained time and place for all things.

Mishnah 4

R. Levitas of Jabneh[1] said, Be[2]
exceedingly humble of spirit, since
the hope of man is but the worm.[3]
R.[4] Jochanan ben Baroka[5] said, Whosoever profanes the name of Heaven
in secret will suffer[6] the penalty
therefor in public; [and] it[7] is all
one whether the profanation of the
Name is [committed] unwittingly or
in wilfulness.

מִשְׁנָה ד

רַבִּי לְוִיטַס אִישׁ יַבְנֶה אוֹמֵר מְאֹד
מְאֹד הֱוֵי שְׁפַל רוּחַ, שֶׁתִּקְוַת אֱנוֹשׁ
רִמָּה. רַבִּי יוֹחָנָן בֶּן בְּרוֹקָא אוֹמֵר
כָּל־הַמְחַלֵּל שֵׁם שָׁמַיִם בַּסֵּתֶר
נִפְרָעִין מִמֶּנּוּ בַּגָּלוּי; אֶחָד שׁוֹגֵג
וְאֶחָד מֵזִיד בְּחִלּוּל הַשֵּׁם.

1 Or *Jamnia*, N.W. of Jerusalem, seat of the Sanhedrin after 80 c.e.   2 הֱוֵה in the
Prayer Book.   3 From *Ben Sira* or *Ecclesiasticus* 7[17].   4 Here begins *Mishnah 5* in
the Prayer Book.   5 Some prefer the vowelled form בְּרוֹקָא, *Beroka.*   6 In the
Prayer Book, נִפְרָעִים.   7 אֶחָד בְּשׁוֹגֵג וְאֶחָד בְּמֵזִיד in the Prayer Book.

Mishnah 5

R.[1] Ishmael his son[2] said, He who
learns in order to teach[3] will be
granted[4] [by Heaven] the means
both to learn and to teach; but he
that learns in order to practise,

מִשְׁנָה ה

רַבִּי יִשְׁמָעֵאל בְּנוֹ אוֹמֵר הַלּוֹמֵד
עַל מְנָת יְלַלֵּמֵד, מַסְפִּיקִין בְּיָדוֹ
לִלְמוֹד וּלְלַמֵּד; וְהַלּוֹמֵד עַל מְנָת

[Heaven] will grant[4] him the opportunity to learn and to teach, to observe and to perform. R.[5] Zadok said, Make[6] not of [the Law] a crown wherewith to aggrandise thyself, nor a spade wherewith to dig. And so also used Hillel to say, He who makes worldly use of[7] the crown [of the Law] shall waste away. Hence thou mayest deduce that whoever derives profit from the words of the Law is promoting his own destruction.[8]

לַעֲשׂוֹת, ⁹מַסְפִּיקִין בְּיָדוֹ לִלְמוֹד
וּלְלַמֵּד, לִשְׁמוֹר וְלַעֲשׂוֹת· ¹רַבִּי
צָדוֹק אוֹמֵר ²אַל תַּעֲשֵׂם עֲטָרָה
לְהִתְגַּדֵּל בָּהֶם, וְלֹא קַרְדּוּם לַחְפּוֹר
בָּהֶם· וְכַךְ הָיָה הִלֵּל אוֹמֵר
³וְדִישְׁתַּמֵּשׁ בְּתָגָא חֲלָף· הָא לָמַדְתָּ
כָּל־הַנֶּהֱנֶה מִדִּבְרֵי תוֹרָה, ⁴נוֹטֵל
חַיָּיו מִן־הָעוֹלָם·

1 *viz.*, R. Ishmael ben R. Jochanan ben Baroka. רַבִּי יִשְׁמָעֵאל בַּר רַבִּי יוֹסֵי is given in some texts. *Mishnah* 6 begins here in the Prayer Book. 2 בְּנוֹ is omitted in the גְּמָרָא. 3 But action (*i.e.*, putting into practice) is implied (see יוֹמָא 72b, תַּעֲנִית 7a). 4 מַסְפִּיקִים is given in the Prayer Book. 5 In the Prayer Book *Mishnah* 7 is given here. 6 In the Prayer Book is given אַל תִּפְרוֹשׁ מִן־הַצִּבּוּר*, וְעַל תַּעַשׂ עַצְמְךָ כְּעוֹרְכֵי הַדַּיָּנִין (or הַדִּינִים) וְעַל תַּעֲשֶׂה עֲטָרָה לְהִתְגַּדֵּל בָּהּ וְלֹא קָרְדֹּם לַחְפָּר בָּהּ, *Separate not thyself from the congregation; and be not like those that lay down the law* (or, *act not on the counsel's part in the office of a judge*, or *act not like those that seek to influence the judges*), *and make not of [the Law] a crown wherewith to aggrandise thyself, nor a spade wherewith to dig.* *Compare 2⁴. 7 The Prayer Book has וּדְאִשְׁתַּמֵּשׁ. 8 Literally *takes his life from the world.* Compare תַּעֲנִית 7a.

Mishnah 6

R. Jose[1] said, He that honours the Law[2] will himself be honoured[3] by his fellow-men,[4] but whosoever dishonours the Law[5] will himself be dishonoured[6] by mankind.

מִשְׁנָה ו

¹רַבִּי יוֹסֵי אוֹמֵר כָּל־הַמְכַבֵּד אֶת־
²הַתּוֹרָה, גּוּפוֹ ³מְכוּבָּד עַל ⁴הַבְּרִיּוֹת,
וְכָל הַמְחַלֵּל אֶת־⁵הַתּוֹרָה, גּוּפוֹ
⁶מְחוּלָּל עַל הַבְּרִיּוֹת·

1 *Mishnah* 8 commences here in the Prayer Book. R. Jose ben Chalafta is referred to here. 2 *i.e.*, fulfils its precepts. 3 מְכַבֵּד in some texts. 4 Compare בְּרָכוֹת 19b. 5 *i.e.*, disregards its moral teachings. 6 In some texts מְחַלָּל.

Mishnah 7

R.[1] Ishmael, his son, said, Whosoever shuns judicial office[2] rids himself of hatred,[3] (and) robbery[4] and

מִשְׁנָה ז

¹רַבִּי יִשְׁמָעֵאל בְּנוֹ אוֹמֵר הַחוֹשֵׂךְ
עַצְמוֹ מִן־הַדִּין, פּוֹרֵק מִמֶּנּוּ אֵיבָה

68

perjury, but he that presumptuously thrusts himself forward[5] to lay down a decision is foolish, wicked and of an arrogant disposition.

יוֹגֵל, וּשְׁבוּעַת שָׁוְא, יְהַגַס לִבּוֹ בְּהוֹרָאָה, שׁוֹטֶה רָשָׁע, וְגַס רוּחַ·

1 Here commences *Mishnah* 9 in the Prayer Book. *sc.*, R. Ishmael ben Jose. *R. Simon* is given in some editions and *Bar Kappara* in others. **2** Or *refrains from passing* [hasty] *judgment* (see סַנְהֶדְרִין 6b). **3** Compare שַׁבָּת 119a. **4** Wrongful judgment deprives an innocent man of what is rightly his. Or יֻגֵּל. **5** Or *he that is shameless, is forward, is presumptuous;* compare סוֹטָה 16.

Mishnah 8

מִשְׁנָה ח

He[1] used to say, Judge not alone,[2] for none may judge alone save One; and say not [to thy fellow judges], 'Adopt my view', for[3] it is for them to choose [to concur], and it is not thou [who mayest enforce accordance].[4]

הוּא הָיָה אוֹמֵר אַל תְּהִי דָן יְחִידִי, שֶׁאֵין דָן יְחִידִי, אֶלָּא אֶחָד, וְאַל תֹּאמַר קַבְּלוּ דַעְתִּי שֶׁהֵן רַשָּׁאִין וְלֹא יַאְתָּה·

1 *viz.*, R. Ishmael ben Jose. Here commences *Mishnah* 10 in the Prayer Book. **2** Compare 3⁶; סַנְהֶדְרִין 5a. **3** שֶׁהֵם רַשָּׁאִים in some texts. **4** A decision follows the opinion of a majority of judges.

Mishnah 9

מִשְׁנָה ט

R.[1] Jonathan said, Whoso fulfils the Law in poverty[2] shall in the end fulfil it in wealth,[3] and he that disregards the Law in wealth shall ultimately neglect it in poverty.

רַבִּי יוֹנָתָן אוֹמֵר כָּל־הַמְקַיֵּם אֶת־ הַתּוֹרָה מֵעוֹנִי סוֹפוֹ לְקַיְּמָה מֵעוֹשֶׁר, וְכָל הַמְבַטֵּל אֶת־הַתּוֹרָה מֵעוֹשֶׁר, סוֹפוֹ לְבַטְּלָה מֵעוֹנִי·

1 In the Prayer Book *Mishnah* 11 commences here. He was probably Jonathan ben Joseph, and a disciple of R. Akiba and R. Ishmael ben Elisha. Some texts give יוֹחָנָן, *Jochanan*, and others נָתָן, *Nathan*. **2** מֵעָנִי in some texts. **3** Contrast 3¹⁷. מֵעֹשֶׁר in some texts.

Mishnah 10

מִשְׁנָה י

R.[1] Meir said, Decrease[2] thy labours in worldly avocations and occupy thyself in the Law;[3] and be[4] humble of spirit before all men; and if thou neglect the Law, many things to

רַבִּי מֵאִיר אוֹמֵר הֱוֵי מְמַעֵט בְּעֵסֶק, וַעֲסֹק בַּתּוֹרָה; וֶהֱוֵי שְׁפַל רוּחַ בִּפְנֵי כָל־אָדָם; וְאִם בָּטַלְתָּ

69

disregard it shall present themselves to thee,[5] but if thou toil in the Law, He[6] has abundant reward to give[7] to thee.[8]

מִן־הַתּוֹרָה, *יֶשׁ־לְךָ בְּטֵלִים הַרְבֵּה
'כְּנֶגְדְּךָ, וְאִם עָמַלְתָּ בַתּוֹרָה, §יֶשׁ־
'לוֹ שָׂכָר הַרְבֵּה 'לִיתֵּן 'לָךְ.

1 *Mishnah* 12 starts here in the Prayer Book. 2 הֲוֵה in some texts. 3 Compare 2[5].
4 In some texts, וֶהֱוֵה. 5 Compare סוּכָּה 28b. 6 לוֹ is omitted in the גְּמָרָא, and
the rendering of יֶשׁ by itself would then be *There is*. 7 לִתֵּן in some texts.
8 Compare 2[14, 16]; בְּרָכוֹת 35b. *Or יֶשׁ לְךָ. § יֶשׁ לוֹ.

Mishnah 11

R.[1] Eliezer[2] ben Jacob said, Whoso performs one good deed acquires for himself one advocate, but whosoever commits one transgression[3] acquires for himself one accuser; repentance and good deeds are as a shield[4] against punishment.[5] R.[6] Jochanan Ha-Sandelar[7] said, Every assembly that is for the sake of Heaven will in the end be established, but that which is not for the sake of Heaven will not in the end be established.

מִשְׁנָה יא

'רַבִּי 'אֱלִיעֶזֶר בֶּן יַעֲקֹב אוֹמֵר
הָעוֹשֶׂה מִצְוָה אַחַת קוֹנֶה לוֹ פְּרַקְלִיט
אֶחָד, וְהָעוֹבֵר 'עֲבֵירָה אַחַת קוֹנֶה
לוֹ קַטֵּגוֹר אֶחָד ; תְּשׁוּבָה וּמַעֲשִׂים
טוֹבִים 'כִּתְרֵיס בִּפְנֵי 'הַפּוּרְעָנוּת.
'רַבִּי יוֹחָנָן 'הַסַּנְדְּלָר אוֹמֵר כָּל־
כְּנֵסִיָּה שֶׁהִיא לְשֵׁם שָׁמַיִם סוֹפָהּ
לְהִתְקַיֵּים, וְשֶׁאֵינָהּ לְשֵׁם שָׁמַיִם, אֵין
סוֹפָהּ לְהִתְקַיֵּים.

1 Here, in the Prayer Book, starts *Mishnah* 13. 2 A disciple of R. Akiba, and not to be confused with the Sage quoted in מִדּוֹת 1[2]. 3 עֲבֵרָה in some texts. 4 Or כְּתָרֵיס, כְּתְרֵיס. 5 God's pardon and favour are not granted if there is no true repentance followed by charitable deeds. 6 Here starts *Mishnah* 14 in the Prayer Book. In some texts הַפְּרְעָנוּת. 7 Literally *the Sandal-maker*. According to one opinion אַלְכְּסַנְדְּרִי = הַסַּנְדְּלָר, *the Alexandrian*.

Mishnah 12

R.[1] Elazar ben Shammua said, Let the honour of thy disciple be as precious to thee as thine own,[2] and the honour of thy colleague[3] be as the reverence for thy master,[4] and the reverence for thy master be like the fear of Heaven.[5]

מִשְׁנָה יב

'רַבִּי אֶלְעָזָר בֶּן שַׁמּוּעַ אוֹמֵר יְהִי
כְבוֹד תַּלְמִידְךָ חָבִיב עָלֶיךָ 'כְּשֶׁלָּךְ,
וּכְבוֹד יַחֲבֵרְךָ כְּמוֹרָא 'רַבָּךְ, וּמוֹרָא
רַבָּךְ כְּמוֹרָא 'שָׁמָיִם.

70

1 *Mishnah* 15 starts here in the Prayer Book.   2 Actually mutual reverence between master and disciple is advocated.   3 Or *associate, fellow.*   4 Or *teacher.*   5 For the master teaches the Law of God.

Mishnah 13

R.[1] Judah said, Be[2] cautious in study[3] [of the Law], for an error in study[4] [of the Law] is accounted presumptuous transgression.[5]   R.[6] Simon said, There are[7] three crowns: the crown of [the study of] the Law, the crown of priesthood,[8] and the crown of royalty, but the crown of a good name surpasses them all.[9]

מִשְׁנָה יג

יַרַבִּי יְהוּדָה אוֹמֵר יֶהֱוֵי זָהִיר
יִבְּתַלְמוּד שֶׁשִּׁגְגַת ילְמוּד עוֹלָה יָזָדוֹן׳
יַרַבִּי שִׁמְעוֹן אוֹמֵר שְׁלֹשָׁה כְתָרִים
יֹהֵם, כֶּתֶר תּוֹרָה, כֶּתֶר יִכְהוּנָה,
וְכֶתֶר מַלְכוּת, וְכֶתֶר שֵׁם טוֹב עוֹלָה
עַל יַגַּבֵּיהֶן׳

1 *Mishnah* 16 begins here in the Prayer Book.   2 הֱוֵה in some texts.   3 Some render it *Be heedful in teaching the Law.* The גְּמָרָא has בְּתַלְמוּד, and thus in the Prayer Book.   4 Or *teaching.** If this is not intentional, for it may lead to false doctrine and wanton sinfulness.   The גְּמָרָא has לָמוּד, and thus in the Prayer Book.   5 Compare בָּבָא מְצִיעָא 33b.   6 *Mishnah* 17 begins here in the Prayer Book.   7 In the Prayer Book, הֵן.   8 See *Exodus* 29, 6.   The Prayer Book has וְכֶתֶר כְּהֻנָּה.   9 See *Proverbs* 23, 1; *Ecclesiastes* 7, 1.   *תַּלְמוּד in the Prayer Book.

Mishnah 14

R.[1] Nehorai[2] said, Wander[3] forth to a place of the Law,[4] and say not that it will come after thee, or that thy colleagues will establish it in thy possession;[5] and lean not upon thine own understanding.[6]

מִשְׁנָה יד

יַרַבִּי יְנְהוֹרַאי אוֹמֵר יֶהֱוֵי גוֹלֶה
לִמְקוֹם יתּוֹרָה וְאַל תֹּאמַר שֶׁהִיא
תָבוֹא אַחֲרֶיךָ, שֶׁחֲבֵירֶיךָ יְקַיְּמוּהָ
יּבְיָדְךָ, וְאֶל בִּינָתְךָ אַל יתִּשָּׁעֵן׳

1 In the Prayer Book *Mishnah* 18 begins here.   2 Or נְהוֹרַי.   See נָזִיר 9⁵, קִדּוּשִׁין 4¹⁴.   He is said to be R. Elazar ben Arach (see 2¹⁰).   3 In some texts, הֱוֵה.   4 Where the Law is studied (see 6⁹).   5 Compare 1¹⁶.   6 Compare *Proverbs* 3,5.

Mishnah 15

R.[1] Jannai[2] said, It is not in our power[3] to explain either the prosperity of the wicked or the tribulations of the righteous.[4]   R. Mattia[5] ben Cheresh[6] said, Be[7] first in the

מִשְׁנָה טו

יַרַבִּי יַנַּאי אוֹמֵר אֵין יּבְיָדֵינוּ לֹא
מִשַּׁלְוַת הָרְשָׁעִים, וְאַף לֹא מִיִּסּוּרֵי
יהַצַּדִּיקִים׳ רַבִּי יּמַתְיָא בֶן יחֶרֶשׁ

71

salutation of peace to all men,[8] and be[9] [rather] a tail to (the) lions than a head to (the) foxes.[10]

אוֹמֵר יֱהֱוֵי מַקְדִּים בְּשָׁלוֹם כָּל־
אָדָם, יֶהֱוֵי זָנָב לָאֲרָיוֹת, וְאַל תְּהִי
רֹאשׁ [10]לַשּׁוּעָלִים.

1 Here begins *Mishnah* 19 in the Prayer Book.   2 Or יַי.   Perhaps the father of R. Dostai quoted in 3[8].   3 Compare תַּעֲנִית 11b.   4 Some render this: *it does not lie with us concerning the security of the ungodly or the afflictions of the righteous*—a reflection on the mediocre status of the Jews during the period 250 C.E. (*circa*).   5 Or מַתְיָה; in some editions מַתִּתְיָה, *Mattathiah*.   See יוֹמָא 86.   In the Prayer Book *Mishnah* 20 begins here.   6 Or חָרַשׁ.   7 In the Prayer Book, הֱוֵי.   8 Particularly good advice in unfriendly surroundings.   9 וֶהֱוֵה in the Prayer Book.   10 לַשְּׁעָלִים in the Prayer Book.

Mishnah 16

מִשְׁנָה טז

R.[1] Jacob[2] said, This world is like a vestibule to the world to come; prepare thyself[3] in the vestibule that thou mayest enter into the (banqueting-) hall.[4]

[1]רַבִּי יִיַעֲקֹב אוֹמֵר הָעוֹלָם הַזֶּה
דוֹמֶה לִפְרוֹזְדוֹר בִּפְנֵי הָעוֹלָם הַבָּא;
[2]הַתְקֵן עַצְמְךָ בִּפְרוֹזְדוֹר כְּדֵי
שֶׁתִּכָּנֵס [4]לִטְרַקְלִין.

1 In the Prayer Book *Mishnah* 21 commences here.   2 See 3[7].   3 By true repentance and good deeds.   Compare 3[11], 4[11].   4 Compare 3[16].

Mishnah 17

מִשְׁנָה יז

He[1] used to say, Better is one hour of repentance and good actions[2] in this world than the whole life of the world to come; and better is one hour of bliss[3] of spirit in the world to come than all the life of this world.

[1]הוּא הָיָה אוֹמֵר יָפָה שָׁעָה אַחַת
בִּתְשׁוּבָה [2]וּמַעֲשִׂים טוֹבִים בָּעוֹלָם
הַזֶּה מִכָּל חַיֵּי הָעוֹלָם הַבָּא; וְיָפָה
שָׁעָה אַחַת שֶׁל [3]קוֹרַת רוּחַ בָּעוֹלָם
הַבָּא מִכָּל חַיֵּי הָעוֹלָם הַזֶּה.

1 *i.e.*, R. Jacob.   *Mishnah* 22 begins here in the Prayer Book.   2 Compare 3[11], 4[11], 4[16].   3 Or קָרַת.

Mishnah 18

מִשְׁנָה יח

R.[1] Simon ben Elazar said, Do not placate thy fellow in the hour of his wrath,[2] and comfort him not in the hour[3] while his dead[4] lies before him,[5] and question him not in the

[1]רַבִּי שִׁמְעוֹן בֶּן אֶלְעָזָר אוֹמֵר אַל
תְּרַצֶּה אֶת־חֲבֵרְךָ בְּשָׁעַת [2]כַּעֲסוֹ,
וְאַל תְּנַחֲמֶנּוּ [3]בְּשָׁעָה שֶׁמֵּתוֹ [4]מוּטָל

72

hour of his vow,* and endeavour not to see him in the hour of§ his disgrace.

י־לְפָנָיו, וְאַל תִּשְׁאַל לוֹ בִּשְׁעַת יּנִדְרוֹ, וְאַל תִּשְׁתַּדֵּל לִרְאוֹתוֹ יּבִשְׁעַת קַלְקָלָתוֹ.

1 *Mishnah* 23 in the Prayer Book starts here. 2 Uncontrollable anger and fury must be first allowed to cool down before any attempt at appeasement and pacification is made. 3 Or the indefinite בְּשָׁעָה, *in an hour*. 4 Or מָשֵׁל. 5 Only after the burial is condolence offered to a mourner. *See ADDENDA at the end of this *Tractate*. §Popularly pronounced בְּשַׁעַת.

Mishnah 19   מִשְׁנָה יט

Samuel[1] the Younger[2] said, *Rejoice[3] not when thine enemy falleth,[4] and let not thine heart be glad when he stumbleth, lest the Eternal see it and it displease Him, and[5] he turn away his wrath from him* [to thee].[6]

יּשְׁמוּאֵל יּהַקָּטָן אוֹמֵר יּיבִּנְפוֹל אוֹיִבְךָ אַל תִּשְׂמָח וּבִכָּשְׁלוֹ אַל יָגֵל לִבֶּךָ פֶּן־יִרְאֶה ה' יּיָרַע בְּעֵינָיו וְהֵשִׁיב מֵעָלָיו אַפּוֹ.

1 *Mishnah* 24 starts here in the Prayer Book. 2 Some render it *the Little*. 3 *Proverbs* 24, 17. 4 בִּנְפֹל in Scripture. 5 *Proverbs* 24, 18. 6 Compare *Job* 31, 29.

Mishnah 20   מִשְׁנָה כ

Elisha[1] ben Abuyah said, If one learn as a child, what is it like? Like ink written on new paper.[2] He that learns as an old man, what is it like? To ink written on blotted paper.[3] R.[4] Jose ben R.[5] Judah of Kephar[6] ha-Babli said, If one learn from the young, to what is he like? To one that eats unripe grapes,[7] or drinks wine[8] from his winepress. And one who learns from the aged, to what is he like? To one that eats ripe grapes and drinks old wine. Rabbi[9] said, Look not at the flask[10] but at what is therein; there may be§ a new flask[10] full of old [wine], and an old [flask] wherein is not even new [wine].[11]   §Or קַנְקָן.

יּאֱלִישָׁע בֶּן אֲבוּיָה אוֹמֵר הַלּוֹמֵד יֶלֶד לְמָה הוּא דוֹמֶה? לִדְיוֹ כְּתוּבָה עַל יְנְיָר חָדָשׁ. וְהַלּוֹמֵד זָקֵן לְמָה הוּא דוֹמֶה? לִדְיוֹ כְּתוּבָה עַל יְנְיָר מָחוּק. יּרַבִּי יוֹסֵי יּבְּרַבִּי יְהוּדָה אִישׁ יּכְּפַר הַבַּבְלִי אוֹמֵר הַלּוֹמֵד מִן־ הַקְטַנִּים, לְמָה הוּא דוֹמֶה? לְאוֹכֵל יּעֲנָבִים קֵהוֹת וְשׁוֹתֶה יַיִן מִגִּתּוֹ. וְהַלּוֹמֵד מִן־הַזְּקֵנִים לְמָה הוּא דוֹמֶה? לְאוֹכֵל עֲנָבִים בְּשׁוּלוֹת וְשׁוֹתֶה יַיִן יָשָׁן. יּרַבִּי אוֹמֵר אַל תִּסְתַּכֵּל יּיּבַּקַנְקַן אֶלָּא בְּמַה־שֶּׁיֶּשׁ בּוֹ; יּיֵשׁ יּיקַנְקַן חָדָשׁ מָלֵא יָשָׁן וְיָשָׁן שֶׁאֲפִילוּ יּיּחָדָשׁ אֵין בּוֹ.

73

1 He was surnamed אַחֵר קָטָן מוֹעֵד 20a, חֲגִיגָה 14b). *Mishnah* 25 in the Prayer
Book begins here. **2** *i.e.*, clean paper. Or נְיָר. **3** Paper from which writing had
been rubbed out. **4** *Mishnah* 26 begins here in the Prayer Book. **5** Or בַּר* in
some texts (as in the Prayer Book). **6** A Galilean village. Compare עֵדוּיוֹת 6[1].
7 They set the teeth on edge. **8** *i.e.*, wine not properly matured. **9** רַבִּי מֵאִיר,
Rabbi Meir, in the Prayer Book. *Mishnah* 27 in the Prayer Book. **10** Popular
reading קַנְקַן, בְּקַנְקַן. **11** Compare עֵירוּבִין 27a. *See ADDENDA, Page 552.

Mishnah 21

R.[1] Elazar ha-Kapar[2] said, Envy,
(and) cupidity[3] and ambition take[4]
a man out of the world.[5]

רַבִּי אֶלְעָזָר הַקַּפָּר אוֹמֵר הַקִּנְאָה
וְהַתַּאֲוָה וְהַכָּבוֹד, מוֹצִיאִין אֶת־
הָאָדָם מִן־הָעוֹלָם.

מִשְׁנָה כא

1 *Mishnah* 28 begins here in the Prayer Book. **2** Or *Hakappar* (בְּרָכוֹת 63a). **3** Or
lust. **4** In the Prayer Book, מוֹצִיאִים. **5** Compare 2[16].

Mishnah 22

He[1] used to say, They that are born
[are destined] to die; and the dead
[are destined] to be brought to life
again;[2] and the living[3] [are destined
after death] to be judged,[4] to know,
to make known,[5] and to understand[6]
that He is God, He is the Maker, He
is the Creator, He is the Discerner,
He is the Judge, He is [the] Witness,
He is the Complainant.[7] And He[8]
it is that shall judge in future,
blessed be He, with Whom there is
no unrighteousness, nor forgetfulness, nor respect of persons,[9] nor
taking of bribes[10] for all is His;[11]
and know that everything is according to the reckoning; and let not
thy [evil] imagination[12] lull thee with
the hope that the grave will be a
refuge for thee;[13] for perforce wast
thou formed, (and[14] perforce wast
thou born), and thou livest despite
thyself, and despite thyself wilt thou

הוּא הָיָה אוֹמֵר הַיִּלּוֹדִים לָמוּת;
וְהַמֵּתִים לְהַחֲיוֹת; וְהַחַיִּים לִידוֹן
לֵידַע, לְהוֹדִיעַ, וּלְהִוָּדַע, שֶׁהוּא
אֵל, הוּא הַיּוֹצֵר הוּא הַבּוֹרֵא, הוּא
הַמֵּבִין, הוּא הַדַּיָּין, הוּא עֵד, הוּא
בַּעַל דִּין, יְהוּא עָתִיד לָדוּן, בָּרוּךְ
הוּא שֶׁאֵין לְפָנָיו לֹא עַוְלָה וְלֹא
שִׁכְחָה, וְלֹא מַשּׂוֹא פָנִים, וְלֹא מִקַּח
שׁוֹחַד שֶׁהַכֹּל שֶׁלּוֹ; וְדַע שֶׁהַכֹּל
לְפִי הַחֶשְׁבּוֹן; וְאַל יַבְטִיחֲךָ יִצְרְךָ
שֶׁהַשְּׁאוֹל בֵּית מָנוֹס יִלָךְ; שֶׁעַל
כָּרְחֲךָ אַתָּה נוֹצָר (וְעַל כָּרְחֲךָ
אַתָּה נוֹלָד), וְעַל כָּרְחַךָ אַתָּה חַי,
וְעַל כָּרְחַךָ אַתָּה מֵת, וְעַל כָּרְחֲךָ

מִשְׁנָה כב

74

die, and perforce in the hereafter wilt thou have to give[15] account and reckoning[16] before the Supreme King of kings,[17] the Holy One, blessed be He.

אַתָּה עָתִיד ¹⁴לִיתֵּן דִּין ¹⁵וְחֶשְׁבּוֹן לִפְנֵי ¹⁷מֶלֶךְ מַלְכֵי הַמְּלָכִים הַקָּדוֹשׁ בָּרוּךְ הוּא.

1 R. Elazar Hakappar. Here begins *Mishnah* 29 in the Prayer Book. 2 A reference to the belief in the resurrection of the dead. 3 *i.e.*, the resurrected. 4 לָדוּן in the Prayer Book. 5 In the Prayer Book, וּלְהוֹדִיעַ, *and to make known.* 6 Literally *and to be made to understand.* 7 Or *accuser, plaintiff.* 8 וְהוּא, *and He,* in the Prayer Book. 9 *i.e.*, partiality, favouritism. 10 Compare *II Chronicles* 19, 7. 11 וְהַכֹּל שֶׁלּוֹ is omitted in the Prayer Book. 12 *i.e.*, evil nature, wicked inclination. Compare 2¹⁶. 13 *viz.*, that there is no hereafter. 14 This phrase in parenthesis is given in the גְּמָרָא. 15 לִתֵּן? in the Prayer Book. 16 Compare 3¹. 17 Literally *the King of kings of kings.*

CHAPTER 5

Mishnah 1

With ten *Sayings*[1] was the world created. And What does this teach? Could it not have been created with one *Saying*? But [the purpose was] to requite the wicked that destroy[2] the world which was created by ten *Sayings*, and to bestow[2] the goodly reward upon the righteous who sustain[2] the world that was created with ten *Sayings*.

פֶּרֶק ה

מִשְׁנָה א

¹בַּעֲשָׂרָה מַאֲמָרוֹת נִבְרָא הָעוֹלָם. וּמַה־תַּלְמוּד לוֹמַר? וַהֲלֹא בְּמַאֲמָר אֶחָד יָכוֹל לְהִבָּרְאוֹת? אֶלָּא לְהִפָּרַע מִן־הָרְשָׁעִים ²שֶׁמְּאַבְּדִין אֶת־הָעוֹלָם שֶׁנִּבְרָא בַּעֲשָׂרָה מַאֲמָרוֹת, ²וְלִיתֵּן שָׂכָר טוֹב לַצַּדִּיקִים ²שֶׁמְּקַיְּמִין אֶת־הָעוֹלָם שֶׁנִּבְרָא בַּעֲשָׂרָה מַאֲמָרוֹת.

1 In *Genesis* 1, 3, 6, 9, 11, 14, 20, 24, 26, 29, and 2, 18* the formula וַיֹּאמֶר אֱלֹהִים, *and God 'said'* occurs ten times. Some consider *Genesis* 1, 1 should also be accounted as a *Saying* paralleled by *Psalm* 33, 6. *Actually וַיֹּאמֶר ה' אֱלֹהִים. See ADDENDA at the end of this *Tractate*. 2 In the Prayer Book, שֶׁמְּקַיְּמִים, וְלִתֵּן, שֶׁמְּאַבְּדִים, respectively.

Mishnah 2

There were ten generations[1] from Adam to[2] Noah[3] to make known how long-suffering* God is,[4] seeing that all the generations continued to provoke Him,[5] until He brought upon

מִשְׁנָה ב

עֲשָׂרָה ¹דוֹרוֹת מֵאָדָם ²עַד ³נֹחַ לְהוֹדִיעַ כַּמָּה אֶרֶךְ אַפַּיִם ⁴לְפָנָיו, שֶׁכָּל הַדּוֹרוֹת הָיוּ ⁵מַכְעִיסִין וּבָאִין,

75

them the waters of the Flood. There[6] were ten generations from Noah[7] to[2] Abraham,[8] to make known how long-suffering God is, for all those generations provoked Him continually,[5] until[9] Abraham came and received the reward they [should] all [have earned].[10]

עַד שֶׁהֵבִיא עֲלֵיהֶם אֶת־מֵי הַמַּבּוּל׃ ²עֲשָׂרָה דוֹרוֹת ³מִנֹּחַ יַעַד ⁸אַבְרָהָם, לְהוֹדִיעַ כַּמָּה ⁴אֶרֶךְ אַפַּיִם לְפָנָיו, שֶׁכָּל הַדּוֹרוֹת הָיוּ ⁵מַכְעִיסִין וּבָאִין יעַד שֶׁבָּא אַבְרָהָם וְקִבֵּל עָלָיו שָׂכַר ¹⁰כּוּלָם׃

1 דּוֹר = 100 years. See *Genesis* 5. 2 וְעַד in the Prayer Book. 3 Including Noah's years of life. 4 God, in His patience, awaited their repentance. 5 The Prayer Book gives מַכְעִיסִים לְפָנָיו instead of מַכְעִיסִין וּבָאִין. 6 Here begins *Mishnah* 3 in the Prayer Book. 7 *viz.*, after Noah's death. 8 See *Genesis* 11, 10ff. 9 The Prayer Book has עַד שֶׁבָּא אַבְרָהָם אָבִינוּ וְקִבֵּל שָׂכַר כֻּלָּם. 10 *sc.*, which they forfeited by their transgressions. *In some texts אֶרֶךְ.

Mishnah 3   מִשְׁנָה ג

With[1] *ten trials* was our father *Abraham*, peace be unto him,[2] tried,[3] yet he stood steadfast in them all,[4] to make manifest how great was the love of Abraham our father,[5] peace be unto him.[2]

¹עֲשָׂרָה נִסְיוֹנוֹת נִתְנַסָּה אַבְרָהָם אָבִינוּ יְעָלָיו הַשָּׁלוֹם וְעָמַד ⁴בְּכֻלָּם, לְהוֹדִיעַ כַּמָּה חִבָּתוֹ שֶׁל ⁵אַבְרָהָם אָבִינוּ יְעָלָיו הַשָּׁלוֹם׃

1 *Mishnah* 4 begins here in the Prayer Book. 2 עָלָיו הַשָּׁלוֹם is omitted in the Prayer Book. 3 They are enumerated in *33.* אָבוֹת דְּרַבִּי יוֹסָן 4 בְּכֻלָּם in the Prayer Book. 5 Compare *Isaiah* 41, 8. *See ADDENDA, Page 552.

Mishnah 4   מִשְׁנָה ד

Ten[1] *miracles** were wrought for our ancestors in Egypt,[2] and ten at the Sea.[3] (Ten[4] plagues did the Holy One, blessed be He, bring upon the Egyptians in Egypt, and ten[5] at the Sea.) With *ten*[6] *temptations*[7] did our forefathers tempt the *Omnipresent*,[8] blessed be He, in the wilderness, as it is said,[9] *yet have they put Me*[10] *to the proof these ten times, and have not hearkened to My voice.*

¹עֲשָׂרָה *נִסִּים נַעֲשׂוּ לַאֲבוֹתֵינוּ ²בְּמִצְרָיִם, וַעֲשָׂרָה עַל ³הַיָּם׃ (⁴עֶשֶׂר מַכּוֹת הֵבִיא הַקָּדוֹשׁ בָּרוּךְ הוּא עַל הַמִּצְרִיִּים בְּמִצְרַיִם וַעֲשָׂרָה עַל הַיָּם)׃ ⁶עֶשֶׂר ⁷נִסְיוֹנוֹת נִסּוּ אֲבוֹתֵינוּ אֶת־⁸הַמָּקוֹם בָּרוּךְ הוּא בַּמִּדְבָּר, ⁹שֶׁנֶּאֱמַר וַיְנַסּוּ¹⁰אוֹתִי זֶה עֶשֶׂר פְּעָמִים וְלֹא שָׁמְעוּ בְּקוֹלִי׃

76

1 *Mishnah* 5 in the Prayer Book commences here. 2 *i.e.*, the Ten Plagues (*Exodus* 7, 14 *et seq.*). 3 Inferred from *Exodus* 15 and enumerated in אֲבוֹת דְּרַבִּי יוֹנָתָן 33. 4 *Mishnah* 6 commences here in the Prayer Book. The part in parentheses is not given in the גְּמָרָא. 5 וְעֶשֶׂר in the Prayer Book. 6 In the Prayer Book עֶשָׂרָה. *Mishnah* 7 begins here in the Prayer Book. 7 See עֲרָכִין 15a.§ 8 The Prayer Book gives אֶת־הַקָּדוֹשׁ, *the* Holy One, instead of אֶת־הַמָּקוֹם. 9 *Numbers* 14, 22. 10 אֹתִי in the Scripture.
*§See ADDENDA, Pages *552, §553.

Mishnah 5

Ten[1] miracles were wrought for our forefathers[2] in the Temple: no woman miscarried from the odour of the holy flesh;[3] (and) the holy flesh never turned putrid; (and) no fly was [ever] seen in the slaughter-house; (and) no pollution[4] [ever] befell* the High Priest on the Day of Atonement; (and) rains[5] [never] quenched the fire of the wood-pile[6] [on the Altar], (and) neither did the wind [ever] prevail over the column of smoke[7] [that arose therefrom]; (and) [never] was there found a disqualifying defect in the *omer*,[8] or in the *two loaves*[9] or in the *shew-bread*;[10] [and though the people] stood pressed closely together, they yet found ample space to prostrate themselves;[11] (and) never did serpent or scorpion cause injury in Jerusalem; and no man ever said to his fellow, '*The*[12] place is too strait for me* that I should lodge [over night] in Jerusalem'.[13]

מִשְׁנָה ה

[1]עֲשָׂרָה נִסִּים נַעֲשׂוּ [2]לַאֲבוֹתֵינוּ בְּבֵית הַמִּקְדָּשׁ, לֹא הִפִּילָה אִשָּׁה מֵרֵיחַ [3]בְּשַׂר הַקֹּדֶשׁ; וְלֹא הִסְרִיחַ בְּשַׂר הַקֹּדֶשׁ מֵעוֹלָם; וְלֹא נִרְאָה זְבוּב בְּבֵית הַמִּטְבָּחַיִם; וְלֹא [4]אֵירַע [4]קֶרִי לְכֹהֵן גָּדוֹל בְּיוֹם הַכִּפּוּרִים; וְלֹא כִבּוּ [5]גְשָׁמִים אֵשׁ שֶׁל [6]עֲצֵי הַמַּעֲרָכָה; וְלֹא נִצְּחָה הָרוּחַ אֶת־עַמּוּד [7]הֶעָשָׁן; וְלֹא נִמְצָא פְּסוּל [8]בָּעֹמֶר, [9]וּבִשְׁתֵּי הַלֶּחֶם, [10]וּבְלֶחֶם הַפָּנִים; עוֹמְדִים צְפוּפִים [11]וּמִשְׁתַּחֲוִים רְוָחִים; וְלֹא הִזִּיק נָחָשׁ וְעַקְרָב בִּירוּשָׁלַיִם מֵעוֹלָם; וְלֹא אָמַר אָדָם לַחֲבֵרוֹ [12]צַר לִי הַמָּקוֹם שֶׁאָלִין [13]בִּירוּשָׁלָיִם.

1 *Mishnah* 8 in the Prayer Book starts here. 2 Compare יוֹמָא 21b. 3 Of the sacrifices. 4 Pollution would have disqualified him from officiating. See יוֹמָא 21[1]. 5 הַגְּשָׁמִים, *the rains*, in the Prayer Book. 6 See פְּסָחִים 59b. 7 See יוֹמָא 21b. 8 Of new barley, offered on the second day of פֶּסַח. *Leviticus* 23, 19ff. 9 The 'first-fruits' of the wheat harvest, offered on שָׁבוּעוֹת. *Leviticus* 23, 17. 10 *Exodus* 25, 30; *Leviticus* 24, 5-9. 11 On the Day of Atonement. 12 *Isaiah* 49, 20. 13 Even during the crowded periods of the שָׁלֹשׁ רְגָלִים. * אֶרֶע in some texts.

77

Mishnah 6

'Ten¹ things were created on the eve
of Sabbath in the twilight,² and
these are: the mouth of the earth,³
(and) the mouth* of the well,⁴ (and)
the mouth* of the she-ass,⁵ (and)
the rainbow,* ⁶ (and) the manna,⁷
(and) the rod,⁸ (and) the Shamir,⁹
(and) the writing,¹⁰ (and) the writing
tool,¹¹ and the Tables [of Stone];¹²
some say, [also] the destroying
spirits,¹³ (and) the sepulchre of
Moses,¹⁴ and the ram¹⁵ of Abraham
our father; and others say, [also]
tongs¹⁶ made with tongs.¹⁷ * The
conjunction ‎ו or ‎וְ is ommited in the
Prayer Book.

מִשְׁנָה ו

‎יְעֲשָׂרָה דְבָרִים נִבְרְאוּ בְּעֶרֶב שַׁבָּת

‎יְבֵין הַשְּׁמָשׁוֹת, וְאֵלּוּ הֵן, ⁱⁱפִי הָאָרֶץ,

‎ⁱⁱⁱוּפִי הַבְּאֵר,   ⁱᵛוּפִי הָאָתוֹן,

‎ⁱⁱⁱⁱוְהַקֶּשֶׁת,   וְהַמָּן,   וְהַמַּטֶּה,

‎ⁱⁱⁱⁱוְהַשָּׁמִיר,   ᵛⁱⁱⁱוְהַכְּתָב,   ⁱⁱⁱⁱⁱוְהַמִּכְתָּב,

‎ⁱⁱⁱⁱוְהַלּוּחוֹת; וְיֵשׁ אוֹמְרִים אַף

‎ⁱⁱⁱⁱⁱהַמַּזִּיקִין, ⁱⁱⁱⁱⁱⁱⁱוּקְבוּרָתוֹ שֶׁל מֹשֶׁה,

‎ⁱⁱⁱⁱⁱⁱⁱוְאֵילוֹ שֶׁל אַבְרָהָם אָבִינוּ ; וְיֵשׁ

‎אוֹמְרִים אַף ⁱⁱⁱⁱⁱⁱⁱⁱצְבָת ⁱⁱⁱⁱⁱⁱⁱⁱⁱבִּצְבָת עֲשׂוּיָה.

---

1 *Mishnah* 9 starts here in the Prayer Book. 2 When the first Sabbath began
(Genesis 2, 3). 3 *Numbers 16, 32*. Where Korah and his associates were engulfed.
4 *Numbers 21, 16-18*. Which supplied the Israelites with water. 5 *Numbers 22, 28*.
Balaam's ass. 6 *Genesis 9, 13*. 7 *Exodus 16, 14, 15*. 8 *Exodus 4, 17*. Moses' rod.
Tradition says it belonged to Adam. 9 Literally *diamond, flint*. See ‎גִּיטִּין 68a;
‎סוֹטָה 48b. The *Shamir* here referred to was a legendary worm, which, when placed
upon the hardest stone, had the power of splitting it instantly, and was used by
King Solomon in the building of the Temple, in the construction of which and of
the Altar no iron tool—the symbol of war and disharmony—was to be employed.§
The *Shamir* was credited with other miraculous properties, and it vanished from earth
at the destruction of the Temple. 10 Some render this by *the writing on the Tables of
Stone*, and others by *the miraculous character of the letters of the Decalogue* which though
cut through the Stone Tablets could be read on both sides (or on the four sides)
and yet did not fall out of their position. 11 *i.e., the engraving instrument, the style.*
Some say this refers to the *miraculous characters* (see the preceding **Note**). Compare
‎מְגִילָה 2a. 12 The first Tablets of Stone (whose fragments were deposited in the
Ark—‎בָּבָא בַּתְרָא 14b—together with the flask of manna—‎יוֹמָא 22b). *Exodus 32,*
15, 16. 13 This must be taken to refer to evil inclinations as the belief in demonology
is forbidden to Jews. 14 *Deuteronomy 34, 6*. God must have made it seeing that
none know its location. 15 *Genesis 22, 13*. Its presence in the thicket was pre-
ordained. 16 Popular pronunciation ‎צְבָת, ‎בִּצְבָת, as given in the Prayer Book.
17 An attempt by the *Mishnah* to explain who fashioned the tongs to hold the first
tongs being made. §Compare *Exodus 20, 22*.

Mishnah 7

There[1,2] are seven characteristics of an uncultured person,[3] and seven of a wise man.[4] A wise man does not speak before one who is superior[5] to him in wisdom; (and) he does not break in upon the words of his fellow; (and) he is not hasty to answer; he questions in accordance with the subject matter, and makes answer to the point;[6] (and) he speaks upon the first thing first, and upon the last thing last;[7] (and) regarding what he has not heard he says, 'I do not understand it';[8] and he admits the truth.[9] And the reverse of [all] these is characteristic of an uncultured man.[10]

מִשְׁנָה ז

שִׁבְעָה דְבָרִים בְּגֹלֶם, וְשִׁבְעָה בְּחָכָם. חָכָם אֵינוֹ מְדַבֵּר בִּפְנֵי מִי שֶׁהוּא גָדוֹל מִמֶּנּוּ בְּחָכְמָה; וְאֵינוֹ נִכְנָס לְתוֹךְ דִּבְרֵי חֲבֵרוֹ; וְאֵינוֹ נִבְהָל לְהָשִׁיב; שׁוֹאֵל כָּעִנְיָן, וּמֵשִׁיב כַּהֲלָכָה; וְאוֹמֵר עַל רִאשׁוֹן רִאשׁוֹן, וְעַל אַחֲרוֹן אַחֲרוֹן; וְעַל מַה־שֶׁלֹּא שָׁמַע אוֹמֵר לֹא שָׁמָעְתִּי; וּמוֹדֶה עַל הָאֱמֶת. וְחִלּוּפֵיהֶן בְּגֹלֶם.

1 *Mishnah* 10 begins here in the Prayer Book. 2 *sc.*, distinguishing marks in conversation. 3 *i.e.*, one not learned, an uneducated person, a boor. 4 *i.e.*, learned, educated, tutored, scholarly. 5 In the Prayer Book, שֶׁגָּדוֹל instead of שֶׁהוּא גָדוֹל. 6 *i.e.*, his reply is relevant to received doctrine (*Halachah*). 7 *viz.*, he is methodical and systematic. 8 Literally '*I have not heard*,' *sc.*, he admits his ignorance. 9 He does not obstinately hold to his opinion when he has been convinced of his error. 10 In the Prayer Book, וְחִלּוּפֵיהֶם בְּגֹלֶם.

Mishnah 8

Seven[1] kinds of retribution[2] come[3] into the world for seven cardinal transgressions. If[3] some give tithes and others do not give tithes,[5] a famine from drought ensues,[4] some suffering hunger while others have sufficient. If[6] they [all] resolve not to give tithes, a dearth from tumult[7] and drought ensues.[8] (And) [if they all determine] not[9] to set apart the *dough-offering*,[10] there comes[8] an exterminating dearth. Pestilence[11] comes into the world because of the

מִשְׁנָה ח

שִׁבְעָה מִינֵי פּוּרְעָנִיּוֹת בָּאִין לָעוֹלָם, עַל שִׁבְעָה גוּפֵי עֲבֵירָה. מִקְצָתָן מְעַשְּׂרִין, וּמִקְצָתָן אֵינָן מְעַשְּׂרִין, רָעָב שֶׁל בַּצֹּרֶת בָּאָה, מִקְצָתָן רְעֵבִים, וּמִקְצָתָן שְׂבֵעִים. גָּמְרוּ שֶׁלֹּא לְעַשֵּׂר, רָעָב שֶׁל מְהוּמָה וְשֶׁל בַּצֹּרֶת בָּאָה. וְשֶׁלֹּא לִטּוֹל אֶת־הַחַלָּה, רָעָב שֶׁל כְּלָיָה

79

death-penalties enjoined in the Law, with[12] whose infliction however the human courts of justice are not empowered, and for [the transgression of the law] regarding the produce of the *Seventh year*.[13] The sword[14] comes[15] into the world because of the delay of justice[16] and for the perversion of justice, and on account of [the offence of] them that interpret the Law not in accordance with strict tradition.[17]

יֶבָּאָה· ¹¹יֶדֶבֶר בָּא לָעוֹלָם, עַל מִיתוֹת הָאֲמוּרוֹת בַּתּוֹרָה ¹²שֶׁלֹּא נִמְסְרוּ לְבֵית דִּין, וְעַל פֵּירוֹת ¹³שְׁבִיעִית· ¹⁴חֶרֶב ¹⁵בָּא לָעוֹלָם, עַל ¹⁶עִנּוּי הַדִּין, וְעַל עִוּוּת הַדִּין, וְעַל הַמּוֹרִים בַּתּוֹרָה שֶׁלֹּא ¹⁷כַהֲלָכָה·

---

1 *Mishnah* 11 in the Prayer Book begins here.   **2** פָּרְעָנִיּוֹת in the Prayer Book. **3** In the Prayer Book, בָּאִים; and likewise מִקְצָתָם מְעַשְּׂרִים וּמִקְצָתָם אֵינָם מְעַשְּׂרִים. **4** The first retribution.   **5** Thus depriving the priests, the Levites and the needy of their just dues. See *Appendix*, **Note 1.**   **6** The second retribution.   **7** *i.e.*, war and destruction.   **8** בָּא, more grammatically correct, in the Prayer Book.   **9** The third retribution.   **10** *Numbers* 15, 20.   *Appendix*, **Note 3.**   **11** The fourth retribution, for failure to punish the criminal and for neglect of the poor.   **12** Some render this: *but are not brought before human tribunals.*   **13** *Leviticus* 25, 1-7, 26, 9; שְׁבִיעִית, INTRODUCTION.   **14** The fifth retribution (see the next *Mishnah*).   **15** In the Prayer Book, בָּאָה more grammatically correct.   **16** And unnecessary, undue postponement of a legal decision.   **17** Confusing prohibitions and permissions (see שַׁבָּת 33).

Mishnah 9

מִשְׁנָה ט

Noxious beasts[1] come into the world because of perjury,[2] and for the profanation of the Divine Name. Captivity[3] ensues[4] in the world on account of idolatry,[5] (and) because of incest, (and) for bloodshed,[6] and on account of [the neglect of the year of] *the release for the land*.[7] At[8] four periods does pestilence increase, in the fourth year, (and) in the seventh year, (and) at the conclusion of the seventh year, and at the conclusion of the Festival of Tabernacles[9] in each year. In the fourth years because of [the disregard

¹חַיָּה רָעָה בָּאָה לָעוֹלָם, עַל ²שְׁבוּעַת שָׁוְא, וְעַל חִלּוּל הַשֵּׁם· יָגָלוּת ³בָּא ⁴לָעוֹלָם, עַל ⁵עֲבוֹדַת כּוֹכָבִים, וְעַל גִּלּוּי עֲרָיוֹת, וְעַל ⁶שְׁפִיכַת דָּמִים, וְעַל ⁷הַשְׁמָטַת הָאָרֶץ· ⁸בְּאַרְבָּעָה פְרָקִים הַדֶּבֶר מִתְרַבֶּה, בָּרְבִיעִית, וּבַשְׁבִיעִית, וּבְמוֹצָאֵי שְׁבִיעִית, וּבְמוֹצָאֵי ⁹הֶחָג שֶׁבְּכָל שָׁנָה וְשָׁנָה· בָּרְבִיעִית, מִפְּנֵי

80

of] *the poor-man's tithe*[10] in the third year; in the seventh year, for default of [giving] *the poor-man's tithe* in the sixth year; (and] at the conclusion of[11] the seventh year, because of [violating the laws] regarding *the produce*[12] *of the seventh year*; and at the conclusion[11] of the Festival of Tabernacles in each year,

מַעֲשַׂר עָנִי שֶׁבַּשְּׁלִישִׁית; בַּשְּׁבִיעִית, מִפְּנֵי מַעֲשַׂר עָנִי שֶׁבַּשִּׁשִּׁית; וּבְמוֹצָאֵי שְׁבִיעִית, מִפְּנֵי פֵּירוֹת שְׁבִיעִית; וּבְמוֹצָאֵי הֶחָג שֶׁבְּכָל שָׁנָה וְשָׁנָה, מִפְּנֵי גֶּזֶל מַתְּנוֹת עֲנִיִּים.

for robbing[13] the poor of the dues [granted to them].[14]

---

1 Literally *an evil beast*. In the Prayer Book, the next two sentences are part of *Mishnah* 11; they are the *sixth* and *seventh retributions* begun in the preceding paragraph. 2 Compare יוֹמָא 86a. Devastated lands become infested by wild, noisome beasts. 3 Or *exile*. 4 בָּאָה, more correct grammatically, in the Prayer Book. 5 עֲבוֹדַת אֱלִילִים in some texts. 6 שְׁפִיכוּת in the Prayer Book. 7 *Leviticus* 25, 3ff., 26, 4ff. *Deuteronomy* 15, 1. It is most difficult to vowelise השמטת to agree with the given rendering, seeing it is a *construct* form with the *definite article* ־ה; שְׁמִטַּת, as given in the Prayer Book, is grammatically correct. Perhaps it might be vocalised הַשְׁמָטַת, the *construct* form of הַשְׁמָטָה, and render the phrase by [*for the non-observance of the law of*] *the restoration of real estate to the vendor in the year of the jubilee*. 8 Here commences *Mishnah* 12 in the Prayer Book. 9 סֻכּוֹת (Feast of Tabernacles) is termed חַג in the *Mishnah*. 10 *Deuteronomy* 14, 28ff. See *Appendix*, **Note 1**; מַעַשְׂרוֹת, INTRODUCTION. 11 בְּמוֹצָאֵי, *at the conclusion of*, in the Prayer Book. 12 Perhaps, preferably, פֵּירוֹת. 13 Or גֵּזֶל, גֵּל. 14 *viz.*, לֶקֶט (gleanings), שִׁכְחָה (*forgotten sheaf*), פֵּאָה (*field corners*). *Leviticus* 19, 9, 10, 23, 22; *Deuteronomy* 14, 28, 29, 24, 19-22. See *Appendix*, **Note 1**; פֵּאָה, INTRODUCTION.

Mishnah 10

There[1] are four [kinds of] characters among men: he that says, 'What is mine is mine and what is thine is thine', this[2] is the average[3] character, and some say this is a characteristic of Sodom;[4] [he who says,] What is mine is thine and what is thine is mine',[5] [such is] an ignoramus; [one that says,] 'What is mine is thine and what is thine is thine',[6] [he is] a saintly person; [and one who says,] 'What[7] is mine is mine and what is thine is mine', [he is] a wicked man.

מִשְׁנָה י

אַרְבַּע מִדּוֹת בְּאָדָם, הָאוֹמֵר שֶׁלִּי שֶׁלִּי וְשֶׁלְּךָ שֶׁלָּךְ· זוֹ מִדָּה בֵּינוֹנִית, וְיֵשׁ אוֹמְרִים זוֹ מִדַּת סְדוֹם; שֶׁלִּי שֶׁלָּךְ וְשֶׁלְּךָ שֶׁלִּי, עַם הָאָרֶץ; שֶׁלִּי שֶׁלָּךְ וְשֶׁלְּךָ שֶׁלָּךְ, חָסִיד; שֶׁלִּי שֶׁלִּי וְשֶׁלְּךָ שֶׁלִּי, רָשָׁע.

§ Or וְיֵשׁ־אוֹמְרִים.

81

1 In the Prayer Book, *Mishnah* 13 commences here. **2** Popular pronunciation זו.*
3 Or *common, ordinary, neutral.* **4** *i.e., selfishness, uncharitableness.* **5** This would be
tantamount to social insecurity and instability, leading to anarchy. Compare 3[2].
6 Charity that knows no bounds. **7** שֶׁלְּךָ שֶׁלִּי וְשֶׁלִּי שֶׁלִּי, '*What is thine is mine and
what is mine is mine,*' in the Prayer Book.*

Mishnah 11

There[1] are four types of tempera-
ments: [one whom it is] easy to
anger and easy to pacify, his gain
disappears in his loss;[2]* [he whom
it is] hard to incense and hard to
appease, his loss vanishes in his
gain;[3]* [one whom it is] hard to
provoke and easy to placate is a
saintly man;[4] [he whom it is] easy
to vex and hard to mollify is a
wicked man.

מִשְׁנָה יא

י‎אַרְבַּע מִדּוֹת בְּדֵעוֹת, נוֹחַ לִכְעוֹס
וְנוֹחַ לִרְצוֹת, יָצָא שְׂכָרוֹ *בְּהֶפְסֵדוֹ ;
קָשֶׁה לִכְעוֹס וְקָשֶׁה לִרְצוֹת, יָצָא
*הֶפְסֵדוֹ בִּשְׂכָרוֹ ; קָשֶׁה לִכְעוֹס וְנוֹחַ
לִרְצוֹת יָחָסִיד ; נוֹחַ לִכְעוֹס וְקָשֶׁה
לִרְצוֹת רָשָׁע.

* Some vocalise these הֶפְסֵדוֹ, בְּהֶפְסֵדוֹ.

1 Here starts *Mishnah* 14 in the Prayer Book. **2** This is the formula in the גְּמָרָא ;
the Prayer Book gives יָצָא הֶפְסֵדוֹ בִּשְׂכָרוֹ, *his loss disappears in his gain.* **3** This is
the formula in the גְּמָרָא ; the Prayer Book has יָצָא שְׂכָרוֹ בְּהֶפְסֵדוֹ, *his gain vanishes
in his loss.* **4** Nevertheless the good man should show his displeasure and indignation
at the violation of truth, justice and righteous conduct of every kind.

Mishnah 12

There[1] are four characteristic qualities[2] in disciples: [he that is] quick[3]
of perception and quick[3] to forget,
his gain disappears in his loss;* [one
who has] difficulty in perceiving
but forgets with difficulty his loss*
vanishes in his gain; [he who is]
swift[3] of perception and forgets with
difficulty is a wise man;[4] [and one
that finds it] difficult to perceive
and quickly[3] forgets, this[5] is an
evil lot.

מִשְׁנָה יב

י‎אַרְבַּע יְמִדּוֹת בְּתַלְמִידִים, יְמַהֵר
לִשְׁמֹעַ יוּמַהֵר לְאַבֵּד, יָצָא שְׂכָרוֹ
בְּהֶפְסֵדוֹ ; קָשֶׁה לִשְׁמֹעַ וְקָשֶׁה
לְאַבֵּד, יָצָא הֶפְסֵדוֹ בִּשְׂכָרוֹ ; יְמַהֵר
לִשְׁמֹעַ וְקָשֶׁה לְאַבֵּד, יָחָכָם ; קָשֶׁה
לִשְׁמֹעַ יוּמַהֵר לְאַבֵּד, יְזֶה חֵלֶק
רָע.

* See the preceding *Mishnah.*

1 *Mishnah* 15 starts here in the Prayer Book. This paragraph does not deal with
any moral principles. **2** *i.e.,* mental abilities. **3** In the Prayer Book, וּמָהִיר, מָהִיר.

4 The Prayer Book gives זוֹ חֵלֶק טוֹב . . . ., *perceiving quickly and forgetting with difficulty, this is a good portion.* **5** זוֹ (זֶה) in the Prayer Book. See Volume II, Page 12.

Mishnah 13

There[1] are four characteristic types among those that give alms: one who desires to give, but not that others should give, his eye is evil towards what pertains to others;[2] he that wishes that others should give, but he himself will not give, his eye is evil towards what appertains to him;[3] one that gives, and [desires that] others should give, he is a saintly man;[4] he who will not give, and [is] not [minded] that others should give, is a wicked man.[5]

מִשְׁנָה יג

יֹֽאַרְבַּע מִדּוֹת בְּנוֹתְנֵי צְדָקָה, הָרוֹצֶה שֶׁיִּתֵּן וְלֹא יִתְּנוּ אֲחֵרִים, עֵינוֹ רָעָה בְּשֶׁל אֲחֵרִים; יִתְּנוּ אֲחֵרִים, וְהוּא לֹא יִתֵּן, עֵינוֹ רָעָה בְּשֶׁלּוֹ; יִתֵּן וְיִתְּנוּ אֲחֵרִים, חָסִיד; לֹא יִתֵּן וְלֹא יִתְּנוּ אֲחֵרִים, רָשָׁע׃

1 In the Prayer Book *Mishnah* 16 starts here. **2** *i.e.*, he grudges others the joy and merit of almsgiving and charitable deeds. **3** He is indifferent to the acquisition for himself of merit for charitable acts. **4** He possesses the disposition of the universal benefactor. **5** He is indifferent and unsympathetic towards human suffering and distress.

Mishnah 14

There[1] are four kinds of dispositions in those that attend the house[2] of study: one who goes[3] but does not practise[4] has the reward for going; he that practises[4] but does not go has the reward for practising; one that goes and practises[4] is a saintly man;[5] [and] he who neither goes nor practises[4] is a wicked man.[6]

מִשְׁנָה יד

יֹֽאַרְבַּע מִדּוֹת בְּהוֹלְכֵי יֹלְבֵית הַמִּדְרָשׁ, הוֹלֵךְ וְאֵינוֹ עוֹשֶׂה, שְׂכַר הֲלִיכָה בְּיָדוֹ; עוֹשֶׂה וְאֵינוֹ הוֹלֵךְ, שְׂכַר מַעֲשֶׂה בְּיָדוֹ; הוֹלֵךְ וְעוֹשֶׂה, חָסִיד; לֹא הוֹלֵךְ וְלֹא עוֹשֶׂה, רָשָׁע׃

1 Here begins *Mishnah* 17 in the Prayer Book. **2** In the Prayer Book, בֵּית Attendance for the acquisition of religious and spiritual knowledge, leading to virtuous conduct. Compare 1¹⁷, 3⁹, 1⁷. **3** Compare בָּבָא קַמָּא 17a. **4** *viz.*, studies the Law and practises good deeds. וְעָשָׂה, עָשָׂה, in the Prayer Book. **5** He makes every effort to acquire knowledge to lead a virtuous life. **6** He possesses no knowledge to distinguish between good and evil and—in consequence—leads an unrighteous existence.

Mishnah 15

There[1] are four characteristic traits among them that sit in the presence of the wise: [they are like] a sponge, a funnel, a strainer, and a sieve.[2] A sponge—which absorbs everything;[3] a funnel[4]—that lets in at one end and discharges at the other; a strainer—which lets out the wine and retains the lees;[5] and a sieve—which lets the coarse flour pass out and retains the fine flour.[6]

מִשְׁנָה טו

ⁱאַרְבַּע מִדּוֹת בְּיוֹשְׁבִים לִפְנֵי חֲכָמִים, סְפוֹג, וּמַשְׁפֵּךְ, מְשַׁמֶּרֶת, יֿוָפָה. סְפוֹג, שֶׁהוּא סוֹפֵג אֶת־הַכֹּל; ⁱמַשְׁפֵּךְ, שֶׁמַּכְנִיס בְּזוֹ וּמוֹצִיא בְזוֹ; מְשַׁמֶּרֶת, שֶׁמּוֹצִיאָה אֶת הַיַּיִן וְקוֹלֶטֶת אֶת־יֿהַשְּׁמָרִים; וְנָפָה, שֶׁמּוֹצִיאָה אֶת־הַקֶּמַח וְקוֹלֶטֶת אֶת־יֿהַסֹּלֶת׃

1 *Mishnah* 18 begins here in the Prayer Book. 2 נָפָה, *a fine sieve or sifter* [כְּבָרָה, *a coarse sieve*]. 3 *i.e.*, the disciple learns the trivial and important without discrimination. 4 וּמַשְׁפֵּךְ, *and a funnel*, in the Prayer Book. Compare 5¹², 'quick to perceive and quick to forget.' בְּזוֹ, חֹו,* in the Prayer Book. Literally *at this, at that.* 5 *i.e.*, the disciple forgets the essentials but retains the unimportant. 6 *i.e.*, the disciple memorises the good and rejects the worthless. *See Volume II, Page 12.

Mishnah 16

If[1] love depend on some material cause,[2] and the material cause passes away, the love vanishes [too]; but if it do not depend upon some material cause, it will never pass away. Which[3] love was it that was dependent[4] on a material cause? This[3] was the love of Amnon and Tamar.[5] And [which love was it] that was not dependent on a material cause? Such[3] was the love of David and Jonathan.[6]

מִשְׁנָה טז

ⁱכָּל־אַהֲבָה שֶׁהִיא תְלוּיָה יֿבְדָבָר, בָּטֵל דָּבָר, בָּטְלָה אַהֲבָה; וְשֶׁאֵינָה תְלוּיָה בְדָבָר, אֵינָה בְּטֵלָה לְעוֹלָם׃ ⁱאֵיזוֹ הִיא אַהֲבָה יֿהַתְּלוּיָה בְדָבָר? ⁱזוֹ אַהֲבַת יֿאַמְנוֹן וְתָמָר׃ וְשֶׁאֵינָה תְלוּיָה בְדָבָר? ⁱזוֹ אַהֲבַת יֿדָוִד וִיהוֹנָתָן׃

1 *Mishnah* 19 in the Prayer Book begins here. Literally *All love that depends.* 2 An absence of morality. 3 Love for self-gratification is immoral and not enduring. 4 In the Prayer Book, שֶׁהִיא תְלוּיָה. 5 *II Samuel* 13, 1ff. 6 *I Samuel* 18, 1; *II Samuel* 1, 26.

Mishnah 17

Every[1] controversy that is for God's sake[2] shall in the end lead to a lasting result, but [any controversy] that is not for God's sake[3] shall not in the end be permanent. Which controversy was it that was for God's sake? This was the controversy[4] of Hillel and Shammai.[5] And which [controversy] was not for God's sake? Such[3] was the controversy[6] of Korah and all his faction.[7]

מִשְׁנָה יז

^יכָּל־מַחֲלוֹקֶת שֶׁהִיא ^בלְשֵׁם שָׁמַיִם סוֹפָהּ לְהִתְקַיֵּים, וְשֶׁאֵינָהּ לְשֵׁם שָׁמַיִם אֵין סוֹפָהּ לְהִתְקַיֵּים· אֵיזוֹ הִיא מַחֲלוֹקֶת שֶׁהִיא לְשֵׁם שָׁמַיִם? זוֹ ^דמַחֲלוֹקֶת הִלֵּל ^הוְשַׁמַּאי· וְשֶׁאֵינָהּ לְשֵׁם שָׁמַיִם? זוֹ ^ומַחֲלוֹקֶת ^זקֹרַח וְכָל־עֲדָתוֹ·

1 In the Prayer Book *Mishnah* 20 commences here. 2 Literally *in the name of Heaven*.
3 There is no sincerity for truth. 4 The search for moral truths. 5 וְשַׁמַּי in the Prayer Book. 6 A political rebellion against established authority.
7 *Numbers* 16, 1ff. וְכָל עֲדָתוֹ, *and all his company*, is omitted in some editions.

Mishnah 18

Whosoever[1] causes the multitude to be righteous, through him shall no sin be brought about,[2] but one that leads the many to sin, to him shall not be given[3] the means to repentance.[4] Moses was righteous and he made the many righteous;[5] the righteousness of the many can be attributed to him, as it is said,[6] *He executed the justice of the Eternal, and His judgments with Israel.* Jeroboam[7] sinned and caused the multitude to sin; the sin of the many was laid upon him, as it is said,[8] *For the sins of Jeroboam, the son of Nebat,*[9] *which he sinned, and wherewith he made Israel to sin.*

מִשְׁנָה יח

^יכָּל־הַמְזַכֶּה אֶת־הָרַבִּים, אֵין חֵטְא ^בבָּא עַל יָדוֹ, וְכָל הַמַּחֲטִיא אֶת־הָרַבִּים אֵין ^גמַסְפִּיקִין בְּיָדוֹ לַעֲשׂוֹת ^דתְּשׁוּבָה· מֹשֶׁה זָכָה ^הוְזִכָּה אֶת־הָרַבִּים זְכוּת הָרַבִּים תָּלוּי בּוֹ, ^ושֶׁנֶּאֱמַר צִדְקַת ה' עָשָׂה וּמִשְׁפָּטָיו עִם יִשְׂרָאֵל· יָרָבְעָם ^זחָטָא וְהֶחֱטִיא אֶת־הָרַבִּים חֵטְא הָרַבִּים תָּלוּי בּוֹ, ^חשֶׁנֶּאֱמַר עַל חַטֹּאות יָרָבְעָם ^טבֶּן נְבָט אֲשֶׁר חָטָא וַאֲשֶׁר הֶחֱטִיא אֶת־יִשְׂרָאֵל·

1 Here commences *Mishnah* 21 in the Prayer Book. 2 Compare יוֹמָא 86a.
3 מַסְפִּיקִים in the Prayer Book. 4 The transgressions of others being beyond the remedial action of his penitence (יוֹמָא 87a). 5 In the Prayer Book, חִכָּה.
6 *Deuteronomy* 33, 21. 7 In the Prayer Book בֶּן נְבָט, *the son of Nebat*, is inserted here.

8 *I Kings* 15, 30. 9 בֶּן נְבָט is not given in Scripture and is omitted in the Prayer Book.

Mishnah 19

מִשְׁנָה יט

Whosoever[1] has[2]* these three qualities is of the disciples[3] of Abraham our father; but [he in whom there are] three other attributes is of the disciples[3] of Balaam the wicked. A good eye,* (and) a lowly mind and a humble soul [are the traits] of the disciples of Abraham our father; an evil eye,§ (and) a haughty[4] mind and a proud soul [are the characteristics] of the disciples of Balaam the wicked. What is the difference[5] between the disciples of our father Abraham and the disciples of the wicked Balaam? The disciples of our father Abraham enjoy[6] this world and inherit[7] the world to come, as it is said,[8] *That I may cause those that love me[9] to inherit substance,[10] and that I may fill their treasuries.[11]* But[12] the disciples of the wicked Balaam inherit *Gehenna*[13] and descend[14] to the pit of destruction, as it is said,[15] *But Thou, O God, wilt bring them down[16] into the pit of destruction; bloodthirsty and deceitful men shall not live out half their days, but as for me, I will trust in Thee.* * Or שֶׁיֶּשׁ־בְּיָדוֹ.

יׄכָּל־מִי *שֶׁיֵּשׁ *בְּיָדוֹ שְׁלֹשָׁה דְבָרִים
הַלָּלוּ, מִתַּלְמִידָיו שֶׁל אַבְרָהָם
אָבִינוּ ; וּשְׁלֹשָׁה דְבָרִים אֲחֵרִים,
יׄמִתַּלְמִידָיו שֶׁל בִּלְעָם הָרָשָׁע· יׄעַיִן
טוֹבָה וְרוּחַ נְמוּכָה וְנֶפֶשׁ שְׁפָלָה
מִתַּלְמִידָיו שֶׁל אַבְרָהָם אָבִינוּ ; יׄ§עַיִן
רָעָה וְרוּחַ יׄגָּבוֹהַּ וְנֶפֶשׁ רְחָבָה
מִתַּלְמִידָיו שֶׁל בִּלְעָם הָרָשָׁע· יׄמַה־
בֵּין תַּלְמִידָיו שֶׁל אַבְרָהָם אָבִינוּ
לְתַלְמִידָיו שֶׁל בִּלְעָם הָרָשָׁע ? יׄ
תַּלְמִידָיו שֶׁל אַבְרָהָם אָבִינוּ יׄאוֹכְלִין
בָּעוֹלָם הַזֶּה יׄוְנוֹחֲלִין בָּעוֹלָם הַבָּא,
יׄשֶׁנֶּאֱמַר לְהַנְחִיל יׄאוֹהֲבַי יׄꞌꞌיֵשׁ
יׄוְאוֹצְרוֹתֵיהֶם אֲמַלֵּא· יׄאֲבָל
תַּלְמִידָיו שֶׁל בִּלְעָם הָרָשָׁע יוֹרְשִׁים
יׄגֵּיהִנָּם יׄוְיוֹרְדִין לִבְאֵר שָׁחַת,
יׄשֶׁנֶּאֱמַר וְאַתָּה אֱלֹהִים יׄתּוֹרִידֵם
לִבְאֵר שַׁחַת אַנְשֵׁי דָמִים וּמִרְמָה
לֹא־יֶחֱצוּ יְמֵיהֶם וַאֲנִי אֶבְטַח בָּךְ·

1 Here in the Prayer Book starts *Mishnah 22*. 2 שֶׁיֵּשׁ־בּוֹ is given in the Prayer Book. 3 The Prayer Book has הוּא מִתַּלְמִידָיו. 4 In the Prayer Book, גְּבוֹהָה, grammatically more correct. 5 In their ultimate destiny. 6 אוֹכְלִים in the Prayer Book. Literally *eat*. 7 וְנוֹחֲלִים in the Prayer Book. 8 *Proverbs* 8, 21. 9 Compare *Isaiah* 41, 8. The Scriptural orthography is אֹהֲבַי. 10 Spiritually, of the Hereafter. 11 The Scriptural orthography is וְאֹצְרֹתֵיהֶם which is given in the Prayer Book. 12 אֲבָל is omitted in the Prayer Book. 13 Compare 1⁵. 14 וְיוֹרְדִים in the Prayer Book. 15 *Psalm* 55, 24. 16 תּוֹרִדֵם is the Scripture orthography. **i.e.*, contented, not covetous. §*i.e.*, discontented, jealous, covetous.

Mishnah 20

Judah[1] ben Tema said, Be strong[2] as the leopard, (and) light* as the eagle (and) fleet as the hart,[3] and mighty as the lion[4] to do the will of thy Father Who is in Heaven. He used to say, The bold-faced[5] are for *Gehenna*, but the shame-faced[6] are for the Garden of Eden.[7] [He said further], May[8] it be Thy will, O Eternal our God and God of our forefathers, that Thy City be rebuilt[9] speedily in our days and grant our portion in Thy Law.[10]

מִשְׁנָה כ

יְהוּדָה בֶּן תֵּימָא אוֹמֵר הֱוֵי ¹עַז
כַּנָּמֵר, וְקַל כַּנֶּשֶׁר, ²וְרָץ יִכַּצְבִי,
וְגִבּוֹר ⁴כָּאֲרִי, לַעֲשׂוֹת רְצוֹן אָבִיךְ
שֶׁבַּשָּׁמַיִם. הוּא הָיָה אוֹמֵר ⁵עַז פָּנִים
לְגֵיהִנָּם, ⁶וּבְשֶׁת פָּנִים ⁷לְגַן עֵדֶן.
⁸יְהִי רָצוֹן מִלְפָנֶיךָ ה׳ ⁹אֱלֹהֵינוּ
יִשְׁתַּבְּנֶה עִירְךָ בִּמְהֵרָה בְיָמֵינוּ וְתֵן
¹⁰חֶלְקֵנוּ בְּתוֹרָתֶךָ.

*רָץ in some texts.

1 Here *Mishnah* 23 starts in the Prayer Book. 2 Nothing must be allowed to stand in the way of leading a righteous life. 3 Compare 4²; *Psalm* 119, 60. 4 Compare *II Samuel* 1, 23. 5 Or *shameless, brazen-faced, impudent*. See 1⁵, **Note 9.** 6 A sense of shame is a preventive for transgression. וּבֹשׁ, instead of וּבְשֶׁת, in the Prayer Book. 7 The abode of the righteous in the Hereafter. Compare נְדָרִים 20a. 8 This prayer is incorporated in the Prayer Book at the end of the עֲמִידָה. 9 In the Prayer Book, שֶׁיִּבָּנֶה בֵּית הַמִּקְדָּשׁ, *that the Temple be rebuilt* (thus, too, at the end of the עֲמִידָה ; and also לְפָנֶיךָ, instead of מִלְפָנֶיךָ, there). 10 Originally *Chapter 5* concluded here. §In some texts אֱלֹהֵינוּ וַאלֹהֵי אֲבוֹתֵינוּ.

Mishnah 21

He[1] used to say, At five years of age [one is ready for [the study of] the *Scripture*, at ten [years] of age[2] [one is fit] for [the study of] the *Mishnah*, at the age of thirteen for [the fulfilment of] the commandments, at the age of fifteen for [the study of] the *Talmud*, at the age of eighteen for marriage,[3] at the age of twenty for pursuing [a vocation],[4] at the age of thirty for entering into one's full vigour, at the age of forty for understanding, at the age of fifty for counsel,[5] at the age of sixty one attains old age,[6] at the age of seventy

מִשְׁנָה כא

¹הוּא הָיָה אוֹמֵר בֶּן חָמֵשׁ שָׁנִים
לַמִּקְרָא, ²בֶּן עֶשֶׂר לַמִּשְׁנָה, בֶּן
שְׁלֹשׁ עֶשְׂרֵה לַמִּצְוֹת, בֶּן חֲמֵשׁ
עֶשְׂרֵה לַתַּלְמוּד, בֶּן שְׁמֹנֶה עֶשְׂרֵה
³לַחוּפָּה, בֶּן עֶשְׂרִים ⁴לִרְדּוֹף, בֶּן
שְׁלֹשִׁים לַכֹּחַ, בֶּן אַרְבָּעִים לַבִּינָה,
בֶּן חֲמִשִּׁים ⁵לָעֵצָה, ⁶בֶּן שִׁשִּׁים
לַזִּקְנָה, בֶּן שִׁבְעִים ⁷לְשֵׂיבָה, בֶּן
שְׁמֹנִים ⁸לִגְבוּרָה, בֶּן תִּשְׁעִים לָשׁוּחַ,

for the hoary head,⁷ at the age of eighty for special strength,⁸ at the age of ninety for bending [beneath the weight of old age], at the age of a hundred one is as though⁹ he were [already] dead and had passed away and ceased from the world.

בֶּן מֵאָה ⁹כְּאִילוּ מֵת וְעָבַר וּבָטֵל מִן־הָעוֹלָם.

1 sc., Judah ben Tema. Miahnah 24 begins here in the Prayer Book. Mishnahs 21, 22, 23 were later supplements to Chapter 5. **2** The Prayer Book has בֶּן עֶשֶׂר שָׁנִים. **3** לַחֻפָּה in the Prayer Book. Here concludes the period of preparation for one's life. **4** Here begins the period of application and activity in one's life. **5** Based on Numbers 8, 25ff. **6** Here commences the period of decline in one's life. **7** Compare I Chronicles **29**, 28. viz., strength to maintain such old age. **8** Compare Psalm **90**, 10. **9** In the Prayer Book, כְּאִלּוּ.

Mishnah 22

מִשְׁנָה כב

Ben¹ Bag Bag² said, Turn³ it [—the Law—] and turn³ it over again, for everything⁴ is therein, and contemplate⁵ it, and wax gray and old over it,⁶ and stir not therefrom,⁷ for thou canst have no better principle than this.

¹בֶּן יָּג בָּג בָּג אוֹמֵר הֲפוֹךְ בַּהּ, יַהֲפוֹךְ בַּהּ, ³דְּכֹלָּא בַּהּ, וּבַהּ ⁵תֶּחֱזֵי, וְסִיב וּבְלֵה ⁶בַהּ, וּמִינַּהּ ⁷לָא תְזוּעַ, שֶׁאֵין לְךָ מִדָּה טוֹבָה הֵימֶנָּה.

1 In the Prayer Book Mishnah 25 commences here. This Mishnah and the next are in Aramaic, and in the אֲבוֹת דְּרַבִּי יוֹתָן they are ascribed to הִלֵּל. Compare 1³, 2⁶. **2** See BIOGRAPHIES. Compare קִדּוּשִׁין 10b. **3** i.e., study it thoroughly from all aspects. In the Prayer Book, וַהֲפָךְ הַפָּךְ. **4** All that pertains for righteous living. דְּכֹלָּה in some editions. **5** תֶּחֱזָא in the Prayer Book. **6** i.e., study it all through life. **7** i.e., do not neglect its study or deviate from its precepts.

Mishnah 23

מִשְׁנָה כג

Ben¹ Hai Hai said, According² to the suffering is the reward.

¹בֶּן הֵא הֵא אוֹמֵר ²לְפוּם צַעֲרָא אַגְרָא.

1 Here starts Mishnah 26 in the Prayer Book. **2** In the Prayer Book, לְפָם. The more one labours at the study of the Law and practises its commandments the greater is his recompense.

נִשְׁלְמָה מַסֶּכֶת אָבוֹת

TRACTATE AVOTH CONCLUDED.

88

CHAPTER 6[1]

The Sages taught [further the following] in the language of the *Mishnah*: Blessed be He Who made choice of them and their *Mishnah*.[2]

פֶּרֶק ו[1]

שָׁנוּ חֲכָמִים בִּלְשׁוֹן הַמִּשְׁנָה בָּרוּךְ
שֶׁבָּחַר בָּהֶם יּבְמִשְׁנָתָם.[2]

1 See INTRODUCTION. **2** Thus far, in the Prayer Book; this paragraph, from a source in the *Talmud*, is indicated as an introduction after which *Mishnah* 1 proper begins. This *Mishnah* is an encomium lauding the Law (compare 6[8, 9]).

Mishnah 1*

R. Meir said, Whosoever engages in [the study of] the Law[1] for its own sake[2] merits many things, and, not only so, he is [as it were] deserving of the whole world[3]—he is called friend, beloved [of God], lover of the Omnipresent, lover of humanity,[4] pleasing the Omnipresent, pleasing humanity [5] (and) it invests him with humility and reverence[6] (and) it fits him to become righteous, pious, upright and faithful (and) it keeps him remote from sin, and draws him nigh to virtue, and through him men enjoy[7] counsel and sound knowledge, understanding and power, as it is said,[8] *Counsel is mine,*[3] and *sound wisdom; I am understanding, I have might;* and it gives him sovereignty and dominion and discernment in judgment (and) to him are revealed[10] the secrets of the Law [11] (and) he is made like a spring that never fails[12] and like a stream that flows on with ever-sustained vigour; (and) he becomes[13] modest,[14] (and) long-suffering, (and) forgiving of insult (toward himself); and it magnifies him and exalts him above all things [here below].

מִשְׁנָה א[*]

רַבִּי מֵאִיר אוֹמֵר כָּל־הָעוֹסֵק
בַּתּוֹרָה יּלִשְׁמָה זוֹכֶה לִדְבָרִים
הַרְבֵּה וְלֹא עוֹד אֶלָּא יֶּשֶׁכָּל הָעוֹלָם
כֻּלּוֹ כְּדַי הוּא לוֹ, נִקְרָא רֵעַ אָהוּב
אוֹהֵב אֶת־הַמָּקוֹם אוֹהֵב אֶת־
הַבְּרִיּוֹת, יּמְשַׂמֵּחַ אֶת־הַמָּקוֹם
מְשַׂמֵּחַ אֶת־הַבְּרִיּוֹת; וּמַלְבַּשְׁתּוֹ
עֲנָוָה יְּיִרְאָה; וּמַכְשַׁרְתּוֹ לִהְיוֹת
צַדִּיק חָסִיד יָשָׁר וְנֶאֱמָן; וּמְרַחַקְתּוֹ
מִן־הַחֵטְא וּמְקָרַבְתּוֹ לִידֵי זְכוּת
יּוְנֶהֱנִין מִמֶּנּוּ עֵצָה וְתוּשִׁיָּה בִּינָה
וּגְבוּרָה יֶּשֶׁנֶּאֱמַר לִי עֵצָה וְתוּשִׁיָּה
אֲנִי בִינָה לִי גְבוּרָה; וְנוֹתֶנֶת לוֹ
מַלְכוּת וּמֶמְשָׁלָה וְחִקּוּר דִּין;
יּוּמְגַלִּין לוֹ רָזֵי יּתוֹרָה; וְנַעֲשֶׂה
כְּמַעְיָן יּשֶׁאֵינוֹ פוֹסֵק וּכְנָהָר
יּהַמִּתְגַּבֵּר וְהוֹלֵךְ; יּוְהֹוֶה יּצָנוּעַ
וְאֶרֶךְ רוּחַ וּמוֹחֵל עַל עֶלְבּוֹנוֹ;
וּמְגַדַּלְתּוֹ וּמְרוֹמַמְתּוֹ עַל כָּל־
הַמַּעֲשִׂים.

89

1 Compare 1[1]. 2 *viz.*, not for honour or gain. 3 Some render this *the whole world is indebted to him.* 4 Compare 1[12]. 5 מִשְׂמֵחַ אֶת־הַמָּקוֹם מְשַׂמֵּחַ אֶת־הַבְּרִיּוֹת is omitted in some texts. 6 For God. 7 וְהֵמָּנִים in some texts. 8 *Proverbs* 8, 14. 9 The תּוֹרָה is, as it were, made to say this. 10 In some texts, וּמְעַלִּים. 11 Compare *Psalm* 25, 14. 12 שֶׁמִּתְגַּבֵּר in some texts. Compare 2[8]. 13 The vocalisation וְהֵוֶה as given in some Prayer Books is grammatically incorrect. 14 Or *humble.* Compare *Micah* 6, 8. *See ADDENDA, Page 552.

Mishnah 2   מִשְׁנָה ב

R. Joshua ben Levi said, Every day a heavenly voice[1] goes forth from Horeb[2] proclaiming and saying, 'Woe to mankind[3] for contempt[4] of the Law!'—for whosoever does not engage in [the study of] the Law is said to be 'rebuked',[5] as it is said,[6] *As a ring of gold in a swine's snout, so is a fair woman that turneth aside from discretion;* and it says,[7] *And the tables were the work of God, and the writing was the writing of God, graven upon the tables.* Read not חָרוּת [*graven*] but חֵרוּת [*freedom*],[8] for no man is free but he who occupies himself with [the study of] the Law. But whoever labours in [the study of] the Law, lo, he shall be exalted, as it is said,[9] *And from Mattanah to Nachaliel, and from Nachaliel to Bamoth.*[10]

אָמַר רַבִּי יְהוֹשֻׁעַ בֶּן לֵוִי בְּכָל יוֹם וָיוֹם י-בַּת קוֹל יוֹצֵאת מֵהַר יחוֹרֵב וּמַכְרֶזֶת וְאוֹמֶרֶת אוֹי יּלָהֶם יּלַבְּרִיּוֹת ימֵעֶלְבּוֹנָהּ שֶׁל תּוֹרָה, שֶׁכָּל מִי שֶׁאֵינוֹ עוֹסֵק בַּתּוֹרָה נִקְרָא נָזוּף, יּשֶׁנֶּאֱמַר נֶזֶם זָהָב בְּאַף חֲזִיר אִשָּׁה יָפָה וְסָרַת טָעַם ; יוְאוֹמֵר וְהַלֻּחוֹת מַעֲשֵׂה אֱלֹהִים הֵמָּה וְהַמִּכְתָּב מִכְתַּב אֱלֹהִים הוּא חָרוּת עַל הַלֻּחֹת• אַל תִּקְרָא חָרוּת אֶלָּא יחֵרוּת שֶׁאֵין לְךָ בֶּן חוֹרִין אֶלָּא מִי שֶׁעוֹסֵק בַּתַּלְמוּד תּוֹרָה• וְכָל מִי שֶׁעוֹסֵק בְּתַלְמוּד תּוֹרָה הֲרֵי זֶה מִתְעַלֶּה, יּשֶׁנֶּאֱמַר וּמִמַּתָּנָה נַחֲלִיאֵל וּמִנַּחֲלִיאֵל יּבָּמוֹת•

1 [בַּת קוֹל] is also used for *echo*]. Literally *daughter of* [the] *voice*—a belief that when Prophecy had ceased Divine pronouncements to mankind were made in this manner. 2 *i.e.*, Mount Sinai, where the Revelation of the Law was made (*Exodus* 19 *et seq.*). 3 The whole human race, irrespective of creed or colour. 4 *i.e.*, neglect of study and practice of its tenets. 5 Or *under divine censure, reprobate;* the term נָזוּף is here connected by the peculiar form of rabbinic interpretation known as *notarikon* with the initial letters of the words נֶזֶם זָהָב and the final letter of the word בְּאַף. 6 *Proverbs* 11, 22. 7 *Exodus* 32, 16. 8 An homiletical interpretation. 9 *Numbers* 21, 19. 10 An homiletic rendering upon the etymological meanings of these place-names: מַתָּנָה, *gift*, *i.e.*, 'from the gift of the Law,' נַחֲלִיאֵל, *inheritance of God*, *i.e.*, 'humanity receives a divine heritance', בָּמוֹת, *high places*, *i.e.*, 'and he is led to high ideals.'

Mishnah 3

He that learns from his fellow[1] a single chapter,[2] or a single rule, or a single verse, or a single expression,[4] or even a single[3] letter,[5] ought to render him honour, for so we find [it the case] with David, King of Israel, who learned only two things[6] from Achitophel, and yet called him his master, his guide[7] and his familiar friend, as it is said,[8] *But it was thou, a man mine equal, my companion, and my familiar friend.* And is it not an inference from minor to major?[9]—If David, the King of Israel, who learnt only two things from Achitophel, regarded him as his teacher, his companion and his familiar friend, then how much more should one who learns from his fellow[1] a single chapter, or a single[3] rule, or a single verse, or a single expression, or even a single[3] letter, pay him honour? And 'honour' is naught but 'the Law', as it is said, *The[10] wise shall inherit honour,* and *The[11] perfect shall inherit good.* And 'good' is nothing but 'the Law', as it is said,[12] *For I give you good doctrine; forsake ye not my Law.*[13]

מִשְׁנָה ג

הַלּוֹמֵד ¹מֵחֲבֵירוֹ ²פֶּרֶק אֶחָד אוֹ
הֲלָכָה ²אַחַת אוֹ פָּסוּק אֶחָד אוֹ
⁴דִּבּוּר אֶחָד אוֹ אֲפִילּוּ ⁴אוֹת ³אַחַת
צָרִיךְ לִנְהָג בּוֹ כָּבוֹד, שֶׁכֵּן מָצִינוּ
בְּדָוִד מֶלֶךְ יִשְׂרָאֵל שֶׁלֹּא לָמַד
מֵאֲחִיתֹפֶל אֶלָּא ⁶שְׁנֵי דְבָרִים בִּלְבַד
קְרָאוֹ רַבּוֹ ⁷אַלּוּפוֹ וּמְיֻדָּעוֹ, ⁸שֶׁנֶּאֱמַר
וְאַתָּה אֱנוֹשׁ כְּעֶרְכִּי אַלּוּפִי וּמְיֻדָּעִי.
וַהֲלֹא דְבָרִים ⁹קַל וָחֹמֶר? וּמַה
דָּוִד מֶלֶךְ יִשְׂרָאֵל שֶׁלֹּא לָמַד
מֵאֲחִיתֹפֶל אֶלָּא שְׁנֵי דְבָרִים בִּלְבָד
קְרָאוֹ רַבּוֹ אַלּוּפוֹ וּמְיֻדָּעוֹ, הַלּוֹמֵד
¹מֵחֲבֵירוֹ פֶּרֶק אֶחָד אוֹ הֲלָכָה ²אַחַת
אוֹ פָּסוּק אֶחָד אוֹ דִּבּוּר אֶחָד אוֹ
אֲפִילּוּ אוֹת ⁴אַחַת עַל אַחַת כַּמָּה
וְכַמָּה שֶׁצָּרִיךְ לִנְהָג בּוֹ כָּבוֹד ? וְאֵין
כָּבוֹד אֶלָּא תּוֹרָה, שֶׁנֶּאֱמַר
¹⁰כָּבוֹד חֲכָמִים יִנְחָלוּ ¹¹וּתְמִימִים
יִנְחֲלוּ טוֹב. וְאֵין טוֹב אֶלָּא
תּוֹרָה, ¹²שֶׁנֶּאֱמַר כִּי לֶקַח טוֹב נָתַתִּי
לָכֶם תּוֹרָתִי אַל תַּעֲזֹבוּ.¹³

---

1 Or מַחֲבֵרוֹ. 2 Or *paragraph, section*—from *Scripture* or the *Mishnah*. 3 The pointing אַחַת is grammatically more correct than אֶחָת as given in some Prayer Books. 4 Or *word*; or, a *Scriptural* or *Mishnaic saying*. 5 With reference to its orthography. 6 Commentators differ widely as to what this expression refers. By combining the two words into one word שֶׁנִּדְבְּרִים, who [on₁y] *conversed together*, a plausible sense can be given to it thus: 'seeing that a king gave honour to one with whom he merely conversed though he gained no knowledge thereby, how much more must an ordinary individual show honour to anyone, from whom he has acquired aught of the Law.' 7 Or *companion*. Literally *chief, prince.* 8 *Psalms* 55, 14. 9 The first of the Thirteen Exegetical Principles of R. Ishmael (בְּרַיְתָא דְּרַבִּי יִשְׁמָעֵאל) given in the Morning Service. 10 *Proverbs* 3, 35. 11 *Proverbs* 28, 10.

12 *Proverbs* **4**, 2.   **13** Or *teaching*.   The deduction is as follows: as *inherit* is common to the first two quotations, these are considered equal and therefore *honour* in the first is the equivalent of *good* in the second; but seeing that *good* occurs in the second and third quotations these two are also thus equated; hence all three are balanced, and so *honour* becomes the equal of *the Law*.

Mishnah 4	מִשְׁנָה ד

This is the way [to acquire knowledge] of the Law: a morsel of bread with salt thou must eat and[1] *water by measure shalt thou drink*,[2] (and) upon the ground must thou sleep and live a life of trouble the while thou toilest in [the study of] the Law. If thou doest thus, *Happy*[3] *shalt thou be, and it shall be well with thee*; 'happy[4] shalt thou be'—in this world 'and it shall be well with thee'—in the world to come.

כַּךְ הִיא דַרְכָּהּ שֶׁל תּוֹרָה, פַּת
בְּמֶלַח תֹּאכֵל ‏[1]וּמַיִם בִּמְשׂוּרָה
‏[2]תִשְׁתֶּה, וְעַל הָאָרֶץ תִּישָׁן וְחַיֵּי צַעַר
תִּחְיֶה וּבַתּוֹרָה אַתָּה עָמֵל· אִם
אַתָּה עֹשֶׂה כֵן ‏[3]יַאַשְׁרֶיךָ לְטוֹב לָךְ;
‏[4]אַשְׁרֶיךָ בָּעוֹלָם הַזֶּה וְטוֹב לָךְ
לָעוֹלָם הַבָּא·

1 *Ezekiel* **4**, 11.   **2** The happy mean (expressed by אִם אֵין קֶמַח אֵין תּוֹרָה in 3[17]) is between the extreme asceticism advocated here and the opposite extreme of wealth as lauded in *Mishnah* 8 of this Chapter.   The *Talmud* considers a poor man's meal to be 'a morsel of bread with salt.'   **3** *Psalm* **128**, 2.   This is also quoted in 4[1].   **4** This last part is also given in 4[1].

Mishnah 5	מִשְׁנָה ה

Seek not [worldly] greatness for thyself,[1] and covet[2] not [earthly] honour; practise more than thy learning;[3] and crave not after the table of kings,[4] for thy table is greater than their table,[5] and thy crown[6] is greater than their crown, and faithful is thy Employer[7] Who shall pay thee the reward of thy work.

אַל תְּבַקֵּשׁ גְּדֻלָּה ‏[1]לְעַצְמְךָ וְאַל
‏[2]תַּחְמֹד כָּבוֹד; יוֹתֵר ‏[3]יִמִלְמוּדְךָ
עֲשֵׂה; וְאַל תִּתְאַוֶּה לְשֻׁלְחָנָם שֶׁל
‏[4]מְלָכִים, שֶׁשֻּׁלְחָנְךָ גָּדוֹל ‏[5]מִשֻּׁלְחָנָם
‏[6]וְכִתְרְךָ גָּדוֹל מִכִּתְרָם, וְנֶאֱמָן ‏[7]הוּא
בַּעַל מְלַאכְתְּךָ שֶׁיְּשַׁלֶּם לְךָ שְׂכַר
פְּעֻלָּתֶךָ·

1 Compare 1[10].   לְעַצְמְךָ in some Prayer Books.   **2** תַּחֲמוֹד in some Prayer Books.
3 Compare 1[17], 3[9], 5[14].   Theory and practice are inseparable to be effective.   The pointing מִלְמוּדְךָ, given in some Prayer Books, is not grammatically correct.
4 Instead of מְלָכִים some Prayer Books have שָׂרִים, *princes*.   **5** Compare 3[3].
6 Compare 4[13].   In some Prayer Books וְכִתְרְךָ גָּדוֹל מִכִּתְרָם is omitted.   **7** *sc.*, God.

Mishnah 6

Greater is the Law than (the) priesthood and than royalty, for *royalty* is
acquired by *thirty qualifications*[1] and
the *priesthood* by *twenty-four*,[2] while
[learning in] *the Law* is acquired
by *forty-eight qualifications*. And
these are they:[3] [1] by audible
study;[4] [2] by utterance with
the lips;[5] [3] by understanding[6] of
the heart and [4] by discernment of
the heart;[7] [5] by awe, [6] by
reverence,[8] [7] by humility,[9] [8] by
cheerfulness,[10] [9] by ministering to
the Sages,[11] [10] by attaching oneself to colleagues,[12] [11] by discussion
with disciples; [12] by sedateness;[13]
[13] by [knowledge of] *Scripture* and
of the *Mishnah*,[14] [14] by moderation in business,[15] [15] by moderation in intercourse with the world,[16]
[16] by moderation in pleasure,[17]
[17] by moderation in sleep,[18] [18]
by moderation in conversation,[19]
[19] by moderation in jesting;[40]
[20] by long-suffering;[21] [21] by a
good heart;[22] [22] by faith in the
wise; [23] by resignation under
suffering;[23] [24] by recognising one's
place,[24]; and [25] rejoicing in one's
lot, and [26] putting a fence round
one's words,[25] and [27] claiming no
merit for oneself;[26] [28] [by] being
beloved,[27] [29] loving the Omnipresent,[28] [30] loving mankind,[28]
[31] loving charitable deeds, and
[32] loving rectitude[29] and loving
reproof;[30] (and) [33] [by] keeping
oneself far from honour;[31] and [34]
[by] not boasting of one's scholarship,[32] or [35] delighting in making

מִשְׁנָה ו

גְּדוֹלָה תּוֹרָה יוֹתֵר מִן־הַכְּהֻנָּה
וּמִן־הַמַּלְכוּת, שֶׁהַמַּלְכוּת נִקְנֵית
בִּשְׁלֹשִׁים מַעֲלוֹת וְהַכְּהֻנָּה
בְּעֶשְׂרִים וְאַרְבַּע וְהַתּוֹרָה נִקְנֵית
בְּאַרְבָּעִים וּשְׁמוֹנָה דְבָרִים. וְאֵלּוּ
הֵן, יִבְּתַלְמוּד בִּשְׁמִיעַת הָאֹזֶן
יִבַּעֲרִיכַת שְׂפָתַיִם; בִּבִינַת הַלֵּב
יִבְּשִׂכּוּל הַלֵּב; בְּאֵימָה, יִבְּיִרְאָה,
יִבַּעֲנָוָה, יִבְּשִׂמְחָה, יִבְּשִׁמּוּשׁ
חֲכָמִים יִבְּדִבּוּק חֲבֵרִים,
בְּפִלְפּוּל הַתַּלְמִידִים; יִבְּיִשּׁוּב;
יִבְּמִקְרָא וּבְמִשְׁנָה; יִבְּמִעוּט
סְחוֹרָה, יִבְּמִעוּט דֶּרֶךְ אֶרֶץ,
יִבְּמִעוּט תַּעֲנוּג, יִבְּמִעוּט שֵׁנָה,
יִבְּמִעוּט שִׂיחָה, יִבְּמִעוּט שְׂדוֹק;
יִבְּאֶרֶךְ אַפַּיִם; יִבְּלֵב טוֹב; בֶּאֱמוּנַת
חֲכָמִים; יִבְּקַבָּלַת הַיִּסּוּרִים;
יִהַמַּכִּיר אֶת־מְקוֹמוֹ, וְהַשָּׂמֵחַ
בְּחֶלְקוֹ יִוְהָעוֹשֶׂה סְיָג לִדְבָרָיו,
יִאֵינוֹ מַחֲזִיק טוֹבָה לְעַצְמוֹ;
יִ אָהוּב, יִ אוֹהֵב אֶת־הַמָּקוֹם,
יִאוֹהֵב אֶת־הַבְּרִיּוֹת, אוֹהֵב אֶת־
הַצְּדָקוֹת, יִאוֹהֵב אֶת־הַמֵּישָׁרִים,
יִאוֹהֵב אֶת־הַתּוֹכָחוֹת; יִוּמִתְרַחֵק
מִן־הַכָּבוֹד; יִוְלֹא מֵגִיס לִבּוֹ

decisions;³³ [36] [by] bearing the yoke with one's fellow,³⁴ and [37] judging him favourably,³⁵ and [38] rendering him steadfast in truth³⁶ and [39] establishing him in peace; (and) [40] [by] concentrating³⁷ in one's study; [41] [by] asking and making answer,³⁸ [42] hearing and [43] adding thereto;³⁹ (and) [44] [by] learning with the object of teaching,⁴⁰ and [45] learning in order to practise;⁴⁰ [46] [by] making one's master wiser, (and) [47] fixing attention upon his discourse, and [48] reporting a thing in the name of him that said it.⁴¹ Behold, thou hast learnt, 'Whosoever quotes a thing in the name of him that said it, brings deliverance into the world, as it is said,⁴², *And Esther told the king thereof in the name of Mordecai*'.⁴³

בְּתַלְמוּדוֹ, ⁱⁱⁱⁱⁱⁱⁱⁱⁱⁱⁱⁱⁱⁱ שָׂמֵחַ בְּהוֹרָאָה ;
ⁱⁱⁱⁱⁱⁱⁱⁱ נוֹשֵׂא בְעֹל עִם חֲבֵרוֹ, ⁱⁱⁱⁱⁱⁱⁱⁱ וּמַכְרִיעוֹ
לְכַף זְכוּת, ⁱⁱⁱⁱⁱⁱⁱⁱ וּמַעֲמִידוֹ עַל הָאֱמֶת,
וּמַעֲמִידוֹ עַל הַשָּׁלוֹם ; ⁱⁱⁱⁱⁱⁱⁱⁱ וּמִתְיַשֵּׁב
בְּתַלְמוּדוֹ ; ⁱⁱⁱⁱⁱⁱⁱⁱ שׁוֹאֵל וּמֵשִׁיב, ⁱⁱⁱⁱⁱⁱⁱⁱ שׁוֹמֵעַ
וּמוֹסִיף ; הַלּוֹמֵד עַל מְנָת ⁱⁱⁱⁱⁱⁱⁱⁱ לְלַמֵּד,
וְהַלּוֹמֵד עַל מְנָת ⁱⁱⁱⁱⁱⁱⁱⁱ לַעֲשׂוֹת ;
הַמַּחְכִּים אֶת־רַבּוֹ, וְהַמְכַוֵּן אֶת־
שְׁמוּעָתוֹ, וְהָאוֹמֵר דָּבָר ⁱⁱⁱⁱⁱⁱⁱⁱ בְּשֵׁם
אוֹמְרוֹ · הָא לָמַדְתָּ כָּל־הָאוֹמֵר
דָּבָר בְּשֵׁם אוֹמְרוֹ מֵבִיא גְאֻלָּה
לָעוֹלָם, ⁱⁱⁱⁱⁱⁱⁱⁱ שֶׁנֶּאֱמַר וַתֹּאמֶר אֶסְתֵּר
לַמֶּלֶךְ בְּשֵׁם ⁱⁱⁱⁱⁱⁱⁱⁱ מָרְדֳּכָי.

judged;   [3] וְלֹא מֵעִיד, he may not testify;   [4] וְלֹא מְעִידִין אוֹתוֹ, nor may evidence be brought against him;   [5] לֹא חוֹלֵץ, he may not submit to leviratic separation;   [6] וְלֹא חוֹלְצִין לְאִשְׁתּוֹ, nor may one submit to leviratical separation at the hands of his [widowed] wife;   [7] לֹא מְיַבֵּם, he may not contract leviratic marriage;   [8] וְלֹא מְיַיבְּמִים לְאִשְׁתּוֹ, nor may one contract leviratical marriage with his [widowed] wife;   [9] וְאֵין נֹשְׂאִין אַלְמָנָתוֹ, and none may wed his widow;   [10]... מֵת לוֹ מֵת אֵינוֹ יוֹצֵא, if one of his near of kin die he must not go forth ....;   [11]... וּכְשֶׁמַּבְרִין אוֹתוֹ כָּל, and when they set before him the funeral meal all ....;   [12] .... וּמוֹצִיא לְמִלְחֶמֶת הָרָשׁוּת עַל פִּי, and he may lead forth [the army] to political warfare by the decision of ....;   [13] וּפוֹרֵץ לַעֲשׂוֹת לוֹ דֶרֶךְ, and he may break through [private property] to make himself a road;   [14] דֶּרֶךְ הַמֶּלֶךְ אֵין לוֹ שִׁעוּר, the king's road has no definite measurements;   [15] וְכָל הָעָם בּוֹזְזִין וְנוֹתְנִין לְפָנָיו, and all the people that take spoil must set it before him;   [16] וְהוּא נוֹטֵל חָלֶק בָּרֹאשׁ, and he takes a portion first;   [17] לֹא יַרְבֶּה לוֹ נָשִׁים, neither shall he multiply wives to himself;   [18] לֹא יַרְבֶּה לוֹ סוּסִים, he shall not multiply horses to himself;   [19] וְכֶסֶף וְזָהָב לֹא יַרְבֶּה לוֹ, neither shall he multiply to himself silver and gold;   [20] וְכוֹתֵב לוֹ סֵפֶר תּוֹרָה לִשְׁמוֹ, And he must write for himself a Scroll of the Law;   [21] וְיוֹצֵא לַמִּלְחָמָה מוֹצִיאָהּ עִמּוֹ, and when he goes forth to battle he takes it with him: [22] נִכְנַס מַכְנִיסָהּ עִמּוֹ, when he returns he brings it back with him;   [23] יוֹשֵׁב בַּדִּין הִיא עִמּוֹ, when he sits in judgment it must be with him;   [24] מֵיסֵב הִיא כְּנֶגְדּוֹ, when he sits [at a meal] it must be with him;   [25] אֵין רוֹכְבִין עַל סוּסוֹ, none may ride upon his horse;   [26] וְאֵין יוֹשְׁבִין עַל כִּסְאוֹ, and none may sit upon his throne;   [27] וְאֵין רוֹאִין אוֹתוֹ, and none may use his sceptre;   [28] וְאֵין מִשְׁתַּמְּשִׁין בְּשַׁרְבִיטוֹ, and none may look on him when he has his hair cut;   [29] וְלֹא כְּשֶׁהוּא עָרוֹם, or when he is naked;   [30] וְלֹא בְּבֵית הַמֶּרְחָץ, or when in the bath-house.   2 Numbers 18, 8ff.;   בָּבָא קַמָּא 110b.   As set out from Scripture: [1] מִקְדַּשׁ הַקֳדָשִׁים, of the most holy things (viz., זִבְחֵי שַׁלְמֵי צִבּוּר, peace-offerings (sacrifices) of the congregation);   [2] מִן־הָאֵשׁ, from the fire (referring to עוֹר הָעוֹלָה, the hide of the burnt-offering, which must be wholly burned);   [3, 4] כָּל־קָרְבְּנָם, all their offerings (viz., שְׁתֵּי הַלֶּחֶם, the two loaves, וְלֶחֶם הַפָּנִים, and the shewbread);   [5, 6] לְכָל מִנְחָתָם, even all their meal-offerings (viz., שִׁירֵי מְנָחוֹת, the remains of the meal-offerings, וְשִׁירֵי מִנְחַת הָעֹמֶר, and the remainder of the meal-offering of the omer);   [7, 8] וּלְכָל חַטָּאתָם, and even all their sin-offerings (viz., בְּשַׂר שֶׁל חַטָּאת בְּהֵמָה, the flesh of the sin-offering of a beast, וְחַטַּאת הָעוֹף, and of the sin-offering of a bird);   [9, 10] וּלְכָל אֲשָׁמָם, and (for) all their guilt-offerings (viz., וְאָשָׁם וַדַּאי, the guilt-offering for the undoubted commission of certain offences, וְאָשָׁם תָּלוּי, and a guilt-offering when in doubt as to having committed a sinful act;   [11] אֲשֶׁר יָשִׁיבוּ לִי, which they may render unto Me (viz., גֶּזֶל הַגֵּר, robbery from the stranger);   [12] קְדָשׁ קָדָשִׁים, most holy (viz., לוֹג שֶׁמֶן שֶׁל מְצוֹרָע, the log of oil of the leper);   [13] חָזֶה וְשׁוֹק, breast and shank;   [14] תְּרוּמָה, priest's-due (or heave-offering);   [15] תְּרוּמַת מַעֲשֵׂר, priest's-due of the first tithe (or תְּרוּמָה קְטַנָּה, minor priest's-due);   [16] רֵאשִׁית הַגֵּז, the first of the fleece;   [17] חַלָּה, priest's share of the dough;   [18] מַתְּנוֹת הַזְּרוֹעַ וְהַלְּחָיַיִם וְהַקֵּבָה, the privileges of the fore-arm and the two weeks and the maw;   [19] בִּכּוּרִים, first-fruits;   [20] שְׂדֵה אֲחֻזָּה, inherited field;   [21] שְׂדֵה חֵרֶם, field for priests' use;   [22] בְּכוֹר אָדָם, firstborn of man;   [23] בְּכוֹר בְּהֵמָה טְהוֹרָה, firstling of a clean beast;

95

[24] בְּכוֹר בְּהֵמָה טְמֵאָה, *firstling of an unclean beast.*. There are *twenty-four* parallel or comparable *qualifications* that apply to the *High Priest* (*Leviticus* **4**, 3ff., 13ff., 22ff., 27ff., **9**, **22**, **10**, 19; *Numbers* **6**, 24-27, **15**, 22ff., 24, 27; *Deuteronomy* **26**, 14; [1] אֵינוֹ חַיָב עַל הוֹרָאָה אֶלָּא אִם 33,5,6: ;22,3,6 הוֹרָיוֹת ;22,3 סַנְהֶדְרִין ;7⁵ יוֹמָא כֵּן הוֹרָה לְבַטֵּל מִקְצָתוֹ, *he is liable only if he gives a decision which in part disannuls* [what the Law enjoins]; [2] אֵינוֹ חַיָב עַל טוּמְאַת מִקְדָּשׁ, *he is not liable for defilement of* (in) *the Sanctuary;* [3] אֵינוֹ חַיָב עַל טוּמְאַת קֳדָשָׁיו, *he is not liable for defilement of his holy things;* [4] שֶׁמֵּבִיא פָּר עַל חַטָּאת, *he brings a bullock, with the sin-offering;* [5] שֶׁמֵּבִיא פָּר בְּיוֹם הַכִּפּוּרִים, *he brings a bullock on the Day of Atonement;* [6] שֶׁמֵּבִיא עֲשִׂירִית הָאֵיפָה, *he brings the tenth of the ephah;* [7] שֶׁאֵין עֲבוֹדַת יוֹה"כ, *the Service on the Day of Atonement is not valid without him;* [8] מְצֻוֶּה עַל כָּשֵׁר אֶלָּא בּוֹ הַבְּתוּלָה, *he is enjoined* [to wed] *a virgin;* [9] וּמֻזְהָר עַל הָאַלְמָנָה שֶׁלֹּא יִשָּׂאֶנָּה, *and he is admonished not to marry a widow;* [10] שֶׁאֵינוֹ מִטַּמֵּא בִּקְרוֹבָיו, *he m\y not become defiled by* [*the dead of*] *his near of kin;* [11] לֹא פוֹרֵס, *he does not spread out* [his hands at the Priestly Blessing]; [12] וְלֹא פוֹרֵעַ, *and he d\es n\t let his hair loose;* [13] מַחֲזִיר אֶת־ הָרוֹצֵחַ, *he brings back the murderer;* [14] מַקְרִיב אוֹנֵן, *he offers up while a mourner before the burial of his kinsm\n;* [15] פָּרוֹ קוֹדֵם לְפַר הָעֵדָה, *his bullock offering precedes the bullock offering of the congregation;* [16] אֵינוֹ חַיָב אֶלָּא עַל הֶעְלֵם דָּבָר, *he is only culpable for 'forgetfulness' of a matter;* [17] אֵין דָּנִין אוֹתוֹ אֶלָּא בְּבֵית דִּין שֶׁל שִׁבְעִים וְאֶחָד, *he is tried only before a court of seventy-one;* [18] אֵינוֹ יוֹצֵא אַחַר הַמִּטָּא, *he does not go forth behind the bier;* [19] כְּשֶׁמְּנַחֵם אֲחֵרִים כו', *when he gives consolation to others, etc.;* [20] כְּשֶׁהוּא מִתְנַחֵם כו', *when he is consoled, etc.;* [21] וּכְשֶׁמַּבְרִין אוֹתוֹ כו', *and when they set before him the meal after a funeral, etc.;* [22] נוֹטֵל חֵלֶק בָּרֹאשׁ, *he takes a share first;* [23] וּמַקְרִיב חֵלֶק בָּרֹאשׁ *he offers a portion first;* [24] וּמְשַׁמֵּשׁ בִּשְׁמֹנָה בְּגָדִים, *and he ministers in eight garments.* **3** *i.e.,* the 48 qualifications. **4** Audible study is an aid to memorising. **5** *i.e.,* clear and distinct pronunciation and revision. **6** Compare 3¹⁷. **7** בְּשִׁכּוּל הַלֵּב is omitted in some Prayer Books and presumably the number 48 is made up by adding בְּטָהֳרָה, *by purity,* after בְּשִׂמְחָה. **8** Of God. Compare *Psalms* **111**, 10. **9** Compare 6¹ (*meekness*). **10** In fulfilling the commandments. **11** To learn and acquire religious practices. **12** For combined study. Compare 1⁶. **13** Or *application, assiduity.* **14** Knowledge of both is essential for the qualified teacher. In some texts, בְּמִשְׁנָה instead of וּבְמִשְׁנָה. **15** Compare 2⁶, 4¹⁰. **16** Compare 2². **17** Compare 6⁴. **18** See 3¹⁰. **19** Compare 1⁵. **20** Or *laughter.* Compare 3¹³. **21** Or *patience.* **22** Compare 2⁹. **23** Or *by submission under affliction.* הַיִּסּוּרִין in some texts. **24** Compare 3¹, 4⁴. **25** Compare 1¹¹. **26** Compare 2⁸. **27** See 3¹⁰, 6¹. **28** See 6¹. **29** Or *uprightness, undeviating adherence to moral standards.* **30** Compare *Proverbs* **9**, 8. **31** Shunning worldly glory and fame. **32** Compare *Proverbs* **27**, 2. **33** Compare 4⁷. **34** To acquire knowledge of the Law and the practice of its precepts. **35** Compare 1⁶. **36** To reach correct decisions and judgments. **37** Or *being assiduous, being composed.* In some texts, וּמִתְיַשֵּׁב לִבּוֹ בְּתַלְמוּדוֹ. **38** See 5⁷. **39** *i.e.,* confining questions to the subject and replying according to the accepted traditional ruling. **40** Knowledge must both be passed on to others and must lead to good deeds. **41** Taking credit

for what is not due is moral theft. **42** *Esther* 2, 22. **43** The theme of this *Mishnah* is continued in the next *Mishnah*. The pointing in the Prayer Book is מָרְדְּכַי.

Mishnah 7

Great is the Law which bestows life upon those that practise it in this world and in the world to come, as it is said,[1] *For they are life unto those that find them, and health to all their flesh;* and it says,[2] *It shall be health to thy navel, and marrow to thy bones;* and it says,[3] *It is a tree of life to them that lay hold upon it, and happy is every one that holdeth it fast;* and it says,[4] *For they shall be a chaplet of grace unto thy head, and chains about thy neck;* and it says,[5] *It shall give to thy head a chaplet of grace; a crown of glory it will bestow on thee;* and it says,[6] *For by me thy days shall be multiplied, and the years of thy life shall be increased;* and it says,[7] *Length of days is in its right hand; in its left hand are riches and honour;* and it says,[8] *For length of days, and years of life, and peace, shall they add to thee.*

מִשְׁנָה ז

גְּדוֹלָה תּוֹרָה שֶׁהִיא נוֹתֶנֶת חַיִּים
לְעוֹשֶׂיהָ בָּעוֹלָם הַזֶּה וּבָעוֹלָם הַבָּא,
שֶׁנֶּאֱמַר כִּי־חַיִּים הֵם לְמֹצְאֵיהֶם
וּלְכָל־בְּשָׂרוֹ מַרְפֵּא; וְאוֹמֵר רִפְאוּת
תְּהִי לְשָׁרֶךָ וְשִׁקּוּי לְעַצְמוֹתֶיךָ;
וְאוֹמֵר עֵץ־חַיִּים הִיא לַמַּחֲזִיקִים
בָּהּ וְתוֹמְכֶיהָ מְאֻשָּׁר; וְאוֹמֵר כִּי
לִוְיַת חֵן הֵם לְרֹאשֶׁךָ וַעֲנָקִים
לְגַרְגְּרוֹתֶיךָ; וְאוֹמֵר תִּתֵּן לְרֹאשְׁךָ
לִוְיַת־חֵן עֲטֶרֶת תִּפְאֶרֶת תְּמַגְּנֶךָ;
וְאוֹמֵר כִּי בִי יִרְבּוּ יָמֶיךָ וְיוֹסִיפוּ
לְךָ שְׁנוֹת חַיִּים; וְאוֹמֵר אֹרֶךְ יָמִים
בִּימִינָהּ בִּשְׂמֹאולָהּ עֹשֶׁר וְכָבוֹד;
וְאוֹמֵר כִּי אֹרֶךְ יָמִים וּשְׁנוֹת חַיִּים
וְשָׁלוֹם יוֹסִיפוּ לָךְ.

1 *Proverbs* 4, 22.   **2** *Proverbs* 3, 8.   **3** *Proverbs* 3, 18.   **4** *Proverbs* 1, 9.   **5** *Proverbs* 4, 9.
6 *Proverbs* 9,11.   **7** *Proverbs* 3, 16.   **8** *Proverbs* 3, 2.

Mishnah 8

R.[1] Simon ben Judah, in the name of[2] R. Simon ben Jochai,[3] said, Beauty, (and) strength, (and) riches, (and) honour, (and) wisdom,[5] old age, (and) a hoary head, and children are comely to the righteous and comely to the world, as it is said,[6] *The hoary head is a crown of glory; it is found in the way of righteousness;* and it says,[7] *The glory of young men is their strength, and the beauty of*

מִשְׁנָה ח

רַבִּי שִׁמְעוֹן בֶּן יְהוּדָה יְמִשּׁוּם רַבִּי
שִׁמְעוֹן בֶּן יוֹחַאי אוֹמֵר הַנּוֹי וְהַכֹּחַ
וְהָעֹשֶׁר וְהַכָּבוֹד יְוְהַחָכְמָה הַזִּקְנָה
וְהַשֵּׂיבָה וְהַבָּנִים נָאֶה לַצַּדִּיקִים וְנָאֶה
לָעוֹלָם, שֶׁנֶּאֱמַר עֲטֶרֶת תִּפְאֶרֶת
שֵׂיבָה בְּדֶרֶךְ צְדָקָה תִּמָּצֵא; וְאוֹמֵר
תִּפְאֶרֶת בַּחוּרִים כֹּחָם וַהֲדַר זְקֵנִים

old men is the hoary head; and it says,[8] *The crown of the wise is their riches;* and it says,[9] *Children's children are the crown of old men, and the glory of children are their fathers;* and it says,[10] *Then the moon shall be confounded and the sun ashamed; for the Eternal of hosts shall reign in Mount Zion, and in Jerusalem, and before His elders shall be glory.* R. Simon ben Menasia said, These seven qualifications which the Sages enumerated as becoming to the righteous were all realised in Rabbi[11] and in his sons.

שֵׂיבָה; יְאֹמֵר עֲטֶרֶת חֲכָמִים עָשְׁרָם; יְאֹמֵר עֲטֶרֶת זְקֵנִים בְּנֵי בָנִים וְתִפְאֶרֶת בָּנִים אֲבוֹתָם; יְאֹמֵר וְחָפְרָה הַלְּבָנָה וּבוֹשָׁה הַחַמָּה כִּי־מָלַךְ ה' צְבָאוֹת בְּהַר צִיּוֹן וּבִירוּשָׁלַיִם וְנֶגֶד זְקֵנָיו כָּבוֹד. רַבִּי שִׁמְעוֹן בֶּן מְנַסְיָא אוֹמֵר, אֵלּוּ שֶׁבַע מִדּוֹת שֶׁמָּנוּ חֲכָמִים לַצַּדִּיקִים כֻּלָּם נִתְקַיְּמוּ בְּרַבִּי וּבְבָנָיו.

1 The panegyric extolling the Law begun in 6¹ and running through 6⁷ is resumed here and concluded in the next *Mishnah*. **2** מִשָּׁם in some texts. **3** In some texts, יוֹחַי. **4** See 6⁴, **Note 2.** **5** Elijah, the Gaon of Wilna, suggests the omission of וְהַחָכְמָה, *wisdom*, not being referred to in the Scriptural quotations, so as to give *seven* qualifications—and not *eight* as here mentioned—in agreement with R. Simon ben Menassia's statement; on the other hand, the תַּלְמוּד יְרוּשַׁלְמִי (the *Jerusalem*, or *Palestinian Talmud*) gives *seven* by omitting הַזִּקְנָה, *old age.* **6** *Proverbs* **16**, 31. 31. **7** *Proverbs* **20**, 29. **8** *Proverbs* **14**, 24. **9** *Proverbs* **17**, 6. **10** *Isaiah* **24**, 23. **11** רַבִּי יְהוּדָה הַנָּשִׂיא. In some editions this last part from רַבִּי שִׁמְעוֹן is attached to the next *Mishnah*.

Mishnah 9

R.[1] Jose ben Kisma said, 'I was once walking by the way when a man met me and greeted me,[2] and I returned his salutation. He said to me, "Rabbi, from what[3] place art thou?"[4] I said to him, "I come from a great city[5] of Sages and Scribes". He said to me, "If thou art willing to dwell with us in our place, I will give thee a thousand thousand golden *denars*[6] and precious stones and pearls". I replied to him, "If thou wert to give me all the silver and gold and precious

מִשְׁנָה ט

אָמַר רַבִּי יוֹסֵי בֶּן קִסְמָא פַּעַם אַחַת הָיִיתִי מְהַלֵּךְ בַּדֶּרֶךְ וּפָגַע בִּי אָדָם אֶחָד וְנָתַן־לִי שָׁלוֹם וְהֶחֱזַרְתִּי לוֹ שָׁלוֹם. אָמַר לִי רַבִּי מֵאֵיזֶה מָקוֹם אַתָּה? אָמַרְתִּי לוֹ מֵעִיר גְּדוֹלָה שֶׁל חֲכָמִים וְשֶׁל סוֹפְרִים אָנִי. אָמַר לִי רַבִּי רְצוֹנְךָ שֶׁתָּדוּר עִמָּנוּ בִּמְקוֹמֵנוּ וַאֲנִי אֶתֶּן לְךָ אֶלֶף אֲלָפִים יְדִינְרֵי זָהָב וַאֲבָנִים טוֹבוֹת וּמַרְגָּלִיּוֹת. אָמַרְתִּי לוֹ אִם אַתָּה נוֹתֵן לִי כָּל־

98

stones and pearls in the world, I
would not dwell elsewhere but in
a place of the Law'' ' and thus it
is written in the *Book of Psalms*[7] by
the hands of David King of Israel,
*The Law of Thy mouth is better unto me
than thousands of gold and silver;*[8] and
not only so, but in the hour of* man's
departure, neither silver nor gold
nor precious jewels nor pearls accom-
pany him, but only [the reputation
of knowledge of] the Law and good
works, as it is said,[9] *When thou walkest
it shall lead thee, when thou liest down
it shall watch over thee; and when thou
awakest it shall talk with thee;* 'when
thou walkest it shall lead thee'—in
this world; 'when thou liest down it
shall watch over thee'—in the grave;
'and when thou awakest it shall talk
with thee'—in the Hereafter. And
it says,[10] *Mine is the silver, and Mine
is the gold, saith the Eternal of hosts.*

כֶּסֶף וְזָהָב וַאֲבָנִים טוֹבוֹת וּמַרְגָּלִיּוֹת
שֶׁבָּעוֹלָם אֵינִי דָר אֶלָּא בִּמְקוֹם
תּוֹרָה; וְכֵן כָּתוּב בְּסֵפֶר תְּהִלִּים עַל
יְדֵי דָוִד מֶלֶךְ יִשְׂרָאֵל טוֹב לִי תּוֹרַת
פִּיךָ מֵאַלְפֵי זָהָב וָכָסֶף; וְלֹא עוֹד
אֶלָּא שֶׁבִּשְׁעַת פְּטִירָתוֹ שֶׁל אָדָם
אֵין מְלַוִּים לוֹ לְאָדָם לֹא כֶסֶף וְלֹא
זָהָב וְלֹא אֲבָנִים טוֹבוֹת וּמַרְגָּלִיּוֹת
אֶלָּא תוֹרָה וּמַעֲשִׂים טוֹבִים בִּלְבָד,
שֶׁנֶּאֱמַר בְּהִתְהַלֶּכְךָ תַּנְחֶה אֹתָךְ
בְּשָׁכְבְּךָ תִּשְׁמֹר עָלֶיךָ וַהֲקִיצוֹתָ הִיא
תְשִׂיחֶךָ; בְּהִתְהַלֶּכְךָ תַּנְחֶה אֹתָךְ
בָּעוֹלָם הַזֶּה; בְּשָׁכְבְּךָ תִּשְׁמוֹר
עָלֶיךָ בַּקֶּבֶר; וַהֲקִיצוֹתָ הִיא
תְשִׂיחֶךָ לָעוֹלָם הַבָּא. ¹⁰וְאוֹמֵר לִי
הַכֶּסֶף וְלִי הַזָּהָב נְאֻם ה׳ צְבָאוֹת.

1 This *Mishnah* concludes the eulogy of the Law from the preceding *Mishnah*. See the foregoing *Mishnah*, **Note 11.** 2 The חָסִיד, *pious man*, should greet first; but R. Jose was so sunk in thought and study of the Law that he did not observe the other's approach and presence. The phrase פַּעַם אַחַת suggests that this was the only case of such lapse on his part. אֶחָת and בַּדֶּרֶךְ given in some texts are not grammatically correct. 3 מֵאֵי־זֶה in some texts. 4 אַתָּה in some texts is not grammatically correct. 5 Probably *Jabneh.* 6 See זְרָעִים, Page 18f. 7 *Psalms* **119,** 72. 8 וָכָסֶף in some texts is not the Scriptural orthography, and besides the *pausal* form is required here. 9 *Proverbs* 6, 22. 10 *Haggai* 2, 8. *Or שֶׁבְּשַׁעַת.

Mishnah 10   מִשְׁנָה י

Five[1] possessions did the Holy One,
blessed be He, make especially His
own in His world, and these are
they, *the Law*—one possession, *heaven
and earth*—one possession, *Abraham*—
one possession, *Israel*—one possession, and the *Holy Temple*—one

¹⁰חֲמִשָּׁה קִנְיָנִים קָנָה לוֹ הַקָּדוֹשׁ בָּרוּךְ
הוּא בְּעוֹלָמוֹ וְאֵלּוּ הֵן, תּוֹרָה קִנְיָן
אֶחָד, שָׁמַיִם וָאָרֶץ קִנְיָן אֶחָד,
אַבְרָהָם קִנְיָן אֶחָד, יִשְׂרָאֵל קִנְיָן

possession. Whence [do we know this] of 'the Law'? Because it is written,[2] *The Eternal made*[3] *me as the beginning of His way, before His works, of old.* Whence [know we this] of 'heaven and earth'? Because it is written,[4] *Thus saith the Eternal, The heaven is My throne, and the earth is My footstool; what manner of house will ye build unto me? And where is the place for My rest?* And it says,[5] *How manifold are Thy works, O Eternal! In wisdom hast Thou made them all; the earth is full of Thy possessions.* Whence [do we know this] of 'Abraham'? Because it is written,[6] *And he blessed him, and said, Blessed be Abram of the Most High God, Possessor of heaven and earth.* Whence [do we learn this] of 'Israel'? Because it is written,[7] *Till Thy people pass over, O Eternal, till the people pass over which Thou hast gotten;* and it says,[8] *As for the saints that are in the earth, they are the excellent in whom is all my delight.* Whence [do we learn this] of 'the Holy Temple'? Because it is written,[9] *The place, O Eternal, which Thou hast made for Thee to dwell in, the sanctuary, O Eternal, which Thy hands have established;* and it says,[10] *And he brought them to the border of His sanctuary, to this mountain which His right hand had gotten.*[11]

אֶחָד, בֵּית הַמִּקְדָּשׁ קִנְיָן אֶחָד׃ תּוֹרָה
מִנַּיִן? יׄדִּכְתִיב ה' קָנָנִי רֵאשִׁית דַּרְכּוֹ
קֶדֶם מִפְעָלָיו מֵאָז׃ שָׁמַיִם וָאָרֶץ
מִנַּיִן? יׄדִּכְתִיב כֹּה אָמַר ה' הַשָּׁמַיִם
כִּסְאִי וְהָאָרֶץ הֲדוֹם רַגְלָי אֵי־זֶה
בַית אֲשֶׁר תִּבְנוּ לִי וְאֵי־זֶה מָקוֹם
מְנוּחָתִי׃ וְיֹאמַר מָה רַבּוּ מַעֲשֶׂיךָ
ה' כֻּלָּם בְּחָכְמָה עָשִׂיתָ מָלְאָה הָאָרֶץ
קִנְיָנֶךָ׃ אַבְרָהָם מִנַּיִן? יׄדִּכְתִיב
וַיְבָרְכֵהוּ וַיֹּאמַר בָּרוּךְ אַבְרָם לְאֵל
עֶלְיוֹן קֹנֵה שָׁמַיִם וָאָרֶץ׃ יִשְׂרָאֵל
מִנַּיִן? יׄדִּכְתִיב עַד־יַעֲבֹר עַמְּךָ ה'
עַד־יַעֲבֹר עַם־זוּ קָנִיתָ׃ וְיֹאמַר
לִקְדוֹשִׁים אֲשֶׁר־בָּאָרֶץ הֵמָּה וְאַדִּירֵי
כָּל־חֶפְצִי בָם׃ בֵּית הַמִּקְדָּשׁ מִנַּיִן?
יׄדִּכְתִיב מָכוֹן לְשִׁבְתְּךָ פָּעַלְתָּ ה'
מִקְדָשׁ אֲדֹנָי כּוֹנְנוּ יָדֶיךָ; יׄוְיֹאמַר
וַיְבִיאֵם אֶל־גְּבוּל קָדְשׁוֹ הַר־זֶה
קָנְתָה יְמִינוֹ׃

---

1 Three, *viz.*, 'the Law', 'Israel', and 'the Sanctuary' (or 'Temple'), is the number given in one version. *Four* is the number given in the *Gemara* and *Mechilta*, *viz.*, 'the Law', 'heaven and earth', 'Israel', and 'the Sanctuary' (or 'Temple'), and to indicate this some Prayer Books give the text thus : (.... אֶחָד קִנְיָן אַבְרָהָם) .... אַרְבָּעָה (חֲמִשָּׁה). **2** Proverbs 8, 22. **3** Or *possessed*, referring to *the Law*. **4** Isaiah 66, 1. **6** Psalms 104, 4. **6** Genesis 14, 19. **7** Exodus 15, 16. **8** Psalms 16, 3. **9** Exodus 15, 17. **10** Psalms 78, 54. **11** See next *Mishnah*, **Note 1**.

Mishnah 11   מִשְׁנָה יא

Whatsoever[1] the Holy One, blessed be He, created in His world He created but for His glory, as it is said,[2] *Everything that is called by My Name, and which I have created for My glory, I have formed it, yea, I have made it;* and it says,[3] *The Eternal shall reign for ever and ever.* R.[4] Chanania ben Akashia said, The Holy One, blessed be He, was pleased to grant merit to Israel, therefore he gave them a copious Law and many commandments, as it is said,[5] *It pleased the Eternal, for His righteousness' sake, to magnify the Law and make it honourable.*[6]

‏כֹּל מַה שֶּׁבָּרָא הַקָּדוֹשׁ בָּרוּךְ הוּא בְּעוֹלָמוֹ לֹא בְרָאוֹ אֶלָּא לִכְבוֹדוֹ, שֶׁנֶּאֱמַר כֹּל הַנִּקְרָא בִשְׁמִי וְלִכְבוֹדִי בְּרָאתִיו יְצַרְתִּיו אַף עֲשִׂיתִיו; וְאוֹמֵר ה' יִמְלֹךְ לְעוֹלָם וָעֶד. רַבִּי חֲנַנְיָא בֶּן עֲקַשְׁיָא אוֹמֵר רָצָה הַקָּדוֹשׁ בָּרוּךְ הוּא לְזַכּוֹת אֶת־יִשְׂרָאֵל לְפִיכָךְ הִרְבָּה לָהֶם תּוֹרָה וּמִצְוֹת, שֶׁנֶּאֱמַר ה' חָפֵץ לְמַעַן צִדְקוֹ יַגְדִּיל תּוֹרָה וְיַאְדִּיר.

---

1 כָּל־מַה in some texts. In some Prayer Books this *Mishnah* is the concluding part of the preceding *Mishnah*. **2** *Isaiah 43, 7.* **3** *Exodus 15, 18.* **4** This last section is also quoted at the conclusion of מַכּוֹת (see INTRODUCTION). **5** *Isaiah 42, 21.* **6** See מַכּוֹת 3¹⁶, **Note 5.** That Israel may feel honoured and privileged to carry out the commandments. Another rendering is *to aggrandise the Torah and make it mighty.* Neither of these renderings seems satisfactory or conveys much sense, for the Torah does not need magnification, aggrandisement, glorification, honour—it already possesses these qualities ; the terms הַגְדִּיל and הַאֲדַר can be used respectively with their meanings *increase, extend,* and *strengthen, promote honourably,* and the Hebrew can then be rendered *to promote* (or *further*) *knowledge* (or *moral teaching*), *but* (or *and*) *for a lofty purpose.*

סְלִיק בָּרַיְיתָא שֶׁל קִנְיַן תּוֹרָה

CONCLUSION OF THE BARAITHA OF

'THE ACQUISITION OF THE LAW'

ADDENDA

[Additional Notes to אָבוֹת]

1¹, Note 2. Many authorities hold the opinion that the זְקֵנִים could hardly have been judges but rather leaders in times of emergency, and it seems probable that they were consulted at times and their advice was accepted and practised in the tradition of the Law.

1⁵, Note 5. Their deduction—that הָאִשָּׁה refers to (בְּ)אִשְׁתּוֹ—depends on the fact that הָאִשָּׁה is prefixed with the *definite article* הָ and thus refers (as in the Talmudic method) to someone well known, *viz.*, his wife.

3⁸, Note *. See 4²⁰, **Note 5** below.

4¹⁸, Note 2. Otherwise any possible loophole for the annulment of the vow might be closed.

4²⁰, Note 5. בְּרַבִּי [דְּבִרְבִּי] is an abbreviation of בֵּי רַבִּי, *belonging to an academy (or a school) of an eminent teacher*. It is a title most often bestowed on disciples of רַבִּי יְהוּדָה הַנָּשִׂיא and his contemporaries; some of his predecessors and occasionally the first אֲמוֹרָאִים (see Volume I, GENERAL INTRODUCTION) were also thus designated. See גִּטִּין 47, בָּבָא מְצִיעָא 73, אֲהָלוֹת 3⁵.

5¹, Note 2. Many maintain that וַיֹּאמֶר אֱלֹהִים occurring 'nine' times is made up to 'ten' with the word בְּרֵאשִׁית, *In the beginning* [*Genesis* 1, 1] as another 'saying'.

5³, Note 3. The *ten trials* to which *Abraham* was subjected were: [1] when he was born Nimrod sought to slay him and he was hidden in an underground shelter for three years; when he emerged he rejected all idolatrous beliefs and practices and worshipped God only (בֵּית הַמִּדְרָשׁ ב · · · שֶׁל יַעֲלִיזְק?); [2] his experience in the burning furnace (*Nehemiah* 9, 7; תָּנָא דְּבֵי אֵלִיָּהוּ ר; פְּסָחִים, קיח; בְּרֵאשִׁית רַבָּא, לח, לט; יַלְקוּט שִׁמְעוֹנִי תְּהִלִּים); [3] his departure from his native land (*Genesis* 12, 1ff.); [4] the famine (*Genesis* 12, 10); [5] Sarai taken by Pharaoh (*Genesis* 12, 15); [6] his battle with the attackers against Sodom (*Genesis* 14, 1ff.); [7] his vision (*Genesis* 15, 1f.); [8] the circumcision (*Genesis* 17, 23, 21, 4); [9] the expulsion of Hagar and Ishmael (*Genesis* 21, 10ff.); [10] the binding of Isaac (*Genesis* 22, 1ff.).

5⁴, Note 3. The *ten miracles on the sea*, inferred from the varying phrases in *Exodus* 15, 1ff., and detailed in אָבוֹת דְּרַבִּי נָתָן: [1] tunnel-like passages were formed through the sea ; [2] the sea-bottom became like a valley (or a level plain); [3] the waters turned into solid blocks; [4] the sea-bottom became clay-like; [5] the sea-bottom was like to ' a wilderness'; [6] the sea-waters were converted into solid 'crumb-like' structure; [7] the sea-waters became 'rock-like'; [8] the sea-bottom was the like of 'dry land'; [9] the sea-waters parted and stood up like 'walls'; [10] the sea-waters stood up as 'a heap,' The same source (אֲבוֹת דְּרַבִּי נָתָן) gives an alternative list deduced from the varying phrases in *Psalm* **18**, 13ff.: [1] the enemy was confused with miraculous thunderings; [2] the terrifying appearance of a wondrous rainbow; [3] showers of arrows from the sky upon the enemy; [4] swords showered down on them from the sky; [5] destruction from showers of spears upon them; [6] shields from the sky showered down upon them; [7] hooks from the sky destroyed them; [8] javelins and lances showered down from the sky to destroy them; [9] hail destroyed them; [10] burning coals from the sky fell upon them.

5⁴, **Note 7.** The *ten provokings* at the *Red Sea* and in the *Wilderness*: [1] *Exodus* **14**, 11: הֲמִבְּלִי אֵין קְבָרִים, *Because there were no graves . . . . ?* [2] *Exodus* **14**, 30: the fear of the people that an Egyptian army might have crossed somewhere to outflank them and so cut them off to be destroyed, and their minds were set at rest when they saw the dead cast up on the shore—וַיַּרְא יִשְׂרָאֵל אֶת־מִצְרַיִם מֵת עַל שְׂפַת הַיָּם, *and Israel saw the Egyptians dead upon the sea-shore;* [3] *Exodus* **16**, 20: וַיּוֹתִרוּ אֲנָשִׁים, *but some of them left of it* [*viz.*, the manna]; [4] *Exodus* **16**, 20: יָצְאוּ מִן־הָעָם לִלְקֹט, *that there went out some of the people to gather* [*viz.*, the manna on the Sabbath]; some connect this with the 'quails' mentioned in *Genesis* **16**, 13; [5] *Exodus* **16**, 3: בְּשִׁבְתֵּנוּ עַל סִיר הַבָּשָׂר, *when we sat by the 'flesh pots';* [6] *Numbers* **11**, 4: וְהָאסַפְסֻף אֲשֶׁר בְּקִרְבּוֹ הִתְאַוּוּ תַּאֲוָה, *And the mixed multitude that was among them fell a lusting*—in connection with the 'quails' (see *Numbers* **11**, 31ff.); [7] *Exodus* **15**, 24: וַיִּלֹּנוּ הָעָם, *And the people murmured*—when they lacked water; [8] *Exodus* **17**, 2: וַיָּרֶב הָעָם, *wherefore the people strove*—when they lacked water; [9] *Exodus* **32**, 1ff.: עֵגֶל מַסֵּכָה, *a molten calf*—the sin of the עֵגֶל הַזָּהָב, the *golden calf*; [10] *Numbers* **13**, 26ff.: וַיּוֹצִיאוּ דִבַּת הָאָרֶץ, *And they spread an evil report of the land*—the iniquity of the *ten spies*.

6¹, **Note *.** The term מִשְׁנָה, *Mishnah*, given as the heading for each of the separate passages here is not used in its *Mishnaic* sense (seeing that the whole Chapter is a בְּרַיְתָא) but in its alternative meaning, *section* or *paragraph*.

103

BIOGRAPHIES
THE MAKERS OF THE MISHNAH

BY
REV. JOSEPH HALPERN, M.A.

Judaica Press, LTD.

Gateshead • 1985

BIOGRAPHIES

THE MAKERS OF THE MISHNAH

Brief supplementary notes on the scholars cited in the *Mishnah*

[Fl. = flourished, c. = circa, b. = *ben* (בן).]

PRE-TANNAITIC (c. 300 B.C.E.-10 C.E.).

1. **Avtalion:** Av-Bet-Din to Shemaia. Fl. c. 50 B.C.E. Of heathen descent. One of the most influential and beloved scholars of his time. Called Pollion by Josephus, who writes of him:

> "Pollion the Pharisee, and Sameas a disciple of his, were honoured by him (Herod) above all the rest; for when Jerusalem was besieged (37 B.C.E.) they advised the citizens to receive Herod."

He and his colleague Shemaia were the first to be known as *Darshanim.* חגיגה 2²; עדיות 1⁵, 5⁶; אבות 1¹⁰,¹¹.

2. **Akavia b. Mahalel:** Fl. c. 40 B.C.E. All that we know of him is found in the *Mishnah.* He maintained his minority opinion to the last, in spite of inducements of office by his colleagues. His dying advice to his son is worthy of note. עדיות 5⁶,⁷; אבות 3¹; בכורות 3⁴; נגעים 1⁴, 5³; נדה 2⁶.

3. **Antigonus of Soko:** Fl. c. 200 B.C.E. *Avot de R. Nathan* mention two disciples of his who are not referred to in the *Mishnah*, Zadok and Boethus, who inferred from their teacher's words a denial of the resurrection and future life. אבות 1³.

4. **Bava b. Buta:** Fl. c. 30 B.C.E. A disciple of Shammai. A judge in Jerusalem. The *Talmud* tells of his piety, meekness and wisdom. Advised Herod to rebuild the Temple as an atonement for slaughtering the sages of Israel. כריתות 6³.

5. **Hillel:** Fl. at beginning of C.E. Native of Babylonia, of Davidic descent, disciple of Shemaia and Avtalion, appointed *Nasi* early in reign of Herod. Responsible for the 'seven rules' for the oral interpretation of the *Written Law.* Famed for his gentle and peace-loving character, his infinite patience, modesty and charitable nature. Head of school known as *Bet Hillel.* ברכות 1³, 8¹⁻⁸; פאה 3¹, 6¹,²,⁵, 7⁶; דמאי 1³, 6⁶; כלאים 2⁶, 4¹,⁵, 6¹; שביעית 1¹, 4³,⁴,¹⁰, 5⁴,⁸, 8³, 10³; תרומות 1⁴, 5⁴; מעשרות 4²; מעשר שני 2³,⁴,⁷,⁸,⁹, 3⁶,⁷,⁹,¹,³, 4⁸, 5³,⁶,⁷; חלה 1⁶; ערלה 2⁴; שבת 1⁴⁻⁹, 3¹, 21³; ערובין 1², 6⁴,⁶, 8⁶; פסחים 1¹, 4⁵, 8⁸, 10³,⁶; שקלים 2³, 8⁶; סוכה 1¹,⁷, 2⁷, 3⁵,⁹; ביצה 1¹⁻³,⁵⁻⁹, 2¹⁻⁵; ראש השנה 1¹; חגיגה 1¹,²,³, 2²,³,⁴; יבמות 1⁴, 3¹,⁵, 4³, 6⁶, 13¹, 15²,³; כתובות 5⁶, 8¹,⁶; נדרים 3²,⁴; נזיר 2¹,², 3⁶,⁷, 5¹⁻³,⁵; סוטה 4²; גיטין 4³,⁵, 8⁴,⁸,⁹, 9¹⁰; בבא מציעא 3¹², 5⁹; בבא בתרא 9⁸,⁹; עדיות 1¹⁻⁴,⁷⁻¹⁴, 4¹⁻¹², 5¹⁻⁵; אבות 1¹²⁻¹⁴, 2⁵,⁶,⁷, 4⁵, 5¹⁷; זבחים 4¹; חולין 1², 8¹, 11³; בכורות 5²; ערכין 9⁴; כריתות 1⁶; כלים 9², 11³, 14², 18¹, 20²,⁶, 22⁴, 26⁶, 28⁴, 29⁸; אהלות 2³, 5¹⁻⁴, 7³, 11¹,³⁻⁶,⁸, 13¹,⁴, 15⁸, 18¹,⁴,⁸; פרה 12¹⁰; טהרות 9¹,⁵,⁷, 10⁴; מקואות 1⁵, 4¹, 5⁶, 10⁶; נדה 1¹, 2⁴,⁶, 4³, 5⁹, 10¹,⁴,⁶⁻⁸; מכשירין 1²⁻⁴, 4⁴,⁵; זבים 1¹,²; טבול יום 1¹; ידים 3⁵; עוקצין 3⁶,⁸,¹¹.

BIOGRAPHIES

6. **Jochanan High Priest:** John Hyrcanus, king of Judea 135-105 B.C.E., grandson of Mattathias who started the revolt against Antiochus Epiphanes. Enlarged the boundaries of his kingdom by subduing the Edomites and Samaritans. Held in very high esteem until towards the end of his reign when he sided with the Sadducees. מעשר שני 5^{15}; סוטה 9^{10}; פרה 3^5; ידים 4^6.

7. **Jose b. Joezer** and 8. **Jose b. Johanan:** The first of the *Zugot* or *"Pairs"*. Fl. c. 170 B.C.E. Accepted rule of Alcimus who was appointed High Priest by the Syrians against Judah the Maccabee. Alcimus was nephew of Jose b. Joezer and murdered his uncle in a massacre of scholars. (7) חגיגה $2^{2,7}$; סוטה 9^9; עדויות 8^4; אבות 1^4 (8) חגיגה 2^2; סוטה 9^9; אבות $1^{4,5}$.

9. **Joshua b. Perachia:** Fl. c. 100 B.C.E. Fled to Alexandria when John Hyrcanus began persecuting the Pharisees. Gave instructions about performance of the ceremony of the Red Heifer. חגיגה 2^2; אבות 1^6.

10. **Judah b. Tabbai:** Fl. c. 70 B.C.E. Executed a plotting witness in order to refute the Sadducean teaching on this subject. On being rebuked for this by Simon b. Shetach he never again gave a legal decision without him. חגיגה 2^2; אבות 1^8.

11. **Measha:** Contemporary of Hillel. פאה 2^6.

12. **Menachem:** Contemporary of Hillel who entered Herod's service. חגיגה 2^2.

13. **Nittai the Arbelite:** Colleague of Joshua b. Perachia. חגיגה 2^2; אבות $1^{6,7}$.

14. **Onias the Circle-maker:** Fl. c. 70 B.C.E. Josephus relates that he was stoned to death by the party of Hyrcanus when they were besieging Aristobulus in Jerusalem in 65 B.C.E. He was asked to pray for the besiegers. Spreading his hands to heaven, he exclaimed: "They are both Thy children. Listen not if they pray against one another for evil, but only for good." He was the Jewish Rip Van Winkle. תענית 3^8.

15. **Shammai:** Colleague of Hillel. Fearless and outspoken, yet warm-hearted man. Head of school known as *Bet Shammai*. ברכות 6^5; דמאי 3^1; כלאים 8^6; עדויות 2^2; חגיגה 2^6; ביצה 2^8; סוכה $2^{5,12}$; ערלה $2^{4,9}$; מעשר שני 4^3; תרומות 5^9. מכשירין 1^1; נדה 22^4; כלים 4^5; מקואות 5^{17}, $1^{12,15}$; אבות 3^{10}, $1^{1-4,7,8,10,11}$.

16. **Shemaia:** Colleague of Avtalion. Of heathen descent. Both highly esteemed in their generation. Both responsible for reviving Hillel when he was almost frozen to death listening to their lecture on a Sabbath. חגיגה 2^2; עדויות 1^3, 5^6; אבות 1^{10}.

17. **Simon b. Shetach:** Colleague of Judah b. Tabbai and brother-in-law of King Alexander Jannai. Introduced schools for adolescents. Principal adviser to Queen in reign of his sister Alexandra Salome. תענית 3^8; חגיגה 2^2; סנהדרין 6^4; אבות $1^{8,9}$.

18. **Simon the Just:** Fl. c. 300 B.C.E. High Priest. Attempted to make Judaism secure against inroads of Hellenism. אבות $1^{2,3}$; פרה 3^5.

BIOGRAPHIES

THE FIRST GENERATION (c. 10 - 80 C.E.).

19. **Admon b. Gaddai:** Contemporary of R. Jochanan b. Zakkai. The chief of three named police-court judges in Jerusalem who received a salary from the Temple treasury. כתובות 13¹,³⁻⁹; בבא בתרא 9¹; שבועות 6³.

20, **Ben Buchri:** Contemporary of R. Johanan b. Zakkai. שקלים 1⁴.

21. **Dositheus or Dostai of Kefar Yathma** — Disciple of Shammai. ערלה 2⁵.

22. **R. Gamliel the Elder:** Grandson of Hillel. First to be styled Rabban. Transferred the College to Yavne. Executed many beneficial ordinances. פאה 2⁶; 1¹⁶ אבות 1⁴²,³; גטין 9¹⁵; סוטה 2⁵; יבמות 16⁷; ראש השנה 3³, 6¹; שקלים 2¹²; ערלה.

23. **Chanan b. Avishalom:** Colleague of Admon. כתובות 13¹,².

24. **Chanania b. Hezekia b. Gorion:** Younger contemporary of Hillel and Shammai. Through him the books of Ezekiel and Megillat Taanit were preserved. שבת 1⁴.

25. **R. Chanina Vice High Priest:** Served in and survived the destruction of the Temple. A lover of peace. Suffered a martyr's death. פסחים 1⁶; שקלים 4⁴, 6¹; עדיות 2¹⁻³; אבות 3²; זבחים 9³, 12⁴; מנחות 10¹; נגעים 1⁴; פרה 3¹.

26. **R. Jochanan b. Gudgada:** A pious Levite, who served in the Temple. גטין 2⁷; יבמות 14²; חגיגה 5⁵.

27. **R. Jochanan b. ha-Horani:** A disciple of *Bet Shammai* who is recorded to have acted according to the view of *Bet Hillel*. סוכה 2⁷.

28. **Rabban Jochanan b. Zakkai:** The last of Hillel's disciples. Succeeded in persuading Vespasian to spare the College at Yavne. Head of that College for decade following the destruction of Jerusalem. Nine ordinances by him enumerated in the Talmud (*Rosh Hashanah* 31b). שבת 16⁷, 22³; שקלים 1⁴; סוכה 2⁵, 3¹²; ראש השנה 4¹,³,⁴; כתובות 13¹,²; סוטה 5²,⁵, 9⁹,¹⁵; סנהדרין 5²; עדיות 8³,⁷; אבות 2⁸,⁹; מנחות 10⁵; כלים 2², 17¹⁶; ידים 4³,⁶.

29. **Joezer of the Bira:** A disciple of *Bet Shammai*. ערלה 2¹².

30. **Jose Choli Kufri, Abba:** Mentioned only once. מכשירין 1³.

31. **Menachem b. Signai:** A dyer. עדיות 7⁸.

32. **Nachum the Mede:** A judge in Jerusalem in the last days of the Temple. שבת 2¹; נזיר 5⁴; בבא בתרא 5².

33. **Nachum the Scrivener:** Mentioned only once. פאה 2⁶.

34. **Samuel the Younger:** A disciple of Hillel. Composed the blessing against heretics in the *Amidah*. אבות 4¹⁹.

35. **Rabban Simon b. Gamliel I:** Succeeded his father as Patriarch. Opposed appointment of Josephus to command of Galilee. Died a martyr's death, possibly at the hands of the Zealots whose extremism he opposed. אבות 1¹⁷; כריתות 1⁷.

36. **Simon of Mizpa:** Probably a priest who served in the Temple. Contemporary of Nahum the Scrivener. פאה 2⁶.

37. **R. Zecharia b. ha-Kazzav:** Lived while Temple still stood. כתובות 2⁹; עדיות 8²; סוטה 5¹.

38. **R. Zecharia b. Kavutal:** Most probably a priest who served in the Temple. יומא 1⁶.

109

BIOGRAPHIES

THE SECOND GENERATION (c. 80-120 C.E.).

39. R. Dosa b. Harkinas: Already an old man when the Temple was destroyed. but still active in the College at Yavne afterwards. Wealthy and influential. שבת 1[7], חולין 3[10]; אבות 3[1-6]; עדיות 13[1,2]; כתובות 2[8,9]; ראש השנה 3[9]; עירובין 20[4]; טהרות 1[4]; נגעים 3[1]; אהלות 7[2]; בכורות 11[2]; 8[8].

40. R. Elazar b. Arach: Considered the greatest and wisest of the disciples of Rabban Jochanan b. Zakkai, but died in obscurity because he retired to Emmaus on the death of his master in the expectation that his colleagues would come to him; they did not. אבות 2[8,9,14].

41. R. Elazar b. Azaria: Appointed Patriarch by the scholars when Rabban Gamliel was deposed, and later shared this office when he was restored to the dignity. Very young on appointment but wealthy, well-born (a priest, tenth in descent from Ezra) and learned. A great Aggadist. Accompanied Rabban Gamliel, R. Joshua and R. Akiva on their second journey to Rome. Died probably just after the outbreak of the Bar-Cochba revolt. ברכות 1[5], 4[7]; שביעית 1[8], 3[8]; מעשרות 5[1]; מועד קטן 1[2]; מעשר שני 5[9]; שבת 4[2], 5[4], 19[3]; עירובין 4[1]; יומא 8[9]; ביצה 2[8]; עדיות 3[12]; כתובות 4[6], 5[1]; נדרים 3[11]; נזיר 6[2]; סוטה 9[15]; בבא קמא 6[4]; מכות 1[10]; נגעים 7[2], 8[9], 13[6]; כלים 3[8]; זבחים 1[8]; מנחות 13[6]; ערכין 8[4]; כריתות 2[5]; אבות 3[17]; טהרות 7[7]; מקואות 3[2], 8[3]; מכשירין 6[6]; ידים 3[5], 4[2,3]; עוקצין 1[5].

42. R. Elazar b. Diglai (or Dilgai): Mentioned only once. תמיד 3[8].

43. R. Eliezer (b. Hyrcanus): Styled 'the Great.' Came of wealthy but ignorant land-owning family. One of the greatest of the pupils of Rabban Johanan b. Zakkai. Remarkable for his retentive memory, but stubborn in maintaining views he had learnt. Married sister of Rabban Gamliel. Was "sent to Coventry" by his colleagues and retired to Lydda, where he became the teacher of R. Akiva. Lived to a very ripe old age, and went to Rome with R. Joshua and Rabban Gamliel before his retirement. More than three hundred of his halakot are quoted in the *Talmud* and the Tannaitic *Midrashim*. ברכות 1[1,2], 4[5], 5[2], 7[5]; פאה 3[6], 4[9], 5[2,4], 7[7]; דמאי 4[3], 5[9], 6[3]; כלאים 2[10], 3[4], 5[3,8], 6[2], 9[3]; שביעית 5[3], 8[9,10], 9[5,9], 10[7]; תרומות 2[1], 4[7-11], 5[2,4-6], 6[6], 8[1-3,8-11], 11[2]; מעשרות 2[4], 4[3,5,6]; חלה 1[3], 2[1,4,8], 4[7]; ערלה 1[7]; שבת 1[10], 2[3], 6[4], 10[6], 12[4], 13[1], 17[7], 19[1,4], 22[1]; עירובין 1[2], 2[5,6], 3[3,6], 4[5,11], 7[10,11], 9[2], 10[10]; פסחים 1[7], 3[1,3], 5[9], 6[1,2,6], 9[2,4]; ראש השנה 4[1]; שקלים 3[1], 4[7], 8[7]; יומא 5[5], 7[3], 8[1]; סוכה 1[11], 2[6], 4[5]; ביצה 4[6,7]; תענית 1[1], 3[9]; מגלה 4[10]; מועד קטן 3[6]; חגיגה 3[8]; יבמות 3[1], 6[3,4], 8[4,6], 12[2,3], 13[2,6,7,11], 16[2,7]; כתובות 1[6-9], 5[5,6], 9[4]; נדרים 4[3], 9[1,2], 10[5-7]; נזיר 3[3-5], 6[7,11], 7[1]; בבא קמא 1[1], 3[4], 6[1], 8[3], 9[2-4]; גטין 1[1], 3[2], 4[7], 6[3,4], 8[8], 9[1,4]; קדושין 1[4,9], 3[18], 4[2,13]; בבא מציעא 1[4], 6[4], 6[8]; בבא בתרא 3[8], 4[4,5], 9[7]; סנהדרין 1[4], 6[4], 10[3]; מכות 3[5]; שבועות 2[5], 5[3]; עדיות 2[7], 5[4,5], 6[2,3], 7[1,5-7], 8[6]; עבודה זרה 1[8], 3[9]; הוריות 2[7]; זבחים 1[1,4], 3[8], 7[4], 8[4,5,7-12], 11[3]; מנחות 3[1,4], 7[3]; חולין 2[6,7], 12[2]; בכורות 1[5,6], 4[7], 5[3], 7[6], 8[10], 9[5]; ערכין 3[2], 6[1,3], 8[4]; תמורה 3[1,3], 6[5]; כריתות 3[10], 4[2,3], 6[1,3]; מעילה 1[2,3]; כלים 1[2,3], 2[8], 3[2], 5[10], 8[1], 10[1], 11[5,8], 14[1,7], 15[2], 17[1], 18[9], 26[2,4,5], 27[5,12], 28[2]; אהלות 2[2,4], 6[1], 9[14,15], 11[7], 12[2,8], 14[4,5], 17[2,5]; נגעים 6[7], 7[4,5], 9[3], 11[7], 13[2,6], 14[9]; פרה 1[1], 2[1,3,5], 4[1,3], 5[4], 7[10], 9[1,3,4,7], 10[1,3], 11[2,7]; טהרות 2[2,7], 8[7], 9[3]; מקואות 2[4,7,8,10], 6[11], 8[1], 9[3]; נדה 1[3,5], 4[4,6], 5[9], 6[12], 10[3]; מכשירין 4[5], 6[6,7]; זבים 2[2], 5[3,7]; ידים 4[2,3]; עוקצין 1[2], 2[3], 3[10].

44. R. Eliezer b. Jacob I: Lived in time of Temple, on which he was considered an authority. Contemporary of R. Eliezer. תמיד 5[2]; מדות 1[2,9], 2[5,6], 5[4].

BIOGRAPHIES

45. R. Eliezer b. Zadok I: Most probably a priest, who lived in Temple times and was an authority on customs in Jerusalem and in the house of the Patriarch Rabban Gamliel at Yavne, as well as on the Temple. מדות 3⁸.

46. Rabban Gamliel II: Grandson of Rabban Gamliel I. Appointed Patriarch on death of Rabban Johanan b. Zakkai, c. 80 C.E. Deposed by scholars at Yavne after he had three times humiliated R. Joshua. Restored to office on reconciliation. The greatest scholars of the age were with him at Yavne. Went on several missions to Rome on behalf of his people and was well received there, first with R. Eliezer and R. Joshua and later with R. Elazar b. Azaria, R. Joshua and R. Akiva. Man of great learning, well acquainted with the wisdom of the Greeks and Romans, and keenly interested in scientific study. ברכות 1¹, 2⁵⁻⁷, 4³, 6⁸; פאה 2⁴, 4⁵, 6⁶; דמאי 3¹; שביעית 9⁵; תרומות 8⁸; מעשרות 4⁶; מעשר שני 2⁷, 5⁹; חלה 4⁷,⁸; בכורים 2⁶; שבת 12⁶, 16⁸; ערובין 4¹,², 6², 10¹,¹⁰; פסחים 1⁶, 3⁴, 7³, 10⁵; סוכה 2¹,⁵, 3⁹; ביצה 1⁸, 2⁶,⁷, 3²; מועד קטן 3⁶; תענית 1³, 2¹⁰; ראש השנה 1⁶, 2⁸,⁹, 4⁹; יבמות 5¹, 13⁷, 16⁷; כתובות 1⁶⁻⁹, 8¹, 12⁴, 13³⁻⁵; סוטה 2¹; גטין 1¹,⁸; בבא מציעא 5⁸,¹⁰; כריתות 9¹; זבחים 3⁴; עבודה זרה 3⁹⁻¹¹, 7⁷; עדיות 6⁸; שבועות 9¹; בבא בתרא 3⁷⁻⁹; כלים 5⁴, 8⁹, 12³,⁶, 17³, 28⁴; נעים 6⁵, 7⁴; פרה 9³, 11¹; טהרות 9¹; ידים 4⁴.

47. R. Chalafta: Descendant of Jonadab the Rechabite. Contemporary of Rabban Gamliel II. Lived in Sepphoris. תענית 2⁵.

48. R. Chanina b. Dosa: A disciple of Rabban Jochanan b. Zakkai, famed for his piety and wonder-working abilities. His poverty was proverbial. ברכות 5⁵; סוטה 9¹⁶; אבות 3¹⁰,¹¹.

49. R. Chanina b. Gamliel: Older brother of the Patriarch Rabban Simon b. Gamliel. Disciple of his father and R. Tarfon. Many of his sayings are reported by the Amoraim in both *Talmuds.* מנחות 3¹⁵; מכות 10¹; בבא בתרא 3⁴; קדושין 5⁸; בכורות 6⁹.

50. R. Chuzpit: Styled 'The Interpreter,' a post he filled in the College at Yavne in the time of Rabban Gamliel II. One of the Ten Martyrs. שביעית 10⁶.

51. R. Jeshevav: Contemporary of R. Huzpit and like him one of the Ten Martyrs. Is in one place called 'The Scribe.' חולין 2⁴.

52. Jose b. Chanan, Abba: Lived in Temple times. מדות 2⁶.

53. Jose b. Onias: Contemporary of R. Eliezer. זבחים 1⁹.

54. R. Jose son of the Damascene: Disciple of R. Eliezer. ידים 4³.

55. R. Jose the Priest: The third disciple of Rabban Jochanan b. Zakkai. עדיות 8²; אבות 2⁸,⁹,¹².

56. R. Joshua b. Bathira: Member of the noble family in Jerusalem which held the office of Patriarch during the interregnum between Shemaia and Hillel. Colleague of R. Joshua. שבת 12⁵; יבמות 8⁴; עדיות 8¹; פרה 2⁵.

57. R. Joshua (b. Chanania): A Levite, of the singers in the Temple. Disciple of Rabban Jochanan b. Zakkai, being one of those who carried his coffin when he escaped from Jerusalem during the siege. Acquired his master's skill in routing heretics. Appointed *Av-Bet-Din* in College of Yavne in Patriarchate of Rabban Gamliel.

BIOGRAPHIES

Friendly with the Romans and went frequently to Rome on behalf of his people, first with Rabban Gamliel and R. Eliezer and later with Rabban Gamliel, R. Akiva and R. Elazar b. Azaria. Went also to Alexandria. A great linguist. Was a poor man and earned a living as a charcoal-burner. Supported Rabban Gamliel in the dispute with R. Eliezer but was himself three times humiliated by Rabban Gamliel for daring to disagree with him. This brought about the revolt of the scholars and the deposition of Rabban Gamliel. After the reconciliation R. Elazar b. Azaria was appointed *Av-Bet-Din* and R. Joshua established a school of his own at Pekiin. He died in Tiberias. ברכות 1², 4³·⁴; פאה 3⁶; כלאים 6⁴; שביעית 1⁸, 2³, 3¹⁰, 5⁸, 9⁶; עורבין 4⁷⁻¹¹, 8¹⁻³·⁸⁻¹¹, 11²; מעשר שני 2⁷, 5⁹; חלה 2⁵; עורלה 1⁷; שבת 12⁴, 19⁴; ראש השנה 2⁸·⁹; 1⁴, 7¹⁰; פסחים 1⁷, 3³, 6³·⁵, 9⁶; שקלים 4⁷; יומא 2⁸; סוכה 3⁹; נדרים 1⁶·⁹, 2²; נזיר 10⁶; 7⁴, 8¹; תענית 1¹, 2⁶, 4⁴; יבמות 4¹³, 8⁴, 13⁷, 16¹·⁷; כתובות 7¹¹; עדיות 2⁷, 3⁷, 6²·³, 7¹·⁵⁻⁷, סוטה 1¹, 3⁴, 5¹·²·⁵, 6¹, 9¹²·¹⁵; בבא בתרא 9⁷; סנהדרין 8³·⁵⁻⁷; עבודה זרה 2⁵; אבות 2⁸·⁹·¹¹; זבחים 1³, 7⁴, 8¹⁰, 9¹; מנחות 3⁴; חולין 2⁴; קנים 3⁶; מעילה 1¹, 4³; כריתות 3⁷⁻⁹, 4²·³; תמורה 3¹; ערכין 6¹; בכורות 1⁶, 9⁴; נגעים 4¹¹, 7⁴, 8², 14¹³; כלים 11⁴, 13⁷, 14⁷, 17¹, 28²; אהלות 2⁴, 9¹⁵, 12⁸·⁸, 14³⁻⁵, 17²; פרה 1¹, 5³·⁴, 9⁴, 10¹·²·⁶; טהרות 2³, 6², 8⁷·⁹; מקואות 2⁷·⁸·¹⁰, 3¹; נדה 1³, 4⁴, 6¹⁴, 10²; מכשירין 1³; זבים 4¹, 5¹; טבול יום 3⁴·⁵, 4⁶; ידים 3¹·², 4³·⁴.

58. R. Joshua b. Hyrcanus: Fl. at the time of the dispute between Rabban Gamliel and R. Joshua. סוטה 5⁵.

59. R. Judah b. Bathira: Contemporary of R. Joshua, R. Eliezer, Rabban Gamliel and R. Tarfon, but outlived them all and survived even R. Akiva. Had school in Nisibis. Doubtless descended from the same family as his colleague R. Joshua b. Bathira. פאה 3⁶; בכורים 1⁶; שבת 9⁷; פסחים 3³; יבמות 4⁹; כתובות 11⁷; אהלות 2⁴; כלים 8⁶; ערכין 8⁶; עדיות 8³; שבועות 3⁶; גטין 2⁴; נדרים 6⁸; 6¹; נגעים 9⁸, 11⁷; מקואות 4⁵.

60. R. Nechunia b. Elinathan: 'Of the Babylonian Village.' Contemporary of R. Eliezer and R. Joshua. עדיות 6²·³.

61. R. Nechunia b. ha-Kana: Contemporary of the disciples of Rabban Jochanan b. Zakkai. Lived to a great age. Reputed to be a mystic. אבות 3⁵; ברכות 4³.

62. R. Papias: Contemporary of R. Joshua. שקלים 4⁷; נזיר 3³; עדיות 7⁵⁻⁷; תמורה 3¹.

63. Saul b. Botnit, Abba: Contemporary and colleague of R. Eliezer b. Zadok I. ביצה 3⁸; שבת 24⁵.

64. R. Simon b. Bathira: Of the same family as his relatives R. Judah and R. Joshua. זבחים 1⁶; עבודה זרה 8¹; עדיות 5⁷; גטין 4³; פסחים 16¹·³; שבת; מנחות 1².

65. R. Simon b. Nethanel: The fourth of the five great disciples of Rabban Jochanan b. Zakkai. A priest. Married a daughter of Rabban Gamliel the Elder. אבות 2⁸·⁹·¹³.

66. Simon brother of Azaria: Regarded by Maimonides as uncle of R. Elazar b. Azaria. So called because his brother, engaged in business, gave him the means to study. זבחים 1²; טהרות 8⁷.

67. R. Simon son of the Vice High Priest: Regarded by Maimonides as son of R. Chanina. שקלים 8^5; כתובות 2^8; מנחות 11^9.

68. R. Yakim of Hadar: Mentioned once only. עדיות 7^5.

69. R. Zadok: Son of R. Eliezer b. Zadok I. Lived in the circle of Rabban Gamliel at Yavne. תרומות 10^9; שבת 20^2, 24^5; פסחים 7^2; סוכה 2^5; נדרים 9^1; מקואות 5^5. כלים $12^{4,5}$; בכורות 1^6; כלים 4^5; אבות 3^3, 7^{1-4}; עדיות

THE THIRD GENERATION (c. 120 - 140 C.E.).

70. Avtolemus: Teacher of R. Jose. עירובין 3^4.

71. Akiva: Son of a proselyte. Born in Jerusalem before the destruction of the city by the Romans. Ignorant shepherd to a rich land-owner, whose daughter Rachel he married. Encouraged by her he went to study at the schools of R. Eliezer and R. Joshua and became the most famous scholar of his generation. He attempted to find the source of the *Halachah* in the words of the *Torah*, even in its letters. Translations of the *Torah* into Greek and Aramaic were made under his influence by the proselyte Aquila. Travelled throughout the Diaspora, acting as scholar-statesman. Supported revolt of Bar-Cochba, greeting him as Messiah. Courageously taught and practised Jewish law even when it was proscribed after the war. Was one of the Ten Martyrs. ברכות 4^3, 5^2, 6^8, 7^3; פאה 1^6, $3^{2,6}$, $4^{5,10}$, 7^7, 8^5; כלאים 1^3, $3^{5,6}$, 5^7, 6^1, 7^5; שביעית 1^8, 3^{10}, 4^6, 6^2, $8^{9,10}$, 9^6; תרומות 3^3, $4^{5,8,13}$, 6^6, 9^2, 10^{11}; מעשרות $3^{5,9}$, 4^6; מעשר שני $2^{4,7,9}$, $5^{8,9}$; חלה $2^{1,3}$, 3^6, $4^{4,5,9}$; ערלה 3^7; בכורים 3^9; שבת 2^3, 8^5, 9^1, 11^1, 15^3, 19^1; עירובין 1^2, $2^{4,5}$, 4^1, $5^{8,9}$, 6^9, 10^{15}; פסחים 1^6, 3^4, 6^2, 7^1, $9^{2,6}$, $10^{6,9}$; שקלים 3^1, $4^{3,4,6,7}$, 8^7; יומא 2^3, 7^3, 8^9; סוכה $3^{4,9}$; ביצה 3^3; ראש השנה 1^6, 2^9, 4^5; תענית $3^{3,4}$, 4^4; יבמות $4^{12,13}$, 8^4, $12^{8,5}$, $15^{6,7}$, 16^7; כתובות 3^3, 5^3, $9^{2,3}$, 11^4; נדרים 11^1; בבא קמא 7^1, $9^{5,6}$, 10^6, 11^4; נזיר 4^5, $6^{1,6}$, 7^4; סוטה 5^{1-4}, 8^5, $9^{3,4,16}$; גטין 8^{10}, 9^{10}; בבא מציעא 3^5, 6^4, 8^6; בבא בתרא 2^7, 3^{12}; סנהדרין 1^6, 2^9, 3^1, $4^{2,9}$, 6^4, 7^3, 9^{10}; 1^4, שבועות 2^5, $3^{1,5}$; עדיות $1^{8,10}$, $2^{1,2,6-10}$, $8^{1,5}$; מכות $1^{7,10}$, 2^7; עבודה זרה 2^3, $3^{5,6}$; אבות 3^{13-16}; הוריות 1^2, 2^5; זבחים 8^{11}, 9^3, 12^4; מנחות 4^3, 9^6, כריתות 1^1; תמורה 1^1; חולין 2^4, 8^4, 9^4; בכורות 2^{6-9}, 3^1, 4^4, 6^6, 7^5, 8^6, 9^6; 10^4, 11^3, 12^5; מעילה $1^{2,3}$, 5^1, 6^6; כלים $2^{3,4}$, 3^8, 11^6, 12^5, 14^1, $17^{5,13,17}$, $20^{4,6}$, $22^{7,9,10}$ $25^{4,7}$, 27^5, $28^{3,7}$, 30^2; אהלות 1^3, $2^{3,6,7}$, 3^6, $5^{1,3,7}$, 13^8, 16^7; נגעים $1^{2,4}$, 2^1, 4^{7-10}, $5^{3,4}$, 6^6, $7^{3,4}$, 10^1, 12^8, 14^{10}; פרה 2^5, $3^{4,9}$, 8^{11}, $10^{4,5}$; טהרות $5^{1,2}$, 7^6; מקואות 3^3, 7^1, 8^5; נדה 2^3, 5^8, 6^{13}, 8^8, 10^3; מכשירין 4^9, 5^4, 6^8; זבים 1^2, 2^2; טבול יום $3^{4,5}$; ידים $3^{1,5}$, 4^1; עוקצין $3^{5,6,9}$.

72. R. Elazar Chisma: Disciple of R. Joshua. Lived in poverty at the College at Yavne. Reputed to excel in mathematics. אבות 3^{18}; בבא מציעא 7^5; תרומות 3^6; נגעים 7^3, 13^3; מקואות 8^3.

73. R. Elazar b. Judah of Bartotha: Disciple of R. Joshua. So charitable that collectors of charity used to hide from him because he would give them all he had. ערלה 1^4; אבות 3^7; אהלות 3^5; זבים 1^1; טבול יום $3^{4,5}$.

74. R. Elazar b. Parta: Colleague of R. Chanania b. Teradion. Arrested during the Hadrianic persecutions but later freed. Lived in Sepphoris. גטין 3^4.

BIOGRAPHIES

75. R. Elazar of Modiim: Active from the time of Rabban Jochanan b. Zakkai until the siege of Bethar. Executed by his nephew Bar-Cochba on wrongful suspicion of treachery. אבות 3¹¹.

76. Elisha b. Avuya: Teacher of R. Meir. Became an apostate and even an informer against his people to the Romans in the days of persecution following the Bar-Cochba revolt. Yet his disciple did not forsake him and hoped till his dying day that he would repent. It says much for the tolerance of the Rabbis that they record his teaching. אבות 4²⁰.

77. R. Chanania b. Chachinai: A distinguished disciple of R. Akiva. One of the youngest students at Rabban Gamliel's College at Yavne. One of the Ten Martyrs. כלאים 4⁸; מכשירין 3⁹; אבות 3⁴.

78. R. Chanania b. Teradion: Disciple of R. Eliezer. Established his school at Sikni. Was an overseer of charity. Taught Torah during the Hadrianic persecution though he was warned that it might lead to his death. Was one of the Ten Martyrs. His daughter Beruria was the wife of R. Meir. אבות 3²; תענית 2⁵.

79. R. Chanina b. Antigonus: Taught in the days of R. Akiva and R. Meir. Rashi regards him as a priest, but he is not so counted by Maimonides. שביעית 6²; נדה 6⁶; תמורה 6⁵; ערכין 2⁴; בכורות 6³,⁴,¹⁰,¹¹, 7²,⁶; קדשין 4⁵; יבמות 13²; עירובין 4⁸.

80. R. Illai: Mentioned only once in the *Mishnah* but several times in the *Talmud*. Disciple particularly of R. Eliezer, though also of the principal scholars at the College at Yavne in the days of Rabban Gamliel. The father of the more famous son R. Judah b. Ilai. עירובין 2⁶.

81. R. Ishmael (b. Elisha): Not to be confused with his grandfather of the same name, the High Priest, who suffered martyrdom at the same time as Rabban Simon b. Gamliel. Taken captive as child to Rome where he was recognised and ransomed by R. Joshua. Studied under R. Nechunia b. ha-Kana, R. Eliezer and R. Joshua, and was principal disputant of R. Akiva. R. Meir was his most distinguished pupil. Took no part in the Bar-Cochba revolt but settled in Usha. During the Hadrianic persecution he lived in the south, by the border of Edom. Attempted to derive new laws from a simple and direct understanding of the Biblical text. Formulated the *Thirteen Principles of Scriptural Interpretation*. Founded a school whose teachings are frequently quoted in the Talmud as 'Tana debe R. Ishmael.' The *Mechilta* is attributed to this school. ברכות 7³; שביעית 1⁴; דמאי 6⁴; כלאים 3³,⁶,⁷,6⁴; פאה 4¹⁰; שקלים 10⁵; פסחים 1² עירובין 1²; שבת 2², 15³; חלה 4⁴; מעשרות 3⁵; תרומות 4⁵; נדרים 5⁸; סוכה 3⁴; מועד קטן 3⁸; כתובות 3¹¹, 9¹⁰; יומא 4¹, 6⁸; עבודה זרה 6⁸; שבועות 2⁵, 3⁵; עדיות 2⁴⁻⁶,5³; סנהדרין 1²; בבא בתרא 3¹, 6⁴, 10⁸; נזיר 6⁸; ערכין 8⁷; בכורות 9⁴; חולין 3⁷, 10¹; מנחות 3¹²; אבות 1², 2⁵, 4¹; פרה 2⁵; מעילה 3³; אהלות 2², 5³, 7²; נגעים 3⁵; כלים 1², 2¹, 8⁵, 11⁵, 12²; עוקצין 2². ידים 4³; מקואות 1²; נדה 3⁷, 6¹²; זבים 1²; טהרות 1³, 3¹¹, 8¹¹; 7¹, 8³, 9⁶.

82. R. Jochanan b. Baroka: A great disciple of R. Joshua. עירובין 8², 10¹⁵; פסחים 7⁹; סוכה 4⁴; יבמות 6⁶; כתובות 2¹; בבא קמא 10³; בבא בתרא 8⁸; כלים 8¹⁰; בכורות 4⁴; אבות 4⁴; שבועות 7⁷; סנהדרין 11¹. 17¹¹.

83. R. Jochanan b. Joshua: Nephew of R. Akiva (grandson of his father-in-law). ידים 3⁶.

114

BIOGRAPHIES

84. **R. Jochanan b. Matthias:** Mentioned only once. ‎בבא מציעא 7¹.

85. **R. Jochanan b. Nuri:** His teachers were R. Chalafta and R. Eliezer. He and R. Elazar Chisma were appointed to a living by Rabban Gamliel when their excellence as scholars and their dire poverty were pointed out to him by R. Joshua. His greatest colleague and friend was R. Akiva. Lived in Nagninar. Died before the destruction of Bethar. ‎ראש השנה 2⁸, 4⁵·⁶; ‎ערובין 4⁵; ‎חלה 4³; ‎תרומות 10¹¹; ‎כלאים 6¹; ‎חולין 9²·³; ‎עדיות 2¹⁰; ‎בבא מציעא 3⁷; ‎נדרים 11⁴; ‎כתובות 1¹⁰; ‎יבמות 14¹; ‎בכורות 6⁵; ‎תמורה 1¹; ‎כריתות 3⁶; ‎כלים 27, 11³, 17⁵·¹⁴·¹⁷, 30³; ‎אהלות 27, 6⁷, 8¹, ‎עוקצין 3⁵·⁶; ‎טבול יום 2⁵·⁶; ‎מקואות 7¹·⁶; ‎טהרות 8⁶; ‎פרה 12⁸; ‎נגעים 10¹, 14¹⁰; 12¹, 14³.

86. **R. Jose b. Chisma:** Colleague of R. Chanania b. Teradion. Lived in Caesaria and was friendly with the Roman government. Died during, but not on account of, the Hadrianic persecution. ‎אבות 6⁹.

87. **R. Jose the Galilean:** Lived in Galilee where he taught R. Elazar b. Azaria when the latter fled there with his father after the destruction of the Temple. Came to Yavne very much later, a ripe scholar, and always counted among the four elders: R. Tarfon, he, R. Elazar b. Azaria and R. Akiva. Appears to have gone back to Galilee before the catastrophe of Bethar. ‎בכורים 1¹⁰; ‎שביעית 4⁵; ‎ברכות 7³; ‎בבא מציעא 8⁶; ‎בבא קמא 8⁶; ‎גטין 2⁵; ‎סוטה 8⁵; ‎כתובות 3³; ‎פסחים 7¹; ‎ערובין 1⁷; ‎מנחות 8¹², 13¹·²; ‎זבחים 2⁵; ‎הוריות 3⁵; ‎עבודה זרה 2⁷; ‎מכות 10⁶; ‎סנהדרין 2¹⁰; ‎חולין 4³, 5³, 8⁴; ‎בכורות 2⁶, 8¹; ‎נדה 1², 3⁴; ‎פרה 5⁸.

88. **R. Joshua b. Mathias:** Mentioned only once. ‎עדיות 2⁵.

89. **R. Judah b. Bava:** Of the circle of Rabban Gamliel, R. Joshua and R. Akiva at Yavne. Very pious. Ordained R. Meir and his four fellow-students during the Hadrianic persecution and urged them to escape while he remained to meet a martyr's death. ‎ערובין 2⁴·⁵; ‎יבמות 16³·⁵·⁷; ‎עדיות 6¹, 8³.

90. **R. Judah the Priest:** Mentioned once, possibly the son of Rabban Jochanan b. Zakkai. ‎עדיות 8³.

91. **R. Levitas of Yavne:** Mentioned once, and only otherwise in *Pirke de-R. Eliezer*. ‎אבות 4⁴.

92. **R. Matthias b. Cheresh:** Disciple of R. Eliezer and R. Elazar b. Azaria. Left Palestine during the Hadrianic persecution to found a school in Rome. ‎יומא 8⁶; ‎אבות 4¹⁵.

93. **Nehemia of Bet Deli:** A Babylonian disciple of Rabban Gamliel the Elder. Contemporary of R. Akiva. ‎יבמות 16⁷; ‎עדיות 8⁵.

94. **R. Simon b. Akashia:** Mentioned only once. ‎קנים 3⁶.

95. **Simon b. Azzai:** Disciple of R. Joshua, but principally of R. Akiva, whose daughter he married. But he desired to spend his life so much in study that he divorced her and lived as a celibate. Had great reputation as a scholar. Lived in Tiberias. One of the four who entered the 'pardes of hidden knowledge.' ‎בבא בתרא 3⁴, 9¹⁵; ‎סוטה 3¹, 4⁵, 5³; ‎שקלים 3¹, 4⁴, 5³; ‎יבמות 4¹³; ‎תענית 4⁴; ‎יומא 2⁵; ‎ברכות 9⁴; ‎נדה 5⁸; ‎פרה 1¹·³; ‎זבחים 1³; ‎בכורות 1; ‎הוריות 1²; ‎קנים 9⁵; ‎אבות 4²·³; ‎הוריות 9¹⁰; ‎ידים 3⁵, 4².

115

BIOGRAPHIES

96. **R. Simon b. Nanos:** Colleague of R. Akiva and R. Ishmael. בכורים 3[9];
שבת 16[5]; ערובין 10[16]; גטין 8[10]; בבא בתרא 7[3], 10[8]; שבועות 7[5].

97. **R. Simon of Teman:** A young student in the great days of Yavne under Rabban Gamliel. Disputed with R. Akiva. תענית 3[7]; יבמות 4[13]; ידים 1[3].

98. **R. Simon b. Zoma:** Disciple of R. Joshua. A great preacher. Another of the four who entered 'the garden of hidden knowledge.' (The others were R. Simon b. Azzai, R. Akiva and Elisha b. Avuya). Died in the lifetime of his teacher.
חולין 11[4]; מנחות 4[1]; אבות 9[15]; סוטה 8[1]; נזיר 1[5]; ברכות 5[5].

99. **R. Tarfon:** A wealthy, scholarly priest who was about 20 years old when the Temple was destroyed. Established a school in Lydda. His disputes are mainly with R. Akiva who was a student-colleague of his. Teacher of the famous scholars of the next generation, the greatest being R. Judah. Died before the Bar-Cochba revolt. מעשר שני 3[3]; מעשרות 9[2]; תרומות 4[5], 9[2]; כלאים 5[8]; פאה 3[6]; ברכות 1[3], 6[8];
יבמות 3[9]; תענית 3[3]; ביצה 3[3]; סוכה 3[4]; פסחים 10[6]; ערובין 4[4]; שבת 2[3]; 2[4,9];
בבא קמא 3[18]; קדושין 5[5], 6[6]; נזיר 6[6]; נדה 9[3,3]; 7[6], 5[3]; כתובות 15[6,7];
מנחות 10[8], 11[7]; זבחים 2[15,16]; אבות 1[10]; עדיות 1[10]; מכות 4[3]; 2[7], 4[3]; בבא מציעא
פרה 1[3]; אהלות 13[3], 16[1]; כלים 11[4,7], 25[7]; 5[3,2]; כריתות 4[4], 2[6,9]; בכורות 12[5];
מקואות 10[5]; מכשירין 5[4]; ידים 4[9].

THE FOURTH GENERATION (c. 140-165 C.E.).

100. **Abba Saul:** His statements about Temple organisation presuppose either first-hand knowledge (in which case he belongs to an earlier generation) or a tradition the source of which is unknown. Was a grave-digger by profession. פאה 8[5];
גטין 5[4]; נדרים 6[5]; כתובות 7[6]; ביצה 3[6]; שקלים 4[2]; שבת 23[3]; כלאים 2[2];
מכות 10[1]; סנהדרין 2[7,13]; בבא בתרא 6[7], 4[13]; בבא מציעא 4[3,14]; קדושין
אבות 2[8]; מנחות 8[3], 11[5]; מדות 2[5], 5[4].

101. **R. Elazar (b. Shammua):** Most frequently mentioned without the name of his father, which gave rise to the opinion that two different persons are meant. A priest. One of the later disciples of R. Akiva. Studied also under R. Joshua. During the Hadrianic persecution he was one of the five students ordained by R. Judah b. Bava when the latter met a martyr's death. They all fled, to assemble again in Usha after the persecution. But R. Elazar was not among them. He went to Galilee and founded a school where Rabbi subsequently studied. Another of his disciples was R. Joseph the Babylonian. Lived to a great age. שקלים 2[8]; שביעית שקלים 2[8]; בבא קמא 3[8]; גטין 7[4]; מיר 7[4]; 2[8], 3[6]; כתובות 10[1]; יבמות 11[1]; ראש השנה 5[7]; יומא 4[9];
כריתות 2[3], 3[3,4]; תמורה 4[4,7,4], 9[1,6]; ערכין 13[4,6]; זבחים 1[3]; הוריות 4[13]; אבות 4[9];
טהרות 3[3]; 6[4,6].

102. **Elazar b. Dolai, Abba:** Contemporary of R. Meir and his colleagues. Mentioned only once. מקואות 2[10].

103. **R. Elazar b. R. Jose the Galilean:** Named among the seven later disciples of R. Akiva. Famous in Aggada and presumed the author of the *Midrashic* work 'The Thirty-Two Methods of Aggadic Interpretation.' Presumably died young, because not mentioned in the re-assembled College at Usha. סוטה 5[3].

104. **R. Elazar b. Mathias:** A disciple of the great scholars of Yavne. Suggested, though hardly likely, that he was the son of R. Mathias b. Heresh. יבמות 10[3].

116

105. R. Elazar b. Pilai (or Piabi): Mentioned only once. ‭טהרות‬ 7[י].

106. R. Eliezer b. Jacob II: One of the seven later disciples of R. Akiva. Possible that like his colleagues he made a *Mishnah* collection which is quoted in the *Talmud* as *Tani R. Eliezer b. Jacob.* ‭כלאים‬ 2[9], 4[8], 5[3], 6[2]; ‭שביעית‬ 2[10]; ‭תרומות‬ 3[5]; ‭בכורים‬ 1[5]; ‭נדרים‬ 3[1], 13[3]; ‭יבמות‬ 1[3]; ‭מועד קטן‬ 1[3]; ‭שקלים‬ 6[3]; ‭ערובין‬ 6[1], 8[10]; ‭שבת‬ 8[6], 15[3]; ‭ערכין‬ 3[1]; ‭בכורות‬ 3[1]; ‭אבות‬ 4[11]; ‭מנחות‬ 5[6], 9[8]; ‭מכות‬ 2[2]; ‭קדושין‬ 4[7]; ‭סוטה‬ 9[4]; 5[1,2]; ‭מכשירין‬ 3[8]; ‭טהרות‬ 9[3]; ‭פרה‬ 9[2]; ‭נגעים‬ 7[1], 10[4], 11[11]; ‭כלים‬ 7[3], 28[9]; ‭כריתות‬ 2[1]; 6[5].

107. R. Chanania b. Akavia: Colleague of R. Judah. Had a school in Tiberias. ‭כתובות‬ 8[1]; ‭ערכין‬ 1[3].

108. R. Chanania b. Akashia: Mentioned with R. Judah and R. Jose. ‭מכות‬ 3[16].

109. R. Chanania of Ono: Mentioned with R. Meir. ‭גטין‬ 6[7].

110. R. Ishmael b. R. Jochanan b. Baroka: Taught by his father. Was at Usha under the presidency of Rabban Simon b. Gamliel. ‭בבא קמא‬ 10[2]; ‭סנהדרין‬ 11[1]; ‭אבות‬ 4[5].

111. R. Jacob (b. Korshai): An authority on the texts of *Mishnaiot* and *Baraitot*. Appointed by Rabban Simon b. Gamliel to teach his son Rabbi. Upset the plan of R. Meir and R. Nathan to bring about the deposition of R. Simon b. Gamliel from the presidency at Usha. ‭אבות‬ 3[7], 4[16,17].

112. R. Jochanan the Sandal-maker: Appears to have come from Alexandria. A distinguished pupil of R. Akiva. Disguised himself as a pedlar in order to learn an *Halachic* decision from R. Akiva while the latter was in prison. Not mentioned in the College at Usha, so presumably died before the re-assembly of the scholars. ‭יבמות‬ 12[5]; ‭כתובות‬ 5[4]; ‭אבות‬ 4[11]; ‭כלים‬ 5[5].

113. R. Jonathan (b. Joseph): Colleague of R. Josiah (the Babylonian, who is not mentioned in the *Mishnah*). Together they studied under R. Ishmael when he was in the south of Palestine during the Hadrianic persecution. A priest. ‭אבות‬ 5[16].

114. R. Joshua b. Korcha: *Tosafot* (particularly Rabbenu Tam) disagrees with the opinion of Rashi and others that he was the son of R. Akiva. His teachers were R. Elazar b. Azaria and R. Johanan b. Nuri. Famous for his Aggadic sayings. Lived to a very advanced age. ‭ברכות‬ 2[2]; ‭ראש השנה‬ 4[4]; ‭נדרים‬ 3[11]; ‭סנהדרין‬ 7[5].

115. R. Jose b. ha-Chotef Efrati: Pupil of R. Ishmael. ‭כלאים‬ 3[7].

116. R. Jose (b. Chalafta): Descendant of Jonadab the Rechabite, and hence of Jethro. Learnt a great deal from his father, whom he greatly respected. His most famous teacher was R. Akiva, though he learned also from all the outstanding scholars of Yavne. Born in Sepphoris, the destruction and rebuilding of which he saw. When he and his colleagues were ordained by R. Judah b. Bava after the death of R. Akiva, they fled separate ways and met again only after Hadrian's death, when they first assembled to intercalate the year, in the valley of Rimmon. The seven scholars who came together on that occasion were R. Meir, R. Judah, R. Jose, R. Simon, R. Nehemia, R. Eliezer b. Jacob II, and R. Jochanan the Sandal-maker. They then went to Usha and again to Yavne where the incident occurred at which R. Judah spoke well of the Romans, R. Simon spoke ill, while R. Jose was silent. The conversation was reproted to the government and for his silence R. Jose was banished to his native Sepphoris, so that he could not at first go to the College at Usha. At Sepphoris he founded a great school. Later, when the harsh decrees were annulled, he went to Usha and persuaded Rabban Simon b. Gamliel to recall R. Meir and R. Nathan from their banishment. Author of *Seder Olam*, a valuable historical work beginning with the Creation and going as far as the time of Alexander the Great, with some additional notes to the destruction of the Second Temple. Famous in *Halachah* and *Aggadah*. Married his deceased brother's wife, who bore him five sons, all of whom distinguished themselves in learning. ברכות 2³; פאה 3⁴,⁷, 6⁹, 7¹,⁸; דמאי 2⁵, 3³,⁵, 7³; כלאים 2¹,⁷, 3⁷, 5⁴, 6⁵,⁷, 7⁴,⁵, 8⁵,⁶, 9⁷,⁹; שביעית 2⁶, 3¹,⁹, 9⁴,⁸, 10¹; תרומות 1³, 3³, 4¹², 7⁶⁻⁷, 8⁵, 10³,⁸,¹¹, 11¹⁰; מעשרות 1⁸, 3⁵,⁷, 5⁸; מעשר שני 3⁶,¹¹, 4⁷,¹¹, 5²,¹⁴; חלה 4⁸; ערלה 1⁶,⁷,⁹; שבת 2⁵, 3³, 5², 6⁸, 8⁷, 12³, 14², 16²,⁴,⁵, 17⁸, 18³; ערובין 1⁶,⁷, 2⁵, 3⁴, 7⁹, 8⁵, 9³, 10⁹,¹⁰; פסחים 1⁷, 8⁷, 9², 10⁸; שקלים 4¹, 7⁷, 8¹,²; יומא 4³ו⁶, 6³; סוכה 1⁹, 3⁷,¹⁴; ביצה 4²; ראש השנה 1⁵,⁷, 3², 4⁶; תענית 2⁸,⁹, 3⁶,⁷; מגלה 2³; מועד קטן 1⁵,⁸, 2¹,²,⁵; יבמות 4¹⁰, 7³, 8⁶, 10¹,⁴; 16⁴; כתובות 1¹⁰, 5⁷,⁸, 6⁷, 7³; נדרים 3¹¹, 4⁸, 6⁵,¹⁰, 8², 11¹,²; נזיר 4⁷, 6², 9¹,⁵; סוטה 2⁵, 4⁵, 8⁵, 9¹²; גטין 5⁸, 6⁷, 7⁴,⁹; קדושין 3⁹, 4⁵,⁷; בבא קמא 3⁴, 5¹, בבא מציעא 4⁴;· 3²,⁴,⁵, 5⁷, 8⁸, 10²; בבא בתרא 1³, 2¹⁰,¹¹, 8⁷, 10⁵,⁶; סנהדרין 1⁸,⁹; אבות 4⁶; עבודה זרה 1⁸, 2⁷, 3³,⁸; עדיות 1², 5²; שבועות 7⁴; מכות 1⁸,⁹; 6⁴, 8², 9⁴; זבחים 4⁵,⁶, 6¹, 7⁶, 13³; מנחות 2¹,², 6⁵, 9⁶, 11⁷; חולין 2⁷, 3⁷, 8¹, 9²; בכורות 2⁶⁻⁸, 3⁴, 4¹, 5⁵; מעילה 3⁶; תמורה 1³, 5³,⁴; כריתות 1⁴, 3⁵, 4², 5⁴⁻⁸, 6¹; ערכין 1⁸, 2⁴, 5¹, 8¹; מדות 2², 3¹; כלים 1⁹, 2⁶, 3⁷,⁸, 8⁸,¹⁰, 12¹, 13¹, 16⁶,⁷, 17⁵,⁶,¹², 18¹,³,⁴, 19³,⁴,⁹, 22², 23²,⁴, 25⁷, 26¹,⁴,⁶, 27⁹,¹⁰, 28³,⁶, 29²,⁴, 30³,⁴; אהלות 2⁷, 3⁶, 4¹,², 7², 8⁵, 10³, 11¹,⁷, 12³,⁸, 14², 17¹, 18¹; נגעים 6⁵, 13¹²; פרה 3¹,²,³,⁷, 5¹,⁶, 7⁷,¹¹, 8⁸, 9⁴, 10⁵, 11¹,⁶,⁹; טהרות 1¹,², 4⁵,⁸,¹⁰, 5²,⁵,⁶, 7¹, 8¹,²,⁸, 9⁷, 10¹,³,⁸; מקואות 2², 3¹, 4¹,³, 5²,⁴,⁵, 6¹¹, 7³, 8²,⁴, 9²,⁶, 10⁶; נדה 1⁵, 2⁶, 4²,⁵, 5⁸, 7¹, 9¹,²,⁹, 10⁵; מכשירין 1⁴,⁵, 3⁹, 5⁶,¹¹, 6⁷; זבים 1⁵, 2³, 4²,⁷; טבול יום 1³,⁴, 3²,³,⁴, 4⁷; ידים 1¹,⁴,⁵, 2¹,⁴, 3⁵; עוקצין 1⁴⁻⁶, 3².

117. R. Judah (b. Illai): Born in Usha, where he studied under his father. His most important teachers were R. Tarfon and R. Akiva. Ordained by R. Judah b. Bava, together with R. Meir, R. Simon, R. Jose, and R. Elazar, and also R. Nehemia, before his martyrdom. The fate and future of Judaism literally depended upon these scholars, who now had to scatter. They re-assembled in the valley of Rimmon to intercalate the year. At Yavne he spoke well of the Roman government and was promoted to be the foremost spokesman among the scholars. The government would not allow the College to remain in Yavne, so it removed again to Usha, Rabban Simon b. Gamliel was brought out of hiding and appointed Patriarch, while R. Judah was appointed by the government to supervise the patriarchal house. He was highly esteemed by the Patriarch. 607 *Halachot* are mentioned in his name in the *Mishnah*. Besides taking such an important share in the work of the College at Usha he had a school at Sikni. His greatest disciple was Rabbi. Was extremely poor and sometimes did not have even a coat to go out in. Lived from his farm. Had great reputation for piety. Outlived most of his colleagues. Left a learned son, R. Jose. ברכות 2¹,³, 3⁴,⁶, 4¹,⁷, 6¹,³,⁴, 7³, 9²; פאה 1³, 2³, 3⁵, 4⁶, 5⁵, 6¹⁰, 7⁴,⁵, 8¹; דמאי 1¹, 2²,³, 3⁶, 4⁷, 5³⁻⁵, 6¹,²,⁵; כלאים 1²,⁷,⁹, 3¹,⁸, 4³,⁷,⁹, 8⁴, 9¹⁰; שביעית 2⁵,⁶, 3¹, 4²,⁵, 5¹,⁵, 7⁴, 9¹,⁴,⁸, 10¹; תרומות 1³, 2²,⁴⁻⁶, 3⁹, 4³, 9⁶,⁷, 10¹,⁸,⁶,¹¹, 11¹,¹⁰; מעשרות 1²,⁷,⁸, 2²,³,⁵,⁸, 3⁵,⁷, 4², 5⁵,⁶; מעשר שני 3¹⁰, 4⁷,¹⁰, 5⁸; חלה 2⁴, 4⁹; ערלה 1²; בכורים 1¹,⁶,⁷,¹¹; שבת 1¹¹, 2⁴, 3⁵, 4¹, 5², 7⁴, 8²,⁴,⁶,⁷, 9⁶⁻⁷, 10⁴, 13⁵, 15², 16⁷, 17⁴,⁶, 18², 19³, 20²,⁶, 21¹, 22¹,³, 24²,³,⁴; ערובין 1¹,⁴,¹⁰, 2¹,³⁻⁵, 3¹,⁴,⁵,⁷,⁸, 4⁴,⁵,⁹,¹⁰, 5⁶, 6²,⁴, 7¹¹, 8²,⁴⁻⁷, 10²,³,⁶,¹¹,¹²,¹³,¹⁶; פסחים 1³,⁴,⁵, 2¹, 3⁵,⁸, 4²,³, 5⁴,⁷,⁸, 8⁷; שקלים 1²,⁴, 2⁴, 6⁵, 7⁴,⁶; יומא 1¹, 4⁵,⁶, 5⁴, 6¹,⁸; סוכה 1¹,²,⁶,⁷, 2¹,³, 3¹,⁶⁻⁸,¹⁶, 4⁵,⁹, 5⁸; ביצה 1¹⁰, 2⁸,¹⁰, 3⁴,⁶,⁸, 4³,⁴, 5⁴;

מועד קטן 1[6,7,9], 2[1,3,5]; מגלה 1[3], 2[3,4], 3[1-3], 4[6,7,10]; תענית 1[2], 2[3], 4[7]; ראש השנה 3[5];
כתובות 2[8], 3[2], 4[2,4], 5[1,7]; יבמות 2[9], 4[7,10], 6[5], 8[6], 11[1], 12[6], 15[1,5], 16[5]; חגיגה 3[7]; 3[4];
נזיר 1[7], 2[1,2], 3[6], 4[3], 6[2,7]; נדרים 1[3,4], 2[4], 4[4], 5[5], 6[3,6,10], 7[3], 8[5], 11[10]; 6[8], 7[1,2], 8[1,5], 9[1];
קדושין 2[8], 4[3,6,8,14]; גטין 1[2], 2[1,4], 3[2,8], 4[7,8], 6[2], 7[4,6], 9[3]; סוטה 1[3,5], 2[2,3], 7[4,6], 8[5,7], 9[1];
בבא מציעא 2[1,6], 3[7,8,11], 4[4,5,9,12], 5[7], 6[7], 7[9], 9[5,6], 10[3,6]; בבא קמא 2[4], 3[1,9], 4[2,7,9], 6[5,6], 8[2,6], 9[4];
סנהדרין 1[3,6], 2[1-4], 3[3,4], 4[3], 5[3], 6[2,3], 7[2-4], 8[4], 9[1,3], 10[2], 11[1,4]; בבא בתרא 1[6], 2[5,14], 3[2,6], 4[1], 5[1,2,8,9], 8[7], 10[5,6];
עדיות 1[4], 7[1-3,6]: שבועות 1[5], 2[3,6,8], 3[4,10,14]; מכות 1[5], 2[3,5,6,8], 3[4,10,14]; עבודה זרה 1[1,5,6,8], 2[5]; אבות 4[13]; הוריות 1[5]; זבחים 2[5], 3[6], 6[7],
חולין 2[1], 3[1,4,7], 5[3], 6[4-6], 7[1-3,6], 9[1,2,6], 10[4], 12[4]; בכורות 3[4], 4[8,9], 5[2], 6[10], 7[1,6], 8[3,4,6], 9[8]; ערכין 1[2],
תמיד 3[6], 6[4,5]; מעילה 3[6], 6[4,5]; מדות 1[7], 3[6], 4[1,3,6]; כלים 1[5], 3[2], 4[1,4], 5[1,2,6,11], 6[1], 7[1,2], 8[8-10], 9[7,8], 10[3,6], 12[2,8], 13[1],
אהלות 3[5,7], 6[3,4], 7[1,4], 10[3], 15[8], 16[2], 17[5]; נגעים 2[1,2,4,5], 6[7], 10[2,4,9,10], 11[3,4,8], 12[4,5], 13[3,10,11], 14[8,9,11,12]; פרה 2[3,4,5], 3[9], 4[1], 5[1,4,6], 7[9], 8[8-11], 9[5], 11[8,9], 12[1,2,5]; טהרות 1[1], 4[1,8,5,6], 6[8], 7[8], 8[1], 9[4], 10[1]; מקואות 2[10], 5[2,4,5], 6[1,5,9], 7[6], 9[1,6,7], 10[5]; נדה 1[7], 3[1], 4[5], 6[11], 7[3,4], 9[5,9,11], 10[3,6]; מכשירין 2[4,5,7,8], 3[1,3,5-7], 6[2,3]; זבים 2[2], 3[1-3]; טבול יום 1[1,2,5], 2[3,7], 3[1]; ידים 3[4,5]; עוקצין 1[2], 2[1,4], 3[3,6].

118. R. Meir: A scribe by profession. Disciple of R. Akiva and R. Ishmael. Ordained by R. Judah b. Bava before his martyrdom. Was pupil also of Elisha b. Avuya, with whom he remained friendly in spite of his apostasy. Was the foremost of the seven scholars who assembled in the valley of Rimmon after the death of Hadrian to intercalate the year. Sent by the scholars when they assembled in Yavne to intercalate the year in Asia Minor (since it was still forbidden to intercalate it in Palestine). When they re-assembled in Usha, Rabban Simon b. Gamliel was appointed *Patriarch*, R. Nathan *Av-Bet-Din* and R. Meir *Haham*. R. Meir was easily the most distinguished of them all in the keenness of his intellect and the clarity of his expression. His generation was responsible for the *Halakic* collections and his own was the basis of Rabbi's *Mishnah*. Humane and kindly man with a firm faith in individual providence. A great *Aggadist* and author of many fables. Married Beruria, daughter of the martyr R. Chanania b. Teradion, the only woman mentioned in the Talmud in connection with *Halachah*. Their two sons died in their lifetime. R. Meir and R. Nathan planned to depose Rabban Simon b. Gamliel, and as a result of the ensuing quarrel he retired to Tiberias, where he founded a school. There his wife committed suicide and he left for Asia Minor where he died. ברכות 2[1]; פאה
2[1], 4[11], 5[3], 7[3,5], 8[5]; דמאי 1[2], 2[5], 5[3,4]; כלאים 2[9,11], 3[7], 4[9], 5[1], 6[5], 7[2]; תרומות 4[1,2],
6[3,5], 7[2,5-7], 10[3], 11[10]; מעשרות 2[3,5], 4[4], 5[8]; מעשר שני 2[8], 5[14]; חלה 1[2]; ערלה 1[5],
3[1,2,6,7]; בכורים 1[6,11]; שבת 6[3,8,10], 8[7], 15[1]; ערובין 1[7], 2[1], 3[4], 4[9,10], 5[2,4], 6[1,4], 8[2,5],
9[1], 10[9]; פסחים 1[4,7], 2[8], 3[6,8], 4[6], 6[5]; שקלים 1[6,7], 2[5], 8[1,2]; יומא 3[6,7], 4[6]; סוכה 1[6,7],
3[6-8]; ביצה 4[3]; תענית 1[2], 2[10]; מגלה 2[3], 3[2]; מועד קטן 1[5]; יבמות 15[5], 16[4]; כתובות 1[3], 5[1,4], 6[7], 7[8,10], 8[3,7], 12[4]; נדרים 1[4], 2[4,5], 3[9], 4[4], 7[2,4,5], 8[2,5,7], 9[3,4,8], 11[7]; נזיר 1[1], 2[6], 6[6], 7[4], 9[1]; סוטה 2[5], 4[3], 9[15]; גטין 1[3,6], 4[7], 5[1], 6[7]; קדושין 1[3,4], 2[8], 3[4,9], 4[14];
בבא בתרא 1[6], 2[1,6], 3[11], 4[5], 6[5], 7[9], 10[6]; בבא קמא 2[4], 3[9], 4[1,4,9], 9[2,4]; בבא מציעא
5[4], 9[6]; סנהדרין 1[1,2], 2[1], 3[1,2], 6[5], 7[8]; מכות 1[2,3], 2[3,5,6]; שבועות 1[4], 4[1,13], 5[1,3], 6[6], 7[4]; עריות 1[9], 3[1]; עבודה זרה 1[3,5,6,8], 2[2,4], 3[1]; אבות 3[8], 4[10]; הוריות 1[5]; זבחים 4[3,5], 7[6],
10[6,7]; מנחות 2[4,5], 5[1], 6[5], 9[1], 10[4,5], 11[5]; חולין 3[2], 4[4,5], 5[3], 6[2,3], 7[1], 9[7,8]; בכורות 2[8],
4[3], 5[4], 8[1,3,4,10], 9[2,5,8]; ערכין 1[2], 2[1,4], 7[5], 9[5]; תמורה 2[1], 5[3,4]; כריתות 1[2,3], 3[1,3,4], 6[1];
מעילה 6[5]; מדות 2[2]; כלים 3[2,5], 5[1,3,7], 7[2,6], 8[10], 13[4], 15[1,4], 16[1], 17[4,5,10,11], 18[4],

BIOGRAPHIES

19³·⁴·⁹·¹⁰, 25¹⁻³·⁵·⁷, 26⁴, 27³, 28⁶; אהלות 2³, 3¹, 6³, 7⁵, 8³, 10³·³, 11⁷, 13⁶, 15⁹, 16³, 18³; נגעים 1¹, 2³·⁵, 4⁴, 6³, 8⁶, 11³, 12⁵, 13¹³; פרה 1¹·³, 2⁵; 3⁵, 5⁶, 6³, 8⁸, 11⁴⁻⁶·⁸; טהרות 1¹, 3³·⁸, 5⁷·⁹, 6⁹, 7²⁻⁴, 8⁴, 9⁴, 10¹·³; מקואות 2¹⁰, 4¹, 5⁴, 6¹⁰; נדה 1⁴, 2⁶, 3³, 4⁵·⁷, 6¹·¹³, 7³, 9¹·⁵; מכשירין 2¹⁰, 3³, 6³·⁵; טבול יום 1⁵, 3¹·⁶, ידים 2¹; עוקצין 1³.

119. R. Menachem (b. R. Jose b. Chalafta): Although mentioned only once in the *Mishnah*, there is a tradition that Rabbi included a number of his opinions anonymously. His father's fifth son. יומא 4⁴.

120. R. Nehemia: Descendant of the Biblical Nehemia. A potter by trade, and very poor. One of the seven disciples of R. Akiva who re-established Jewish learning after the catastrophe of Bethar. Ordained by R. Judah b. Bava. Present at the valley of Rimmon to intercalate the year, as well as at Usha and Yavne. But not mentioned in the later assembly at Usha, and presumably died before that. Author of the original *Tosefta*. תרומות 8⁷; מעשרות 3⁵; שבת 8⁴, 17⁴; יבמות 5⁶; נדרים 3¹¹; מיר 9⁴; סוטה 5⁴; סנהדרין 1⁶, 9¹, 10³; זבחים 13⁶; כלים 18⁵; נגעים 11⁵; טבול יום 4³·⁷; זבים 3³; מכשירין 9³; נדה 3¹.

121. Rabban Simon b. Gamliel II: Observed many traditions in his father's house at Yavne. Was not appointed *Patriarch* on father's death because many of the famous scholars of that generation were still alive. Then came the troubles, the rebellion and the persecution, during which he was in hiding because the Romans would have executed him as a member of the ruling house. When the scholars re-assembled the second time in Usha, R. Judah's influence with the government enabled Rabban Simon to come out of hiding and be appointed *Patriarch*, the sixth in descent from Hillel. Although a modest man, he insisted upon the authority of his office, thereby offending his *Av-Bet-Din* R. Nathan and his *Haham* R. Meir. He came out triumphant in the subsequent quarrel, R. Nathan submitting to him and R. Meir going into exile. Learned in Greek. Was very friendly with the aged R. Joshua b. Korcha. His most famous pupil was his son, Rabbi. מאה 5¹; ברכות 2⁸; שבת 1⁹; דמאי 7³; שביעית 1⁵·⁷, 3⁴, 4¹⁰; ערלה 1⁴; מעשר שני 3⁵, 5¹; מעשרות 5⁵; מעלה 4⁷·⁶; תעניח 3¹; ביצה 8⁵; שקלים 8⁵; פסחים 2³, 4⁵; ערובין 8⁶; כתובות 1⁸; נזיר 6⁸; סוטה 9¹⁵·¹⁶; יצב 1¹, 4⁴·⁶, 6¹·⁶, 7⁵·⁶; בבא קמא 3³, 5⁴; בבא מציעא 1⁸, 3⁶, 5⁵, 7¹, 8⁴·⁸, 9⁴·¹³, 10⁵; שבועות 7⁷; מכות 1¹⁰; סנהדרין 1², 3⁸; בבא בתרא 1⁵, 4⁷, 5¹⁰·¹¹, 6¹·⁴·⁸, 8⁵, 10¹·⁴·⁷; מנחות 11⁹; אבות 1¹⁸; עבודה זרה 2³, 3¹·³, 5³·⁴·¹⁰; עדיות 8³; חולין 2⁶, 3³, 6³, 8³; תמורה 5³; כלים 7⁶, 11¹, 17⁴, 26¹, 28⁵; בכורות 2⁴, 3³, 5⁴, 6⁹, 7⁶; ערכין 6¹; אהלות 18⁹; מקואות 6⁷, 9⁵; ידים 2³, 3¹.

122. R. Simon of Shezur: Disciple of R. Tarfon and disputant with R. Meir and R. Jose. דמאי 4¹; שביעית 2⁸; גטין 6⁵; חולין 4⁵; כריתות 4³; כלים 18¹; טהרות 3³; טבול יום 4⁵.

123. R. Simon (b. Yochai): The student whose innocent question to R. Joshua about the evening service started the revolt of the scholars at Yavne. Studied under R. Akiva at Bnei Brak, and still begged to learn from him even in prison. One of the five ordained by R. Judah b. Bava before his martyrdom. One of the seven scholars who assembled in the valley of Rimmon to intercalate the year after the death of Hadrian. Was also present at Usha and then at Yavne, where he spoke ill of the Roman government in answer to R. Judah's praise. For this he was condemned to

120

death by the Romans, but he fled with his son Elazar and hid for thirteen years in a cave. Then did not return to Usha but founded a school in Tekoa, where he taught Rabbi. Went on a successful mission to Rome with R. Elazar, son of R. Jose. פאה $1^3, 3^3, 4^1$; דמאי $3^4, 5^2$; כלאים $2^{1,3,7}, 4^9, 5^2, 7^{4,8}$; שביעית $1^8, 2^{1,3,5,6,8,10}, 3^{2,3}, 6^{4,6}$, $7^6, 8^{4,7}, 9^{1,8,8}$; תרומות $3^{3,9}, 4^{12}, 5^8, 10^{11}, 11^{10}$; מעשרות $1^4, 2^4, 3^8$; מעשר שני 2^2, $3^{3,11,13}, 5^6$; ערלה $2^{4,9,10,14-16}$; בכורים $2^2, 3^{3,10}$; שבת $3^6, 8^1, 10^{5,6}, 13^6, 14^4$; ערובין $3^4, 4^{6,11}, 5^6, 6^6, 8^{3,5}, 9^1, 10^{3,8,13}$; פסחים $5^4, 8^3, 9^8$; שקלים $2^4, 3^1, 7^6, 8^5$; יומא $5^7, 6^{6,7}$; סוכה 2^1; ביצה $1^6, 3^4$; ראש השנה $1^{1,7}$; חגיגה 1^7; יבמות $2^2, 3^{4,9}, 6^{3,4}, 8^{3,6}, 10^{1,7-9}$, $12^5, 15^6$; כתובות $4^1, 8^{3,4}, 9^6, 10^3, 11^2$; נזיר $2^{4,8}, 5^6, 6^{9,10}$; סוטה $3^{3,5}$; גטין $1^6, 2^2$; בבא בתרא $2^3, 4^{12}$; בבא קמא $4^1, 6^{2,4}, 7^{3,4}$; בבא מציעא $2^{10}, 4^{3,5,9}, 5^{10}, 10^6$; שבועות $1^{4,7}, 3^4$, $2^{3,14}, 4^9, 6^8$; סנהדרין $1^3, 2^4, 3^3, 7^1, 9^{3,3}, 10^6$; מכות $1^7, 2^3, 3^{2,6,15}$; עדיות $5^3, 8^7$; עבודה זרה $3^7, 4^{10}$; אבות $3^3, 4^{13}$; הוריות $1^{3,5}, 2^7, 3^3$; זבחים $1^4, 2^1, 4^{2-5}, 8^{3,13}, 9^{1,3}, 10^{7,8}, 11^7, 12^6, 13^{3,7}, 14^2$; מנחות $3^4, 4^{2-5}, 5^{8,7,9}, 6^{1,4,7}$, $9^{3,7}, 10^8, 11^3, 12^{3,4}, 13^{10}$; חולין $2^{3,5,6,10}, 3^1, 5^3, 9^{7,8}$; בכורות $4^9, 5^3, 8^3, 9^6$; ערכין $7^{4,5}, 8^5, 9^5$; מעילה $3^{3,4,6}$, תמורה $1^{3,9}, 2^3, 3^{1,3,5}, 7^{3,4}$; כריתות $1^5, 3^9, 4^3, 5^{4-8}, 6^9$; 4^6; כלים $3^{2,6}, 5^7, 7^5, 9^{4,6}, 14^3, 15^2, 17^{3,4,11,17}, 18^4, 22^6, 24^{17}, 25^6, 26^9, 27^{4,11,12}, 28^{6,7}$, 30^6; אהלות $2^{3,7}, 3^2, 7^2, 9^{14}, 10^3, 11^7, 13^1, 16^5, 18^5$; נגעים $4^{4,6}, 6^6, 10^{3,4,6,9}, 11^{3,9}$, $12^5, 13^{11}, 14^{9-11}$; פרה $2^3, 5^1, 6^3, 9^3, 11^6, 12^1$; טהרות $4^8, 6^1, 9^{1,3,4}, 10^{1,3}$; מקואות $1^{3,5}, 2^{5,6,10}, 8^5$; נדה $3^4, 4^5, 5^1, 7^3, 9^3$; מכשירין $1^6, 3^5, 4^{10}, 5^{3,10}, 6^{5,6,8}$; זבים 3^3, $4^{3-5,7}, 5^{4,5}$; טבול יום $3^4, 4^7$; ידים $3^{3,5}$; עוקצין $2^9, 3^{2-4}$.

THE FIFTH GENERATION (c. 165 - 200 C.E.).

124. Abba Gorion of Zaidan: Mentioned only once more, in a *Midrash*. קדושין 4^{14}.

125. R. Dositheus b. Yannai: Pupil of R. Meir and colleague of Rabbi. Had pupils of his own. ערובין 5^4; אבות 3^9.

126. R. Elazar b. R. Simon (b. Yochai): Hid with his father for thirteen years in a cave on account of the Romans. Became one of the greatest disciples at his father's school at Tekoa. After his father's death he studied with Rabbi under Rabban Simon b. Gamliel and R. Joshua b. Korcha. Married a daughter of R. Simon b. Jose b. Lakonia. Appointed by the government to catch thieves, an occupation disapproved of by his colleagues. A big-built man. On his death Rabbi wanted to marry his widow but she refused. נגעים 12^3; תמורה 4^4; ביצה 4^5.

127. R. Elazar ha-Kappar: Lived and taught in Lydda. His pupil was the famous R. Joshua b. Levi. אבות $4^{\text{let seq.}}$

128. R. Eliezer b. Zadok II: Pupil of R. Meir. פאה 2^4; כלאים 7^3; שביעית 7^2; מעשרות 4^4; פסחים $3^6, 10^3$; ראש השנה 2^7; סנהדרין 7^2; עדיות 2^6; מנחות 2^4; נדה 8^4; מקואות $2^{10}, 6^{10}$; טהרות 2^8; כלים $2^{5,6}, 26^6$; מעילה 3^7; חולין 3^6; עוקצין $1^6, 2^7$.

129. R. Chalafta b. Dosa of Kefar Chanania: Pupil of R. Meir. אבות 3^6.

130. R. Ishmael b. R. Jose (b. Chalafta): The greatest of his father's five sons. Succeeded his father as head of the school at Sepphoris, and was the teacher of most of the famous scholars of the next generation. Highly esteemed by Rabbi. Was a flax merchant and a wealthy landowner. Died before Rabbi. אבות $4^{7,8}$.

BIOGRAPHIES

131. Jaddua the Babylonian: Mentioned once only. ‏בבא מציעא‎ 7[9].

132. R. Jose b. R. Judah: Son of R. Judah b. Ilai, from whom he received his learning. Colleague of Rabbi, with whom he studied under his father. Probably died before Rabbi. ‏בבא מציעא‎ 7[3]; ‏גטין‎ 4[7]; ‏נדרים‎ 8[6]; ‏פסחים‎ 4[6]; ‏עירובין‎ 1[10]; ‏תמורה‎ 9[7]; ‏בכורות‎ 1[3]; ‏חולין‎ 8[7]; ‏מנחות‎ 6[1]; ‏זבחים‎ 4[20]; ‏אבות‎ 2[3,6]; ‏מכות‎ 8[3]; ‏סנהדרין‎ 2[3].

133. R. Jose b. Judah of Kefar Bavli: Mentioned only once. ‏אבות‎ 4[20].

134. R. Jose b. Meshullam: Colleague of R. Simon b. Elazar and R. Simon b. Menasia. ‏תרומות‎ 4[7]; ‏בכורות‎ 3[3], 6[1].

135. R. Judah the Patriarch: Known more familiarly as **Rabbi** and **Rabbenu the Saintly.** The seventh in direct descent from Hillel. Among his teachers were R. Jacob b. Korshai, R. Meir, R. Judah, R. Elazar, R. Simon, R. Jose, R. Nathan, R. Joshua b. Korcha, besides his own father. To these scholars he went in their own schools, spending much time at each. Fixed the College at Beth Shearim when he became *Patriarch* on the death of his father. Transferred the College to Sepphoris in the last seventeen years of his life. A friend of the Antonine emperors. Travelled widely in Palestine and the Diaspora to regulate communal life and to teach. Skilled in medicine and natural science. Blessed with beauty, power, wealth and wisdom. Used his wealth to support scholars and students in time of need. Called together the scholars from Palestine and all parts of the Diaspora to sift the material of the Oral Law and prepare an authoritative text-book and code, divided into six orders containing 63 tractates, known as the *Mishnah*. By form and arrangement, as well as brevity of expression, it was designed to be learnt by memory. Had two sons, Rabban Gamliel, who succeeded him as *Patriarch*, and R. Simon, whom he appointed as *Haham* on account of his brilliant scholarship. Died 219 C.E., after acting as *Patriarch* for almost fifty years. ‏נדרים‎ 2[4]; ‏כתובות‎ 2[4]; ‏שבת‎ 6[5], 12[3]; ‏מעשרות‎ 5[5]; ‏שביעית‎ 6[4]; ‏עבודה זרה‎ 1[8], 2[1]; ‏סוטה‎ 3[5], 5[1], 9[15]; ‏גטין‎ 5[6]; ‏בבא קמא‎ 5[3]; ‏מכות‎ 1[8], 2[1]; ‏מיר‎ 1[4], 4[6]; 3[11]; ‏ערכין‎ 7[6]; ‏בכורות‎ 3[4]; ‏חולין‎ 6[3], 8[6], 13[3,5,8,9]; ‏מנחות‎ 2[1,3], 4[20]; ‏אבות‎ 2[6], 4[5], 5[11]; ‏מקואות‎ 18[9]; ‏אהלות‎ 3[4]; ‏מדות‎ 5[3]; ‏מעילה‎ 4[3], 6[2]; ‏תמורה‎ 8[5], 9[8,8]; 2[10].

136. R. Judah b. Tema: From the few references in the *Talmud* very little is known of him. ‏אבות‎ 5[20,21].

137. R. Nathan, 'The Babylonian:' Actually a colleague of R. Meir, but also colleague of Rabbi in the compilation of the *Mishnah*. Probably son of the *Resh Galuta* in Babylon. Studied in Palestine but returned to Babylon during the Hadrianic persecution. Came back to the College at Usha, where he was appointed *Av-Bet-Din* by Rabban Simon b. Gamliel. He and R. Meir planned to depose Rabban Simon, but he finally submitted to the latter's authority and was restored to his office. Travelled a great deal, and was well versed in astronomy and civil law. Author of *Avot de R. Nathan*. ‏ברכות‎ 9[5]; ‏שקלים‎ 2[5].

138. R. Nehorai: One of the scholars at Usha. ‏מיר‎ 9[5]; ‏קדושין‎ 4[14]; ‏אבות‎ 4[14].

139. R. Phineas b. Jair: Son-in-law of R. Simon b. Yochai. A saintly scholar of whom marvellous tales are told in the *Talmud*. ‏סוטה‎ 9[15].

140. R. Simon b. Elazar: Pupil of R. Meir and colleague of Rabbi. Lived in Tiberias to a ripe old age. ‏בבא מציעא‎ 2[1]; ‏כלאים‎ 9[8]; ‏סוטה‎ 9[11]; ‏קדושין‎ 4[14]; ‏מכשירין‎ 4[18]; ‏אבות‎ 4[11]; ‏עבודה זרה‎ 4[1], 6[7].

BIOGRAPHIES

141. R. Simon b. Chalafta: Probably grandson of R. Jose. A great friend of Rabbi. Was very poor. עוקצין 3[12].

142. R. Simon b. Judah: Pupil of R. Simon b. Yochai and an older contemporary of Rabbi. מעשר שני 3[6]; מכות 3[6]; שבועות 1[5]; נגעים 10[8].

143. R. Simon b. Menasia: Pupil of R. Meir. Thought very highly of Rabbi and his family. חגיגה 1[7].

144. Symmachos (b. Joseph): Pupil of R. Meir with as brilliant an intellect as his teacher. ערובין 3[1]; בבא מציעא 6[5]; חולין 5[3].

[Historians are not agreed in the correct chronological placement of several of the less well-known *Tannaim*. There is also some confusion and uncertainty regarding the exact identity of several *Tannaim*. The Hebrew letter ח occurring in *proper names* has been rendered generally by the (German guttural) *ch* in preference to *h* favoured by some writers.—*Philip Blackman.*]

תרי"ג מצות
THE 613 COMMANDMENTS

BY

PHILIP BLACKMAN F.C.S.

Judaica Press, LTD.

Gateshead • 1985

The תַּרְיַ"ג מִצְוֹת, the **613 Commandments.**

These are based on the תּוֹרָה and comprise **248 positive commandments** and **365 negative commandments.**

מִצְוַת עֲשֵׂה,* briefly and popularly termed עֲשֵׂה,* = 'a positive commandment.'

מִצְוַת לֹא תַעֲשֶׂה§, always referred to in short as לֹא תַעֲשֶׂה and also alternatively as לָאו§ or לַאו§, = 'a negative commandment.'

In the Table following the numbers in the right-hand column show seriatim the relative positions of *all* the **613 commandments**; the numbers in the left-hand column give the serial order of the positive commandments and of the *negative* commandments among themselves respectively (the latter set in *italics*), thus | 3 | 4 | = the '3rd positive commandment' and is the '4th commandment of the **613 commandments**,' | *2* | *7* | = the '*2nd negative commandment*' and is the '*7th commandment of the* **613 commandments**'.

* Literally 'the commandment of *do thou*.' The *plural* forms are respectively מִצְוֹת עֲשֵׂה rarely used) and עֲשִׂין.

§ Literally respectively 'the commandment of *thou shalt not do*' and 'not' or 'no' or 'negative.' The corresponding respective *plural* forms are מִצְוֹת לֹא תַעֲשֶׂה (rarely used) and לָאוִין or לָאוִין.

Basis in the Pentateuch	positive, *negative*	of the 613	Basis in the Pentateuch	positive, *negative*	of the 613
Genesis **1**, 22	1	1	*Exodus* **20**, 3	14	26
Genesis **17**, 9, 10 ..	2	2	*Exodus* **20**, 4	15	27
Genesis **32**, 33	*1*	*3*	*Exodus* **20**, 5	*16*	*28*
Exodus **12**, 2	3	4	*Exodus* **20**, 5	*17*	*29*
Exodus **12**, 7	4	5	*Exodus* **20**, 7	*18*	*30*
Exodus **12**, 8	5	6	*Exodus* **20**, 8	13	31
Exodus **12**, 9	*2*	*7*	*Exodus* **20**, 10	*19*	*32*
Exodus **12**, 10	*3*	*8*	*Exodus* **20**, 12	14	33
Exodus **12**, 15	6	9	*Exodus* **20**, 13	*20*	*34*
Exodus **12**, 18	7	10	*Exodus* **20**, 13	*21*	*35*
Exodus **12**, 19	*4*	*11*	*Exodus* **20**, 13	*22*	*36*
Exodus **12**, 20	*5*	*12*	*Exodus* **20**, 13	*23*	*37*
Exodus **12**, 43	*6*	*13*	*Exodus* **20**, 14	*24*	*38*
Exodus **12**, 45	*7*	*14*	*Exodus* **20**, 20	*25*	*39*
Exodus **12**, 46	8	15	*Exodus* **20**, 22	*26*	*40*
Exodus **12**, 46	*9*	*16*	*Exodus* **20**, 23	*27*	*41*
Exodus **12**, 48	*10*	*17*	*Exodus* **21**, 2	15	42
Exodus **13**, 2	8	18	*Exodus* **21**, 8	16	43
Exodus **13**, 3	*11*	*19*	*Exodus* **21**, 8	17	44
Exodus **13**, 7	*12*	*20*	*Exodus* **21**, 8	*28*	*45*
Exodus **13**, 8	9	21	*Exodus* **21**, 10	*29*	*46*
Exodus **13**, 13	10	22	*Exodus* **21**, 15	*30*	*47*
Exodus **13**, 13	11	23	*Exodus* **21**, 15, 16, 17 ..	*18*	*48*
Exodus **16**, 29	*13*	*24*	*Exodus* **21**, 18	*19*	*49*
Exodus **20**, 2	12	25	*Exodus* **21**, 20	*20*	*50*

127

Basis in the Pentateuch			positive, *negative*	of the 613	Basis in the Pentateuch			positive, *negative*	of the 613
Exodus **21**, 28	..	..	21	51	Exodus **30**, 37	..	..	64	*110*
Exodus **21**, 28	..	..	*31*	*52*	Exodus **34**, 12	..	..	65	*111*
Exodus **21**, 33	..	..	22	53	Exodus **34**, 21	..	..	47	112
Exodus **21**, 37	..	..	23	54	Exodus **34**, 26	..	..	66	*113*
Exodus **22**, 4	..	..	24	55	Exodus **35**, 3	..	..	67	*114*
Exodus **22**, 5	..	..	25	56	Leviticus **1**, 3	..	..	48	115
Exodus **22**, 6	..	..	26	57	Leviticus **2**, 1	..	..	49	116
Exodus **22**, 8	..	..	27	58	Leviticus **2**, 11	..	..	68	*117*
Exodus **22**, 9	..	..	28	59	Leviticus **2**, 13	..	..	69	*118*
Exodus **22**, 13	..	..	29	60	Leviticus **2**, 13	..	..	50	119
Exodus **22**, 15	..	..	30	61	Leviticus **4**, 13, 14	..		51	120
Exodus **22**, 17	..	..	*32*	*62*	Leviticus **4**, 27, 28	..		52	121
Exodus **22**, 20	..	..	*33*	*63*	Leviticus **5**, 1	..	..	53	122
Exodus **22**, 20	..	..	*34*	*64*	Leviticus **5**, 6	..	..	54	123
Exodus **22**, 21	..	..	*35*	*65*	Leviticus **5**, 8	..	..	70	*124*
Exodus **22**, 24	..	..	*31*	66	Leviticus **5**, 11	..	..	71	*125*
Exodus **22**, 24	..	..	*36*	*67*	Leviticus **5**, 11	..	..	72	*126*
Exodus **22**, 24	..	..	*37*	*68*	Leviticus **5**, 16	..	..	55	127
Exodus **22**, 27	..	..	*38*	*69*	Leviticus **5**, 18	..	..	56	128
Exodus **22**, 27	..	..	*39*	*70*	Leviticus **5**, 23	..	..	57	129
Exodus **22**, 27	..	..	*40*	*71*	Leviticus **5**, 25	..	..	58	130
Exodus **22**, 28	..	..	*41*	*72*	Leviticus **6**, 3	..	..	59	131
Exodus **22**, 30	..	..	*42*	*73*	Leviticus **6**, 5	..	..	60	132
Exodus **23**, 1	..	..	*43*	*74*	Leviticus **6**, 5	..	..	73	*133*
Exodus **23**, 1	..	..	*44*	*75*	Leviticus **6**, 9	..	..	61	*134*
Exodus **23**, 2	..	..	*45*	*76*	Leviticus **6**, 10	..	..	74	*135*
Exodus **23**, 2	..	..	*46*	*77*	Leviticus **6**, 13	..	..	62	136
Exodus **23**, 2	..	..	*32*	*78*	Leviticus **6**, 16	..	..	75	*137*
Exodus **23**, 3	..	..	*47*	*79*	Leviticus **6**, 18	..	..	63	138
Exodus **23**, 5	..	..	*33*	80	Leviticus **6**, 23	..	..	76	*139*
Exodus **23**, 6	..	..	*48*	*81*	Leviticus **7**, 1	..	..	64	140
Exodus **23**, 7	..	..	*49*	*82*	Leviticus **7**, 11	..	..	65	141
Exodus **23**, 8	..	..	*50*	*83*	Leviticus **7**, 15	..	..	77	*142*
Exodus **23**, 11	..	..	*34*	84	Leviticus **7**, 17	..	..	66	143
Exodus **23**, 12	..	..	*35*	85	Leviticus **7**, 18	..	..	78	*144*
Exodus **23**, 13	..	..	*51*	86	Leviticus **7**, 19	..	..	79	*145*
Exodus **23**, 13	..	..	*52*	87	Leviticus **7**, 19	..	..	67	146
Exodus **23**, 14	..	..	*36*	88	Leviticus **7**, 23	..	..	80	*147*
Exodus **23**, 18	..	..	*53*	89	Leviticus **7**, 26	..	..	81	*148*
Exodus **23**, 18	..	..	*54*	*90*	Leviticus **10**, 6	..	..	82	*149*
Exodus **23**, 19	..	..	*37*	91	Leviticus **10**, 6	..	..	83	*150*
Exodus **23**, 19	..	..	*55*	*92*	Leviticus **10**, 7	..	..	84	*151*
Exodus **23**, 32	..	..	*56*	*93*	Leviticus **10**, 9	..	..	85	*152*
Exodus **23**, 33	..	..	*57*	*94*	Leviticus **11**, 2	..	..	68	153
Exodus **25**, 8	..	..	*38*	95	Leviticus **11**, 4	..	..	86	*154*
Exodus **25**, 15	..	..	*58*	*96*	Leviticus **11**, 9	..	..	69	155
Exodus **25**, 30	..	..	39	97	Leviticus **11**, 11	..	..	87	*156*
Exodus **27**, 21	..	..	40	98	Leviticus **11**, 13	..	..	88	*157*
Exodus **28**, 4	..	..	41	99	Leviticus **11**, 21	..	..	70	158
Exodus **28**, 28	..	..	*59*	*100*	Leviticus **11**, 29	..	..	71	159
Exodus **28**, 32	..	..	*60*	*101*	Leviticus **11**, 34	..	..	72	160
Exodus **29**, 33	..	..	42	102	Leviticus **11**, 39	..	..	73	161
Exodus **30**, 7	..	..	43	103	Leviticus **11**, 41	..	..	82	*162*
Exodus **30**, 9	..	..	*61*	*104*	Leviticus **11**, 42	..	..	90	*163*
Exodus **30**, 13	..	..	44	105	Leviticus **11**, 43	..	..	91	*164*
Exodus **30**, 19	..	..	45	106	Leviticus **11**, 44	..	..	92	*165*
Exodus **30**, 25	..	..	46	107	Leviticus **12**, 2	..	..	74	166
Exodus **30**, 32	..	..	*62*	*108*	Leviticus **12**, 4	..	..	93	*167*
Exodus **30**, 32	..	..	*63*	*109*	Leviticus **12**, 6	..	..	75	168

Basis in the Pentateuch	positive, negative	of the 613	Basis in the Pentateuch	positive, negative	of the 613
Leviticus 13, 2	76	169	Leviticus 19, 13	132	228
Leviticus 13, 33	94	170	Leviticus 19, 13	133	229
Leviticus 13, 45	77	171	Leviticus 19, 13	134	230
Leviticus 13, 47	78	172	Leviticus 19, 14	135	231
Leviticus 14, 2	79	173	Leviticus 19, 14	136	232
Leviticus 14, 8	80	174	Leviticus 19, 15	137	233
Leviticus 14, 9	81	175	Leviticus 19, 15	138	234
Leviticus 14, 10	82	176	Leviticus 19, 15	97	235
Leviticus 14, 35	83	177	Leviticus 19, 16	139	236
Leviticus 15, 3	84	178	Leviticus 19, 16	140	237
Leviticus 15, 14	85	179	Leviticus 19, 17	141	238
Leviticus 15, 16	86	180	Leviticus 19, 17	98	239
Leviticus 15, 19	87	181	Leviticus 19, 17	142	240
Leviticus 15, 25	88	182	Leviticus 19, 18	143	241
Leviticus 15, 29	89	183	Leviticus 19, 18	144	242
Leviticus 16, 2	95	184	Leviticus 19, 18	99	243
Leviticus 16, 3	90	185	Leviticus 19, 19	145	244
Leviticus 17, 4	96	186	Leviticus 19, 19	146	245
Leviticus 17, 13	91	187	Leviticus 19, 23	147	246
Leviticus 18, 6	97	188	Leviticus 19, 24	100	247
Leviticus 18, 7	98	189	Leviticus 19, 26	148	248
Leviticus 18, 7	99	190	Leviticus 19, 26	149	249
Leviticus 18, 8	100	191	Leviticus 19, 27	150	250
Leviticus 18, 9	101	192	Leviticus 19, 27	151	251
Leviticus 18, 10	102	193	Leviticus 19, 28	152	252
Leviticus 18, 10	103	194	Leviticus 19, 30	153	253
Leviticus 18, 10	104*	195*	Leviticus 19, 31	101	254
Leviticus 18, 11	105	196	Leviticus 19, 31	154	255
Leviticus 18, 12	106	197	Leviticus 19, 32	155	256
Leviticus 18, 13	107	198	Leviticus 19, 35	102	257
Leviticus 18, 14	108	199	Leviticus 19, 36	156	258
Leviticus 18, 14	109	200	Leviticus 20, 9	103	259
Leviticus 18, 15	110	201	Leviticus 20, 14	157	260
Leviticus 18, 16	111	202	Leviticus 20, 23	104	261
Leviticus 18, 17	112	203	Leviticus 21, 1	158	262
Leviticus 18, 17	113	204	Leviticus 21, 3	159	263
Leviticus 18, 17	114	205	Leviticus 21, 6	105	264
Leviticus 18, 18	115	206	Leviticus 21, 7	160	265
Leviticus 18, 19	116	207	Leviticus 21, 7	161	266
Leviticus 18, 21	117	208	Leviticus 21, 7	162	267
Leviticus 18, 22	118	209	Leviticus 21, 8	163	268
Leviticus 18, 23	119	210	Leviticus 21, 11	106	269
Leviticus 18, 23	120	211	Leviticus 21, 11	164	270
Leviticus 19, 3	92	212	Leviticus 21, 13	165	271
Leviticus 19, 4	121	213	Leviticus 21, 14	107	272
Leviticus 19, 4	122	214	Leviticus 21, 15	166	273
Leviticus 19, 6	123	215	Leviticus 21, 17	167	274
Leviticus 19, 9	124	216	Leviticus 21, 18	168	275
Leviticus 19, 10	93	217	Leviticus 21, 23	169	276
Leviticus 19, 9	125	218	Leviticus 22, 2	170	277
Leviticus 19, 10	94	219	Leviticus 22, 4	171	278
Leviticus 19, 10	126	220	Leviticus 22, 10	172	279
Leviticus 19, 10	95	221	Leviticus 22, 10	173	280
Leviticus 19, 10	127	222	Leviticus 22, 10	174	281
Leviticus 19, 10	96	223	Leviticus 22, 10	175§	282§
Leviticus 19, 11	128	224	Leviticus 22, 12	176	283
Leviticus 19, 11	129	225	Leviticus 22, 15	177	284
Leviticus 19, 11	130	226	Leviticus 22, 20	178	285
Leviticus 19, 12	131	227	Leviticus 22, 21	108	286

Basis in the Pentateuch	positive, negative	of the 613	Basis in the Pentateuch	positive, negative	of the 613
Leviticus 22, 21	179	287	Leviticus 25, 43	212	346
Leviticus 22, 22	180	288	Leviticus 25, 46	135	347
Leviticus 22, 22	181	289	Leviticus 25, 53	213	348
Leviticus 22, 24	182	290	Leviticus 26, 1	214	349
Leviticus 22, 24	183	291	Leviticus 27, 2	136	350
Leviticus 22, 25	184	292	Leviticus 27, 10	215	351
Leviticus 22, 27	109	293	Leviticus 27, 10	137	352
Leviticus 22, 28	185	294	Leviticus 27, 11, 12 ..	138	353
Leviticus 22, 32	186	295	Leviticus 27, 14	139	354
Leviticus 22, 32	110	296	Leviticus 27, 16	140	355
Leviticus 23, 7·	111	297	Leviticus 27, 26	216	356
Leviticus 23, 7	187	298	Leviticus 27, 28	141	357
Leviticus 23, 8	112	299	Leviticus 27, 28	217	358
Leviticus 23, 8	113	300	Leviticus 27, 28	218	359
Leviticus 23, 8	188	301	Leviticus 27, 32	142	360
Leviticus 23, 10	114	302	Leviticus 27, 33	219	361
Leviticus 23, 14	189	303	Numbers 5, 2	143	362
Leviticus 23, 14	190	304	Numbers 5, 3	220	363
Leviticus 23, 14	191	305	Numbers 5, 7	144	364
Leviticus 23, 16	115	306	Numbers 5, 15	145	365
Leviticus 23, 17	116	307	Numbers 5, 15	221	366
Leviticus 23, 21	117	308	Numbers 5, 15	222	367
Leviticus 23, 21	192	309	Numbers 6, 3	223	368
Leviticus 23, 24	118	310	Numbers 6, 3	224	369
Leviticus 23, 25	193	311	Numbers 6, 3	225	370
Leviticus 23, 25	119	312	Numbers 6, 4	226	371
Leviticus 23, 27	120	313	Numbers 6, 4	227	372
Leviticus 23, 27	121	314	Numbers 6, 5	228	373
Leviticus 23, 28	194	315	Numbers 6, 5	146	374
Leviticus 23, 29	195	316	Numbers 6, 6·	229	375
Leviticus 23, 32	122	317	Numbers 6, 7	230	376
Leviticus 23, 34, 35 ..	123	318	Numbers 6, 13, 14, 18 ..	147	377
Leviticus 23, 35	196	319	Numbers 6, 23	148	378
Leviticus 23, 36	124	320	Numbers 7, 9	149	379
Leviticus 23, 36	125	321	Numbers 9, 11	150	380
Leviticus 23, 36	126	322	Numbers 9, 11	151	381
Leviticus 23, 36	197	323	Numbers 9, 12	231	382
Leviticus 23, 40	127	324	Numbers 9, 12	232	383
Leviticus 23, 42	128	325	Numbers 10, 10	152	384
Leviticus 25, 4	198	326	Numbers 15, 20, 21 ..	153	385
Leviticus 25, 4	199	327	Numbers 15, 38	154	386
Leviticus 25, 5	200	328	Numbers 15, 39	233	387
Leviticus 25, 5	201	329	Numbers 18, 3	155	388
Leviticus 25, 8	129	330	Numbers 18, 3	234	389
Leviticus 25, 9	130	331	Numbers 18, 4	235	390
Leviticus 25, 10	131	332	Numbers 18, 5	236	391
Leviticus 25, 11	202	333	Numbers 18, 15	156	392
Leviticus 25, 11	203	334	Numbers 18, 17	237	393
Leviticus 25, 11	204	335	Numbers 18, 23	157	394
Leviticus 25, 14	132	336	Numbers 18, 24	158	395
Leviticus 25, 14	205	337	Numbers 18, 26	159	396
Leviticus 25, 17	206	338	Numbers 19, 2	160	397
Leviticus 25, 23	207	339	Numbers 19, 14	161	398
Leviticus 25, 24	133	340	Numbers 19, 19, 21 ..	162	399
Leviticus 25, 29	134	341	Numbers 27, 8	163	400
Leviticus 25, 34	208	342	Numbers 28, 2, 3	164	401
Leviticus 25, 37	209	343	Numbers 28, 9	165	402
Leviticus 25, 39	210	344	Numbers 28, 11·.. ..	166	403
Leviticus 25, 42	211	345	Numbers 28, 26, 27 ..	167	404

Basis in the Pentateuch	positive, negative	of the 613	Basis in the Pentateuch	positive, negative	of the 613
Numbers 29, 1	168	405	Deuteronomy 13, 17	193	464
Numbers 30, 3	169	406	Deuteronomy 13, 17	272	465
Numbers 30, 3	238	407	Deuteronomy 13, 18	273	466
Numbers 35, 2	170	408	Deuteronomy 14, 1	274	467
Numbers 35, 12	239	409	Deuteronomy 14, 1	275	468
Numbers 35, 25	171	410	Deuteronomy 14, 3	276	469
Numbers 35, 30	240	411	Deuteronomy 14, 11	194	470
Numbers 35, 31	241	412	Deuteronomy 14, 19	277	471
Numbers 35, 32	242	413	Deuteronomy 14, 21	278	472
Deuteronomy 1, 17	243	414	Deuteronomy 14, 22	195	473
Deuteronomy 1, 17	244	415	Deuteronomy 14, 28	196	474
Deuteronomy 5, 18	245	416	Deuteronomy 15, 2	279	475
Deuteronomy 6, 4	172	417	Deuteronomy 15, 3	197	476
Deuteronomy 6, 5	173	418	Deuteronomy 15, 3	198	477
Deuteronomy 6, 7	174	419	Deuteronomy 15, 7	280	478
Deuteronomy 6, 7	175	420	Deuteronomy 15, 8	199	479
Deuteronomy 6, 8	176	421	Deuteronomy 15, 9	281	480
Deuteronomy 6, 8	177	422	Deuteronomy 15, 13	282	481
Deuteronomy 6, 9	178	423	Deuteronomy 15, 14	200	482
Deuteronomy 6, 16	246	424	Deuteronomy 15, 19	283	483
Deuteronomy 7, 2	179	425	Deuteronomy 15, 19	284	484
Deuteronomy 7, 2	247	426	Deuteronomy 16, 3	285	485
Deuteronomy 7, 3	248	427	Deuteronomy 16, 4	286	486
Deuteronomy 7, 25	249	428	Deuteronomy 16, 5	287	487
Deuteronomy 7, 26	250	429	Deuteronomy 16, 14	201	488
Deuteronomy 8, 10	180	430	Deuteronomy 16, 16	202	489
Deuteronomy 10, 19	181	431	Deuteronomy 16, 16	288	490
Deuteronomy 10, 20	182	432	Deuteronomy 16, 18	203	491
Deuteronomy 10, 20	183	433	Deuteronomy 16, 21	289	492
Deuteronomy 10, 20	184	434	Deuteronomy 16, 22	290	493
Deuteronomy 10, 20	185	435	Deuteronomy 17, 1	291	494
Deuteronomy 12, 2	186	436	Deuteronomy 17, 10	204	495
Deuteronomy 12, 4	251	437	Deuteronomy 17, 11	292	496
Deuteronomy 12, 5, 6	187	438	Deuteronomy 17, 15	205	497
Deuteronomy 12, 13	252	439	Deuteronomy 17, 15	293	498
Deuteronomy 12, 14	188	440	Deuteronomy 17, 16	294	499
Deuteronomy 12, 15	189	441	Deuteronomy 17, 16	295	500
Deuteronomy 12, 17	253	442	Deuteronomy 17, 17	296	501
Deuteronomy 12, 17	254	443	Deuteronomy 17, 17	297	502
Deuteronomy 12, 17	255	444	Deuteronomy 17, 18	206	503
Deuteronomy 12, 17	256	445	Deuteronomy 18, 1	298	504
Deuteronomy 12, 17	257	446	Deuteronomy 18, 2	299	505
Deuteronomy 12, 17	258	447	Deuteronomy 18, 3	207	506
Deuteronomy 12, 17	259	448	Deuteronomy 18, 4	208	507
Deuteronomy 12, 17	260	449	Deuteronomy 18, 4	209	508
Deuteronomy 12, 19	261	450	Deuteronomy 18, 7	210	509
Deuteronomy 12, 21	190	451	Deuteronomy 18, 10	300	510
Deuteronomy 12, 23	262	452	Deuteronomy 18, 10	301	511
Deuteronomy 12, 26	191	453	Deuteronomy 18, 11	302	512
Deuteronomy 13, 1	263	454	Deuteronomy 18, 11	303	513
Deuteronomy 13, 1	264	455	Deuteronomy 18, 11	304	514
Deuteronomy 13, 4	265	456	Deuteronomy 18, 11	305	515
Deuteronomy 13, 9	266	457	Deuteronomy 18, 15	211	516
Deuteronomy 13, 9	267	458	Deuteronomy 18, 20	306	517
Deuteronomy 13, 9	268	459	Deuteronomy 18, 20	307	518
Deuteronomy 13, 9	269	460	Deuteronomy 18, 22	308	519
Deuteronomy 13, 9	270	461	Deuteronomy 19, 2, 3	212	520
Deuteronomy 13, 12	271	462	Deuteronomy 19, 13	309	521
Deuteronomy 13, 15	192	463	Deuteronomy 19, 14	310	522

Basis in the Pentateuch	positive, negative	of the 613	Basis in the Pentateuch	positive, negative	of the 613
Deuteronomy 19, 15	311	523	Deuteronomy 23, 17	340	569
Deuteronomy 19, 19	213	524	Deuteronomy 23, 18	341	570
Deuteronomy 20, 3	312	525	Deuteronomy 23, 19	342	571
Deuteronomy 20, 2	214	526	Deuteronomy 23, 21	230	572
Deuteronomy 20, 11	215	527	Deuteronomy 23, 20	343	573
Deuteronomy 20, 16	313	528	Deuteronomy 23, 22	344	574
Deuteronomy 20, 19	314	529	Deuteronomy 23, 24	231	575
Deuteronomy 21, 1, 4	216	530	Deuteronomy 23, 25	232	576
Deuteronomy 21, 4	315	531	Deuteronomy 23, 25	345	577
Deuteronomy 21, 11	217	532	Deuteronomy 23, 26	346	578
Deuteronomy 21, 14	316	533	Deuteronomy 24, 1	233	579
Deuteronomy 21, 14	317	534	Deuteronomy 24, 4	347	580
Deuteronomy 21, 22	218	535	Deuteronomy 24, 5	348	581
Deuteronomy 21, 23	318	536	Deuteronomy 24, 5	234	582
Deuteronomy 21, 23	219	537	Deuteronomy 24, 6	349	583
Deuteronomy 22, 1	220	538	Deuteronomy 24, 8	350	584
Deuteronomy 22, 3	319	539	Deuteronomy 24, 10	351	585
Deuteronomy 22, 4	320	540	Deuteronomy 24, 12	352	586
Deuteronomy 22, 4	221	541	Deuteronomy 24, 13	235	587
Deuteronomy 22, 5	321	542	Deuteronomy 24, 15	236	588
Deuteronomy 22, 5	322	543	Deuteronomy 24, 16	353	589
Deuteronomy 22, 6	323	544	Deuteronomy 24, 17	354	590
Deuteronomy 22, 7	222	545	Deuteronomy 24, 17	355	591
Deuteronomy 22, 8	223	546	Deuteronomy 24, 19	237	592
Deuteronomy 22, 8	324	547	Deuteronomy 24, 19	356	593
Deuteronomy 22, 9	325	548	Deuteronomy 25, 2	238	594
Deuteronomy 22, 9	326	549	Deuteronomy 25, 3	357	595
Deuteronomy 22, 10	327	550	Deuteronomy 25, 4	358	596
Deuteronomy 22, 11	328	551	Deuteronomy 25, 5	359	597
Deuteronomy 22, 13	224	552	Deuteronomy 25, 5	239	598
Deuteronomy 22, 19	225	553	Deuteronomy 25, 9	240	599
Deuteronomy 22, 19	329	554	Deuteronomy 25, 12	241	600
Deuteronomy 22, 24	226	555	Deuteronomy 25, 12	360	601
Deuteronomy 22, 26	330	556	Deuteronomy 25, 13	361	602
Deuteronomy 22, 29	227	557	Deuteronomy 25, 17	242	603
Deuteronomy 22, 29	331	558	Deuteronomy 25, 19	243	604
Deuteronomy 23, 2	332	559	Deuteronomy 25, 19	362	605
Deuteronomy 23, 3	333	560	Deuteronomy 26, 5	244	606
Deuteronomy 23, 4	334	561	Deuteronomy 26, 13	245	607
Deuteronomy 23, 7	335	562	Deuteronomy 26, 14	363	608
Deuteronomy 23, 8	336	563	Deuteronomy 26, 14	364	609
Deuteronomy 23, 8	337	564	Deuteronomy 26, 14	365	610
Deuteronomy 23, 11	338	565	Deuteronomy 28, 9	246	611
Deuteronomy 23, 13	228	566	Deuteronomy 31, 12	247	612
Deuteronomy 23, 14	229	567	Deuteronomy 31, 19	248	613†
Deuteronomy 23, 16	339	568			

Note *. *Negative commandment 104 (195th of the* **613 commandments**), שֶׁלֹּא לְגַלּוֹת עֶרְוַת הַבַּת, *not to uncover the nakedness of a daughter,* is not directly stated in the תּוֹרָה but is inferred by an exegetical deduction (קַל וָחוֹמֶר, *minor to major*) from מֶעֶרְוַת בַּת בִּנְךָ and the penalty is further inferred by the logical principle גְּזֵרָה שָׁוָה (*similarity of phrases*) as explained in the *Tractate* יְבָמוֹת *3ab* (*Babylonian Talmud,* תַּלְמוּד בַּבְלִי).

132

Note §. *Negative commandment 175 (282nd of the* **613 commandments**)*,* שֶׁלֹּא יֹאכַל
עָרֵל קֹדֶשׁ, *one uncircumcised may not eat of aught holy, is not derived from a direct
quotation in the* תּוֹרָה *but is deduced by an exegetical principle known as*
גְּזֵרָה שָׁוָה, *similarity of phrases, thus, the phrase* תּוֹשָׁב וְשָׂכִיר *occurs in connection
with both subjects of* פֶּסַח *and* תְּרוּמָה, *hence the formula* כָּל עָרֵל אָסוּר בּוֹ
coupled with the first also applies to the latter. (עָרֵל *here refers to one who
has not been circumcised because a brother of his had died as a result of
circumcision.)*

Note †. Some authorities add seven Rabbinical commandments making a total
of 620:

‡וְאֵלּוּ שֶׁבַע מִצְוֹת דְּרַבָּנָן

(א) לְבָרֵךְ עַל כָּל־מַה־שֶׁנֶּהֱנֶה [חוּץ מִבִּרְכַּת הַמָּזוֹן שֶׁסּוֹף מִדְּאוֹרַיְיתָא]

(ב) לִיטוֹל אֶת־הַיָּדַיִם׃

(ג) לְהַדְלִיק נֵר בַּשַּׁבָּת׃

(ד) לַעֲשׂוֹת עֵירוּב׃

(ה) לִקְרוֹא אֶת־הַהַלֵּל׃

(ו) לְהַדְלִיק נֵר חֲנוּכָּה׃

(ז) לִקְרוֹא אֶת־הַמְּגִילָה׃

And ‡these are the seven commandments instituted by the Sages: (1)
To recite a *Benediction* over every thing that one enjoys. *Grace after Meals* is
not included here as it is one of the תרי"ג מצות, *viz.*, number 430 (the 180th
positive commandment). (2) To wash the hands. (3) To kindle the *Sabbath
light*. (4) To prepare the *Erub*. (5) To recite the *Hallel*. (6) To kindle the
Chanukah light(s). (7) To read the *Megillah* on Purim.

‡**References:** (1) בְּרָכוֹת 61ᵃ, 36a *et seq.* (2) בְּרָכוֹת 8², 60b. (3) שַׁבָּת 21 ᵗᵒ ⁷, 35b.
38b; סוּכָּה 2:; עֵירוּבִין 121ᵃ *et seq.*; בֵּיצָה 2¹. (5) פְּסָחִים 118a, 5:, 9³; בְּרָכוֹת (4)
רֹאשׁ הַשָּׁנָה 4:; מְגִלָּה 2⁵, 4¹, 21b; תַּעֲנִית 28b, 44:⁵. (6) שַׁבָּת 21b, 22a, 23a. (7)
שְׁקָלִים 1¹; רֹאשׁ הַשָּׁנָה 3:; מְגִלָּה 11:⁴, 21 ᵗᵒ ⁵, 4¹, 21b.

Note: There are variations in the numberings of some of the 613 *Commandments*
according to some authorities, and also others give variant bases; see **Notes**
in the ADDENDA.

The 613 Pentateuchal bases.

100. ויברך אתם אלהים ויאמר להם פרו ורבו· 2. את בריתי תשמר המול לכם כל זכר·
3. על כן לא יאכלו בני ישראל את גיד הנשה. 4§. החדש הזה לכם ראש חדשים. 5. ושחטו
אתו כל קהל עדת ישראל בין הערבים. 6. ואכלו את הבשר בלילה הזה צלי אש ומצות על
מררים יאכלהו. 7. אל תאכלו ממנו נא ובשל מבשל במים. 8. ולא תותירו ממנו עד בקר.
9. אך ביום הראשון תשביתו שאר מבתיכם. 10. בערב תאכלו מצת. 11. שבעת ימים שאר
לא ימצא בבתיכם. 12. כל מחמצת לא תאכלו. 13. כל בן נכר לא יאכל בו. 14. תושב
ושכיר לא יאכל בו. 15. לא תוציא מן הבית מן הבשר חוצה. 16. ועצם לא תשברו בו.
17. וכל ערל לא יאכל בו. 18. קדש לי כל בכור פטר כל רחם בבני ישראל באדם ובבהמה
לי הוא. 19. ולא יאכל חמץ. 20. ולא יראה לך חמץ ולא יראה לך שאר בכל גבולך. 21. והגדת
לבנך ביום ההוא. 22. וכל פטר חמר תפדה בשה. 23. ואם לא תפדה וערפתו. 24. אל יצא
איש ממקומו ביום השביעי 25. אנכי ה' אלהיך אשר הוצאתיך מארץ מצרים. 26. לא יהיה
לך אלהים אחרים. 27. לך תעשה לך פסל וכל תמונה. 28. לא תשתחוה להם. 29. ולא
תעבדם. 30. לא תשא את שם ה' אלהיך לשוא כי לא ינקה את . . . 31. זכור את יום השבת
לקדשו. 32. לא תעשה כל מלאכה. 33. כבד את אביך ואת אמך למען יארכון ימיך. 34. לא
תרצח. 35. לא תנאף. 36. לא תגנב. 37. לא תענה ברעך עד שקר. 38. לא תחמד. 39. לא
תעשון אתי אלהי כסף. 40. לא תבנה אתהן גזית. 41. ולא תעלה במעלות על מזבחי.
42. כי תקנה עבד עברי. 43. עם רעה בעיני אדניו אשר לא יעדה. 44. והפדה.
45. לא ימשל למכרה. 46. שארה כסותה וענתה לא יגרע. 47. ומכה אביו ואמו.
48. מות יומת. 49. וכי יריבן אנשים. 50. נקם ינקם. 51. וכי יגח שור איש. 52. ולא
יאכל את בשרו. 53. וכי יפתח איש בור. 54. כי יגנב איש שור או שה. 55. כי יבער
איש שדה או כרם. 56. כי תצא אש ומצאה קצים ונאכל גדיש או הקמה. 57. כי יתן
איש אל רעהו כסף או כלים לשמר ונגב. 58. על כל דבר פשע. 59. כי יתן איש אל רעהו
חמור או שור. 60. וכי ישאל איש מעם רעהו ונשבר. 61. וכי יפתה איש בתולה אשר לא
ארשה. 62. מכשבה לא תחיה. 63. וגר לא תונה. 64. ולא תלחצנו. 65. כל אלמנה ויתום
לא תענון. 66. אם כסף תלוה את עמי. 67. לא תהיה לו כנשה. 68. לא תשימון עליו נשך.
69. אלהים לא תקלל. 70. אלהים לא תקלל. 71. ונשיא בעמך לא תאר. 72. מלאתך ודמעך
לא תאחר. 73. ובשר בשדה טרפה לא תאכלו. 74. לא תשא שמע שוא. 75. אל תשת ידך עם
רשע להית עד חמס. 76. לא תהיה אחרי רבים לרעת. 77. לא תענה על ריב לנטת.
78. אחרי רבים להטת. 79. ודל לא תהדר בריבו. 80. כי תראה חמור שנאך רבץ תחת
משאו . . . עזב תעזב עמו. 81. לא תטה משפט אבינך בריבו. 82. ונקי וצדיק אל תהרג. 83.
ושחד לא תקח. 84. והשביעה תשמטנה ונטשתה. 85. וביום השביעי תשבת. 86. ושם
אלהים אחרים לא תזכירו. 87. לא ישמע על פיך. 88. שלש רגלים תחג לי בשנה. 89. לא
תזבח על חמץ דם זבחי. 90. ולא ילין חלב חגי. 91. ראשית בכורי אדמתך תביא בית ה'
אלהיך. 92. לא תבשל גדי בחלב אמו. 93. לא תכרת להם ולאלהיהם ברית. 94. ולא
ישבו בארצך. 95. ועשו לי מקדש ושכנתי בתוכם. 96. בטבעת הארן יהיו הבדים לא יסרו
ממנו. 97. ונתת על השלחן לחם פנים לפני תמיד. 98. מחוץ לפרכת אשר על העדת יערך
אתו אהרן ובניו. 99. ועשו בגדי קדש לאהרן אחיך ולבניו. 100. ולא יזח החשן מעל האפוד.
101. שפה יהיה לפיו סביב מעשה ארג . . . לא יקרע. 102. ואכלו אתם אשר כפר בהם. 103.
והקטיר עליו אהרן קטרת סמים בבקר. 104. לא תעלו עליו קטרת זרה. 105. זה יתנו כל
העבר אל הפקדים מחצית השקל. 106. ורחצו אהרן ובניו ממנו את ידיהם ואת רגליהם.
107. ועשית אתו שמן משחת קדש. 108. על בשר אדם לא ייסך. 109. ובמתכנתו לא תעשו
כמהו. 110. והקטרת אשר תעשה במכנתה לא תעשו לכם. 111. פן תכרת ברית ליושב
הארץ. 112. וביום השביעי תשבת בחריש ובקציר תשבת. 113. לא תבשל גדי בחלב אמו.
114. לא תבערו אש בכל משבתיכם ביום השבת. 115†. אם עלה קרבנו מן הבקר זכר תמים
יקריבנו. 116. ונפש כי תקריב קרבן מנחה. 117. כי כל שאר וכל דבש לא תקטירו ממנו אשה
לה'. 118. ולא תשבית מלח ברית אלהיך מעל מנחתך. 119. על כל קרבנך תקריב מלח.
120. ואם כל עדת ישראל ישגו . . . והקריבו פר בן בקר. 121. ואם נפש אחת תחטא בשגגה מעם
הארץ . . . והביא קרבנו שעירת עזים . . . 122. אם†לא יגיד ונשא עונו (is given int
לואו† scripture text) 123. והביא את אשמו לה' על חטאתו אשר חטא. 124. ומלק את ראשו ממול

134

ערפו ולא יבדיל. 125. לא ישים עליו שמן. 126. ולא יתן עליה לבנה. 127. ואת חמישתו
יוסף עליו. 128. והביא איל תמים מן הצאן בערכך לאשם. 129. והשיב את הגזלה אשר גזל
130. ואת אשמו־יביא לה' איל תמים מן הצאן. 131. והרים את הדשן אשר תאכל האש את העלה
132. ... והאש על המזבח תוקד בו. 133. לא תכבה. 134. והנותרת ממנה יאכלו אהרן
ובניו. 135. לא תאפה חמץ חלקם נתתי אתה מאשי. 136. זה קרבן אהרן ובניו אשר יקריבו
לה'. 137. וכל מנחת כהן כליל תהיה לא תאכל. 138. זאת תורת החטאת. 139. וכל חטאת
אשר יובא מדמה אל אהל מועד לכפר בקדש לא תאכל באש תשרף. 140. וזאת תורת האשם
קדש קדשים הוא. 141. וזאת תורת זבח השלמים. 142. לא יניח ממנו עד בקר. 143. והנותר
מבשר הזבח ביום השלישי באש ישרף. 144. לא יחשב לו פגול יהיה. 145. והבשר אשר יגע
בכל טמא לא יאכל. 146. באש ישרף. 147. כל חלב שור וכשב ועז לא תאכלו. 148. וכל
דם לא תאכלו בכל מושבתיכם לעוף ולבהמה. 149. ראשיכם אל תפרעו. 150. ובגדיכם
לא תפרמו. 151. וממפתח אהל מועד לא תצאו. 152. יין ושכר אל תשת אתה ובניך אתך בבאכם
אל אהל מועד. 153. זאת החיה אשר תאכלו מכל הבהמה. 154. אך את זה לא תאכלו ממעלי
הגרה. 155. את זה תאכלו מכל אשר במים. 156. מבשרם לא תאכלו ואת נבלתם תשקצו.
157. ואת אלה תשקצו מן העוף לא יאכלו שקץ הם. 158. אך את זה תאכלו מכל שרץ העוף
ההלך על ארבע אשר ¹לו כרעים ממעל לרגליו (ולא†‡The scripture gives). 159. זה לכם הטמא
בשרץ השרץ על הארץ החלד ... 160. מכל האכל אשר יאכל אשר יבא עליו מים יטמא.
161. וכי ימות מן הבהמה אשר היא לכם לאכלה. 162. וכל השרץ השרץ על הארץ שקץ הוא
לא יאכל. 163. לא תאכלום כי שקץ הם. 164. אל תשקצו את נפשתיכם בכל השרץ השרץ.
165. ולא תטמאו את נפשתיכם בכל השרץ הרמש על הארץ. 166. אשה כי תזריע וילדה זכר
וטמאה שבעת ימים. 167. בכל קדש לא תגע ואל המקדש לא תבא. 168. ובמלאת ימי טהרה
לבן או לבת ... או תר לחטאת. 169. אדם כי יהיה בעור בשרו שאת. 170. ואת הנתק לא
יגלח. 171. בגדיו יהיו פרמים וראשו יהיה פרוע ועל שפם יעטה. 172. והבגד כי יהיה בו נגע
צרעת. 173. וזאת תהיה תורת המצרע ביום טהרתו. 174. וגלח את כל שערו. 175. ורחץ את
בשרו במים. 176. וביום השמיני יקח שני כבשים תמימם. 177. ובא אשר לו הבית הגיד לכהן.
178. וזאת תהיה טמאתו בזובו. 179. וביום השמיני יקח לו שתי תרים. 180. ואיש כי תצא ממנו
שכבת זרע. 181. ואשה כי תהיה זבה דם יהיה זבה בבשרה שבעת ימים תהיה בנדתה.
182. ואשה כי יזוב זוב דמה ימים רבים. 183. וביום השמיני תקח לה שתי תרים. 184. ואל יבא
בכל עת אל הקדש. 185. בזאת יבא אהרן אל הקדש בפר בן לחטאת. 186. ואל פתח
אהל מועד לא הביאו. 187. ושפך את דמו וכסהו בעפר. 188. איש איש אל כל שאר בשרו
לא תקרבו לגלות ערוה. 189. ערות אביך לא תגלה. 190. ערות אמך לא תגלה אמך הוא
לא תגלה ערותה. 191. ערות אשת אביך לא תגלה. 192. ערות אחותך בת אביך או בת אמך
מולדת בית ... 193. ערות בת בנך לא תגלה. 194. או בת בתך לא תגלה ערותן כי ערותך
הנה. 195. ערות הבת. 196. ערות בת אשת אביך ... לא תגלה ערותה. 197. ערות אחות
אביך לא תגלה שאר אביך הוא. 198. ערות אחות אמך לא תגלה כי שאר אמך הוא. 199.
ערות אחי אביך לא תגלה. 200. אל אשתו לא תקרב דדתך הוא. 201. ערות כלתך
לא תגלה· 202. ערות אשת אחיך לא תגלה. 203. ערות אשה ובתה לא תגלה.
204. את בת בנה. 205. ואת בת בתה לא תקח. 206. ואשה אל אחתה לא תקח
לצרור. 207. ואל אשה בנדת טמאתה לא תקרב. 208. ומזרעך לא תתן להעביר
למלך. 209. ואת זכר לא תשכב משכבי אשה. 210. ובכל בהמה לא תתן שכבתך
לטמאה בה. 211. ואשה לא תעמד לפני בהמה לרבעה תבל הוא. 212. איש אמו
ואביו תיראו. 213. אל תפנו אל האלילים. 214. ואלהי מסכה לא תעשו לכם. 215. והנותר
עד יום השלישי באש ישרף. 216. לא תכלה פאת שדך לקצר. 217. לעני ולגר תעזב אתם.
218. ולקט קצירך לא תלקט. 219. לעני ולגר תעזב אתם. 220. וכרמך לא תעולל. 221. לעני
ולגר תעזב אתם. 222. ופרט כרמך לא תלקט. 223. לעני ולגר תעזב אתם. 224. לא תגנבו.
225. ולא תכחשו. 226. ולא תשקרו איש בעמיתו. 227. ולא תשבעו בשמי לשקר. 228. לא
תעשק את רעך. 229. ולא תגזל. 230. לא תלין פעלת שכיר אתך עד בקר. 231. לא תקלל
חרש. 232. ולפני עור לא תתן מכשל. 233. לא תעשו עול במשפט. 234. ולא תהדר פני גדול.
235. בצדק תשפט עמיתך. 236. לא תלך רכיל. 237. לא תעמד על דם רעך. 238. לא
תשנא את אחיך בלבבך. 239. הוכח תוכיח את עמיתך. 240. ולא תשא עליו חטא.

135

241. לא תקם. 242. ולא תטר. 243. ואהבת לרעך כמוך. 244. בהמתך לא תרביע
כלאים. 245. שדך לא תזרע כלאים. 246. שלש שנים יהיה לכם ערלים לא יאכל. 247. ובשנה
הרביעת יהיה כל פריו קדש הלולים. 248. לא תאכלו על הדם. 249. לא תנחשו. 250. ולא
תעוננו. 251. לא תקפו פאת ראשכם. 252. ולא תשחית פאת זקנך. 253. וכתבת קעקע לא
תתנו בכם. 254. ומקדשי תיראו אני ה'. 255. אל תפנו אל האבת. 256. ואל הידענים. 257.
מפני שיבה תקום. 258. לא תעשו עול במשפט במדה במשקל ובמשורה. 259. מאזני צדק אבני
צדק איפת צדק והין צדק יהיה לכם. 260. כי איש איש אשר יקלל את אביו ואת אמו מות יומת.
261. באש ישרפו אתו ואתהן. 262. ולא תלכו בחקת הגוי אשר אני משלח מפניכם. 263. לנפש
לא יטמא בעמיו. 264. לה יטמא. 265. ולא יחללו שם אלהיהם. 266. אשה זנה לא יקחו.
267. וחללה לא יקחו. 268. ואשה גרושה מאישה לא יקחו. 269. וקדשתו. 270. ועל כל נפשת
מת לא יבא. 271. לאביו ולאמו לא יטמא. 272. והוא אשה בבתוליה יקח. 273. אלמנה
וגרושה וחללה זנה את אלה לא יקח. 274. ולא יחלל זרעו בעמיו. 275. איש מזרעך לדרתם
אשר יהיה בו מום. 276. כי כל איש אשר בו מום לא יקרב. 277. אך על הפרכת לא יבא.
278. ולא יחללו את שם קדשי. 279. איש איש מזרע אהרן והוא צרוע או זב בקדשים לא יאכל.
280. וכל זר לא יאכל קדש. 281. תושב כהן ושכיר לא יאכל קדש. 282. כל ערל לא יאכל
קדש. 283. ובת כהן כי תהיה לאיש זר הוא בתרומת הקדשים לא תאכל. 284. ולא יחללו
את קדשי בני ישראל אשר ירימו לה'. 285. כל אשר בו מום לא תקריבו. 286. תמים יהיה
לרצון. 287. כל מום לא יהיה בו. 288. עורת או שבור או חרוץ או יבלת או גרב או ילפת לא
תקריבו. 289. ואשה לא תתנו מהם על המזבח. 290. ומעוך וכתות ונתוק וכרות לא תקריבו
לה'. 291. ובארצכם לא תעשו. 292. ומיד בן נכר לא תקריבו. 293. והיה שבעת ימים תחת
אמו ומיום השמיני והלאה ירצה. 294. אתו ואת בנו לא תשחטו ביום אחד. 295. ולא תחללו
את שם קדשי. 296. ונקדשתי בתוך בני ישראל. 297. ביום הראשון מקרא קדש יהיה לכם.
298. כל מלאכת עבדה לא תעשו. 299. והקרבתם אשה לה' שבעת ימים. 300. ביום
השביעי מקרא קדש. 301. כל מלאכת עבדה לא תעשו. 302. והבאתם את עמר ראשית
קצירכם. 303. ולחם וקלי וכרמל לא תאכלו עד עצם היום הזה. 304. וקלי ... לא תאכלו.
305. וכרמל לא תאכלו. 306. וספרתם לכם ממחרת השבת ... שבע שבתות. 307. ממושבתיכם
תביאו לחם תנופה שתים. 308. וקראתם בעצם היום הזה מקרא קדש ... 309. כל מלאכת
עבדה לא תעשו. 310. בחדש השביעי באחד לחדש יהיה לכם שבתן. 311. כל מלאכת
עבדה לא תעשו. 312. והקרבתם אשה לה'. 313. אך בעשור לחדש השביעי ... ועניתם את
נפשתיכם. 314. והקרבתם אשה לה'. 315. וכל מלאכה לא תעשו בעצם היום הזה. 316. כי
כל הנפש אשר לא תענה בעצם היום הזה ונכרתה מעמיה. 317. שבת שבתון הוא לכם. 318
בחמשה עשר ... ביום הראשון מקרא קדש. 319. כל מלאכת עבדה לא תעשו. 320. שבעת
ימים תקריבו אשה לה'. 321. ביום השמיני מקרא קדש יהיה לכם. 322. והקרבתם אשה לה'
עצרת היא. 323. כל מלאכת עבדה לא תעשו. 324. ולקחתם לכם ביום הראשון פרי עץ
הדר כפת תמרים וענף עץ עבת וערבי נחל. 325. בסכת תשבו שבעת ימים. 326. ובשנה
השביעית ... שדך לא תזרע. 327. וכרמך לא תזמר. 328. את ספיח קצירך לא תקצור.
329. ואת ענבי נזירך לא תבצר. 330. וספרת לך שבע שבתות שנים ... שבע פעמים.
331. והעברת שופר תרועה ... ביום הכפרים. 332. וקדשתם את שנת החמשים שנה. 333.
יובל הוא ... לא תזרעו. 334. ולא תקצרו את ספיחיה. 335. ולא תבצרו את נזריה. 336.
וכי תמכרו ממכר לעמיתך או קנה מיד עמיתך. 337. אל תנו איש את אחיו. 338. ולא תנו
איש את עמיתו. 339. והארץ לא תמכר לצמתת. 340. ובכל ארץ אחזתכם גאלה תתנו לארץ.
341. ואיש כי ימכר בית מושב עיר חומה. 342. ושדה מגרש עריהם לא ימכר. 343. את כספך
לא תתן לו בנשך. 344. לא תעבד בו עבדת עבד. 345. לא ימכרו ממכרת עבד. 346. לא
תרדה בו בפרך. 347. לעלם בהם תעבדו. 348. לא ירדנו בפרך לעיניך. 349. ואבן משכית
לא תתנו בארצכם להשתחות עליה. 350. איש כי יפלא נדר בערכך נפשת לה'. 351. לא
יחליפנו ולא ימיר אתו. 352. והיה הוא ותמורתו יהיה קדש. 353. והעמיד את הבהמה לפני
הכהן והעריך. 354. ואיש כי יקדש את ביתו קדש לה'. 355. ואם משדה אחזתו יקדיש. 356. אך
בכור אשר יבכר לה' בבהמה לא יקדיש. 357. אך כל חרם אשר יחרם איש לה'. 358. לא
ימכר. 359. ולא יגאל כל חרם. 360. וכל מעשר בקר וצאן ... העשירי יהיה קדש לה'.
361. לא יגאל. 362.‡ וישלחו מן המחנה כל צרוע וכל זב ... 363. ולא יטמאו את מחניהם.

136

364. והתודו את חטאתם. 365. והביא האיש את אשתו אל הכהן. 366. לא יצק עליו שמן.
367. ולא יתן עליו לבנה. 368. מיין ושכר יזיר חמץ יין וחמץ שכר לא ישתה. 369. וענבים
לחים . . . לא יאכל. 370. ורבשים לא יאכל. 371. מחרצנים . . . לא יאכל. 372. ועד
זג לא יאכל. 373. תער לא יעבר על ראשו. 374. גדל פרע שער ראשו. 375. על
נפש מת לא יבא. 376. לאביו ולאמו לאחיו ולאחתו לא יטמא להם במתם.
377. ביום מלאת ימי נזרו . . . והקריב את קרבנו . . . וגלח הנזיר . . . 378. כה תברכו
את בני ישראל. 379. עבדת הקדש עליהם בכתף ישאו. 380. בחדש השני בארבעה
עשר יום בין הערבים יעשו אתו. 381. על מצות ומררים יאכלהו. 382. לא ישאירו
ממנו עד בקר. 383. ועצם לא ישברו בו. 384. וביום שמחתכם ובמועדיכם ובראשי
חדשכם ותקעתם בחצצרות על עלתיכם. 385. מראשית ערסתיכם . . . תתנו לה' תרומה.
386. ועשו להם ציצת. 387. ולא תתורו אחרי לבבכם ואחרי עיניכם. 388. ושמרו משמרתך
ומשמרת כל האהל. 389. אך אל כלי הקדש ואל המזבח לא יקרבו. 390. זר לא יקרב
אליכם. 391. ושמרתם את משמרת הקדש. 392. אך פדה תפדה את בכור האדם . . .
393. אך בכור שור או בכור כשב או בכור עז לא תפדה. 394. ועבד הלוי הוא את
עבדת אהל מועד. 395. כי את מעשר בני ישראל . . . 396. ואל הלוים תדבר . . .
והרמתם ממנו תרומת ה' מעשר מן המעשר. 397. ויקחו אליך פרה אדמה תמימה.
398. אדם כי ימות באהל כל הבא אל האהל וכל אשר באהל יטמא שבעת ימים.
399. והוה הטהר על חטמא . . . ומזה מי הנדה יכבס בגדיו. 400‏' איש כי ימות ובן אין
לו. 401. את קרבני לחמי . . . כבשים בני שנה תמימם שנים ליום עלה תמיד. 402'
וביום השבת שני כבשים . . . 403. ובראשי חדשכם תקריבו עלה לה'. 404. וביום
הבכורים בהקריבכם . . . 405. יום תרועה יהיה לכם. 406. איש כי ידר נדר. 407. לא יחל
דברו. 408. ותנו ללוים מנחלת אחזתם ערים לשבת. 409. ולא ימות הרצח עד עמדו לפני
העדה. 410. והשיבו אתו העדה אל עיר מקלטו. 411. ועד אחד לא יענה בנפש למות.
412. ולא תקחו כפר לנפש רצח אשר הוא רשע למות. 413. ולא תקחו כפר לנוס אל
עיר מקלטו. 414‏'. לא תכירו פנים במשפט. 415. לא תגורו מפני איש. 416. ולא תתאוה
בית רעך. 417. שמע ישראל ה' אלהינו ה' אחד. 418. ואהבת את ה' אלהיך. 419.
ושננתם לבניך. 420. ודברת בם בשבתך בביתך ובלכתך בדרך ובשכבך ובקומך.
421. וקשרתם לאות על ידך. 422. והיו לטטפת בין עיניך. 423. וכתבתם על מזוזת
ביתך ובשעריך. 424. לא תנסו את ה' אלהיכם. 425. החרם תחרים אתם. 426. ולא
תחנם. 427. ולא תתחתן בם. 428. לא תחמד כסף וזהב עליהם. 429. ולא תביא
תועבה אל ביתך. 430. ואכלת ושבעת וברכת את ה' אלהיך. 431. ואהבתם את הגר.
432. את ה'אלהיך תירא. 433. אתו תעבד. 434. ובו תדבק. 435‏'. ובשמו תשבע. 436. אבד
תאבדון את כל המקמות. 437. לא תעשון כן לה' אלהיכם. 438. ובאת שמה והבאתם שמה
עלתיכם וזבחיכם. 439. השמר לך פן תעלה עלתיך בכל מקום. 440. שם תעלה עלתיך.
441. רק בכל אות נפשך תזבח ואכלת בשר. 442. לא תוכל לאכל בשעריך מעשר דגנך.
443. ותירשך. 444. ויצהרך. 445. ובכרת. 446. בקרך וצאנך. 447. וכל נדריך אשר תדר.
448. ונדבתיך. 449. ותרומת ידך. 450. השמר לך פן תעזב את הלוי. 451. וזבחת מבקרך
ומצאנך. 452. ולא תאכל הנפש עם הבשר. 453. רק קדשיך אשר יהיו לך ונדריך תשא ובאת
אל המקום . . . 454. לא תסף עליו. 455. ולא תגרע ממנו. 456. לא תשמע אל דברי הנביא.
457. לא תאבה לו. 458. ולא תשמע אליו. 459. ולא תחוס עינך עליו. 460. ולא תחמל.
461. ולא תכסה עליו. 462. ולא יוספו לעשות כדבר הרע הזה בקרבך. 463. ודרשת וחקרת
שאלת היטב. 464. ושרפת באש את העיר. 465. לא תבנה עוד. 466. ולא ידבק בידך
מאומה מן החרם. 467. לא תתגודדו. 468. ולא תשימו קרחה בין עיניכם למת. 469.
לא תאכל כל תועבה. 470. את צפר טהרה תאכלו. 471. וכל שרץ העוף טמא הוא
לכם לא יאכלו. 472. לא תאכלו כל נבלה. 473. עשר תעשר את כל תבואת זרעך
474. מקצה שלש שנים תוציא את כל מעשר תבואתך . . . 475. לא יגש את רעהו.
476. את הנכרי תגש. 477. ואשר יהיה לך את אחיך תשמט. 478. לא תאמץ את לבבך
ולא תקפץ את ידך מאחיך האביון. 479. פתח תפתח את ידך לו. 480. השמר לך פן
יהיה דבר עם לבבך בליעל לאמר קרבה שנת השבע . . . 481. לא תשלחנו ריקם.
482. העניק תעניק לו. 483. לא תעבד בבכר שורך. 484. ולא תגז בכור צאנך

485. לא תאכל עליו חמץ. 486. ולא ילין מן הבשר אשר תזבח בערב. 487. לא תוכל לזבח את הפסח באחד שעריך. 488. ושמחת בחגך. 489. שלש פעמים בשנה יראה. 490. ולא יראה את פני ה׳ ריקם. 491. שפטים ושטרים תתן לך בכל שעריך. 492. לא תטע לך אשרה כל עץ אצל מזבח... 493. ולא תקים לך מצבה. 494. לא תזבח לה׳ אלהיך שור ושה אשר יהיה בו מום. 495. ועשית על פי הדבר אשר יגידו לך. 496. לא תסור מן הדבר אשר יגידו לך. 497. שום תשים עליך מלך. 498. לא תוכל לתת עליך איש נכרי. 499. לא ירבה לו סוסים. 500. לא תספון לשוב בדרך הזה עוד. 501. ולא ירבה לו נשים. 502. וכסף וזהב לא ירבה לו מאד. 503. וכתב לו את משנה התורה הזאת. 504. לא יהיה לכהנים הלוים כל שבט לוי חלק ונחלה. 505. ונחלה לא יהיה לו. 506. ותן לכהן הזרע והלחיים והקבה. 507. ראשית דגן תירשך ויצהרך... תתן לו. 508. וראשית גז צאנך תתן לו. 509. ושרת בשם ה׳ אלהיו. 510. לא ימצא בך... קסם קסמים. 511. מעונן ומנחש ומכשף. 512. וחבר חבר. 513. ושאל אוב. 514. וידעני. 515. ודרש אל המתים. 516. נביא מקרבך... אליו תשמעון. 517. אך הנביא אשר יזיד לדבר דבר בשמי. 518. ואשר ידבר בשם אלהים אחרים. 519. לא תגור ממנו. 520. שלש ערים תבדיל לך בתוך ארצך... תכין לך הדרך. 521. לא תחוס עינך עליו. 522. לא תסיג גבול רעך. 523. לא יקום עד אחד באיש. 524. ועשיתם לו כאשר זמם. 525. ואל תערצו מפניהם. 526. והיה כקרבכם אל המלחמה ונגש הכהן. 527. והיה אם שלום תענך... ועבדוך. 528. לא תחיה כל נשמה. 529. לא תשחית את עצה לנדח עליו גרזן. 530. כי ימצא חלל... וערפו שם את העגלה. 531. אשר לא יעבד בו ולא יזרע. 532. וראית בשביה אשת יפת תאר. 533. ומכר לא תמכרנה בכסף. 534. לא תתעמר בה תחת אשר עניתה. 535. ותלית אתו על עץ. 536. לא תלין נבלתו על העץ. 537. כי קבור תקברנו ביום ההוא. 538. השב תשיבם לאחיך. 539. לא תוכל להתעלם. 540. לא תראה את חמור אחיך או שורו נפלים בדרך. 541. הקם תקי ם עמו. 542. לא יהיה כלי גבר על אשה. 543. ולא ילבש גבר שמלת אשה. 544. לא תקח האם על הבנים. 545. שלח תשלח את האם. 546. ועשית מעקה לגנך. 547. ולא תשים דמים בביתך. 548. לא תזרע כרמך כלאים. 549. פן תקדש המלאה הזרע אשר תזרע ותבואת הכרם. 550. לא תחרש בשור ובחמר יחדו. 551. לא תלבש שעטנז צמר ופשתים יחדו. 552. כי יקח איש אשה ובא אליה. 553. ולו תהיה לאשה. 554. לא יוכל לשלחה כל ימיו. 555. וסקלתם באבנים. 556. ולנערה לא תעשה דבר. 557. ותן האיש השכב עמה לאבי הנער [the reading is הנערה] חמשים כסף ולו תהיה לאשה. 558. תחת אשר ענה לא יוכל שלחה כל ימיו. 559. לא יבא פצוע דכה וכרות שפכה בקהל ה׳. 560. לא יבא ממזר בקהל ה׳. 561. לא יבא עמוני ומואבי בקהל ה׳. 562. לא תדרש שלמם וטבתם. 563. לא תתעב אדמי כי אחיך הוא. 564. לא תתעב מצרי כי גר היית בארצו. 565. כי יהיה בך איש אשר לא יהיה טהור. 566. ויד תהיה לך. 567. ויתד תהיה לך על אזנך. 568. לא תסגיר עבד אל אדוניו. 569. לא תונו. 570. לא תהיה קדשה מבנות ישראל. 571. לא תביא אתנן זונה ומחיר כלב בית ה׳ אלהיך. 572. לנכרי תשיך. 573. ולאחיך לא תשיך. 574. כי תדר נדר לה׳ אלהיך לא תאחר לשלמו. 575. מוצא שפתיך תשמר ועשית כאשר נדרת... בפיך. 576. כי תבא בכרם רעך ואכלת... 577. ואל כליך לא תתן. 578. וחרמש לא תניף על קמת רעך. 579. וכתב לה ספר כריתת. 580. לא יוכל בעלה הראשן אשר שלחה לשוב לקחתה. 581. כי יקח איש אשה חדשה לא יצא בצבא. 582. נקי יהיה לביתו שנה אחת ושמח את אשתו. 583. לא יחבל רחים ורכב. 584. השמר בנגע הצרעת. 585. לא תבא אל ביתו לעבט עבטו. 586. לא תשכב בעבטו. 587. השב תשיב לו את העבוט כבוא השמש. 588. ביומו תתן שכרו. 589. לא יומתו אבות על בנים. 590. לא תטה משפט גר יתום. 591. ולא תחבל בגד אלמנה. 592. וזכחת עמר בשדה לא תשוב לקחתו לגר ליתום ולאלמנה יהיה. 593. לא תשוב לקחתו. 594. והכהו לפניו כדי רשעתו במספר. 595. ארבעים יכנו לא יסיף. 596. לא תחסם שור בדישו. 597. לא תהיה אשת המת החוצה. 598. יבמה יבא עליה ולקחה. 599. וחלצה נעלו מעל רגלו. 600. וקצתה את כפה. 601. לא תחוס עינך. 602. לא יהיה לך בכיסך אבן ואבן גדולה וקטנה. 603. זכור את אשר עשה לך עמלק. 604. תמחה את זכר עמלק. 605. לא תשכח. 606. וענית ואמרת... ארמי אבד אבי. 607. ואמרת לפני ה׳ אלהיך בערתי הקדש. 608. לא אכלתי באני ממנו. 609. ולא בערתי ממנו בטמא. 610. ולא נתתי ממנו למת. 611. והלכת בדרכיו. 612. הקהל את העם האנשים והנשים והטף. 613. ועתה כתבו לכם את השירה הזאת.

TARYAG MITZVOTH

* *Genesis*, 1, 2. 3, בְּרֵאשִׁית.

§ *Exodus*, 4 to *114*, שְׁמוֹת.

† *Leviticus*, 115 to *361*, וַיִּקְרָא.

‡ *Numbers*, 362 to *413*, בְּמִדְבָּר.

¶ *Deuteronomy*, *414* to 613, דְּבָרִים.

The import of each of the **613 Commandments** is stated very briefly.

NOTE.—Each statement is so worded as to bring out its 'positive' or '*negative*' character as the case may be. See also additional **Notes** in the ADDENDA.

Genesis
1: A man must take a wife and beget offspring. 2: A male child must be circumcised on the eighth day after its birth. 3: Not to eat the sinew of the thigh vein.

Exodus
4: To sanctify [*viz.*, fix] the months and to intercalate the leap-year months. 5: The *Passover-offering* must be slaughtered on the 14th day of Nisan at dusk (see 6 *et seq.*, 380 *et seq.*, *486*, *487*). 6: To eat of the *Passover-offering*, which has been roasted over the fire, on the night of the 15th day of Nisan and to eat unleavened bread and bitter herbs (see 5, 7, 10). 7: Not to eat of the *Passover-offering* raw or sodden at all with water but roast with fire (see 5, 6, 8, 16). 8: Naught of the *Passover-offering* may be left to the morning, aught remaining must be burnt (see 5, 6, 7, 16). 9: All leaven must have been cleared out by the eve of Passover [the 14th day of Nisan] (see 10 *et seq.*, 485). 10: Unleavened bread must be eaten on the night of the 15th day of Nisan (see 6, 11, 12). 11: There must not be aught leavened in one's possession during the whole of Passover (see 5, 10, 12). 12: Naught leavened—whether mingled or not with aught else—may be eaten (see 10 11, 19, 20). 13: No alien—an apostate Israelite or a pagan—may eat of the *Passover-offering* (see 5 *et seq.*, 13, 14 *et seq.*). 14: No sojourner or hired servant may eat of the *Passover-offering* (see 13, 17). 15: Naught of the flesh of the *Passover-offering* may be taken outside the place assigned for its eating. 16: Not to break any bone of the *Passover-offering* (see 8). 17: No uncircumcised person—not even an uncircumcised Israelite—may eat of the *Passover-offering* (see 13, 14). 18: To sanctify the *firstborn of man* and the *firstling of beast* (see 22, 392, 393). 19: No leavened bread may be eaten during Passover (see *12*, 20). 20: No leavened bread may be seen in our dwellings or borders during Passover (see 12, 19). 21: The history of the redemption and exodus from Egypt must be narrated on the night of the 15th day of Nisan (and also on the night of the 16th day of Nisan outside the Holy Land). 22: The *firstling of an ass* must be redeemed with a *lamb* (see 18, 23, *393*). 23: If the *firstling of an ass* is not redeemed its neck must be broken (see 18, 22, *393*). 24: None may go beyond 2,000 cubits—the *Sabbath limit*—on the Sabbath. 25: To know that there is **God the Eternal** (see *26*, 417). 26: There is no other god besides the **Only One God the Eternal** (see 25, 417). 27: Not to make any kind of image or likeness or the like for idolatrous purposes (see *28*, *29*, *39*, *429*). 28: Not to practise idolatry or take part in any way in idolatrous practices (see 27, 29, 39). 29: Not to engage in any idol worship whatsoever (see 27, 28, 39). 30: Not to swear falsely, not to take an oath for no valid reason, not to utter the Name of God to no purpose. 31: To bear in mind that the Sabbath must be observed in all its sanctity (see *32*). 32: No manner of work may be performed on the Sabbath (see 31, 85). 33: One must honour his [her] parents. 34: Not to commit murder. 35: Not to commit adultery—not to have any illicit relations with the opposite sex (see *188 et seq.*). 36: Not to steal [and not to kidnap or deceive (see *522*)]. 37: Not to give false testimony [and not to slander or spread false rumours (see *227*, 524)]. 38: Not to covet (see *416*). 39: Not to make idols [and not to believe in them] (see 27, 28, 29). 40: Not to build an altar of hewn stones. 41: Not to ascend unto the altar by steps [but by a ramp]. 42: To deal justly with a Hebrew bondman. 43: The law of the espousal of a Hebrew maid-servant rejected by her master (see 44, 45). 44: A man must aid in the redemption of his espoused Hebrew hand-maid whom he rejected and his son also then refuses to espouse her (see 43, 45). 45: A man may not sell his Hebrew hand-maid whom he espoused and then rejected (see 43, 44). 46: If one take another wife—whether a freewoman or a bondwoman—he must not fail to provide for her proper support. 47: Not to strike a parent. 48: The penalty for striking a parent

139

is strangulation; the penalty for kidnapping is strangulation; the penalty for cursing a parent is stoning. 49: The laws of indemnity in cases of personal physical injury. 50: The penalty for slaying a bondman with a blow is execution with the sword. 51: The laws of indemnity in cases of injury or damage caused by any animal (domestic or wild) or bird. 52: Not to eat the flesh of an ox that had been killed by stoning. 53: The laws concerning indemnity for injury caused by a pit. 54: The laws concerning indemnity from one who stole an ox or lamb. 55: The laws concerning indemnity for setting fire to field or vineyard. 56: The laws concerning indemnity for the spread of fire to shocks of corn or standing corn or field. 57: The laws concerning the *unpaid* guardian and loss of or damage to property (see 59). 58: The laws concerning the litigant, the one pleading guilty, the one pleading not guilty. 59: The laws concerning the *hired* guardian and loss of or damage to property (see 57). 60: The laws concerning the borrower and loss of or damage to property. 61: The laws concerning the case of the seducer of a virgin that is not betrothed. 62: A sorceress or witch must not escape the penalty of death (see 510-515). 63: Not to wrong a stranger (see 64). 64: Not to oppress a stranger (see 63). 65: Not to afflict the widow or orphan. 66: To lend to the poor and needy (see 67, 68, 572, 573). 67: Not to lend to the poor and needy on harsh conditions (see 66, 68, 572, 573). 68: Not to lend to the poor and needy on usurious terms (see 66, 67, 572, 573). 69: Not to blaspheme. 70: Not to curse judges. 71: Not to curse the ruler of the people. 72: Not to delay to separate methodically and systematically in correct order *the first ripe fruits, the priest's-dues,* and *the tithes.* 73: Not to partake of any kinds of *terefah* foodstuffs or drinks. 74: Not to repeat any false report or slander or calumny. 75: Not to aid the sinner with testimony to confirm him in his unrighteousness. 76: Not to join a majority to effect evil (see 77). 77: Not to give evidence to lead to unrighteous co-operation with a majority (see 78). 78: To forbear with such testimony that would lead to co-operation and collaboration with a majority to pervert justice (see 76, 77). 79: Not to favour a poor man in a law-suit (see 81, 233, 234, 235). 80: To assist anyone whose beast is lying helpless under its load (see 540, 541). 81: Not to show favouritism to any litigant (see 79). 82: Not to condemn to death on circumstantial evidence. 83: A judge must not accept a gift or bribe from a suitor. 84: The land must lie fallow in the seventh year [the *Sabbatical year*]. 85: All manner of work must cease on the Sabbath (see 31, 32). 86: Not to mention matters of idolatry (see 87). 87: Not to talk about subjects of idolatry (see 86). 88: To observe the *Three Pilgrim Festivals.* 89: Not to slaughter the *Passover-offering* before all leaven is removed from the home. 90: Not to leave over to the morning the fat of the *Passover-offering* (and of the *pilgrims' offerings*). 91: The *first-fruits* must be separated and taken to the Temple. 92: Meat and milk must not be mingled together or cooked together or any benefit derived from such mixture (see 113, 472). 93: Not to make any covenant with the nations of the land of Canaan or have any dealings with their idolatrous practices. 94: Not to allow idolaters to dwell in the Holy Land (see 93). 95: To build a Temple in the Holy Land. 96: Not to remove the staves of the Ark from the rings. 97: The *showbread* had to be always present on the *table.* 98: The lamps in the Temple were to be kept alight continually [regularly]. 99: The priests were to wear special priestly garments at the services. 100: The *breastplate* must not be loosed from the *ephod*—it must be firmly attached. 101: The robe of the *ephod* must have a binding of woven work about the hole that it be not rent. 102: Priests eat of the things wherewith atonement is made (*e.g.,* sin-offerings, guilt-offerings). 103: Incense must be offered every morning. 104: Not to offer on the Golden Altar in the Sanctuary other than the incense as enjoined every day and not omit the tossing of the blood on the Day of Atonement. 105: To give the *half-shekel due* every year. 106: The priests must wash their hands and feet before officiating at a service. 107: The *holy anointing oil* had to be kept in readiness for anointing high priests, kings and Temple utensils (see 108). 108: Not to use the *holy anointing oil* to anoint a non-priest (see 107). 109: No oil may be made the like of the *holy anointing oil.* 110: No incense may be made the like of the *Temple incense.* 111: Not to eat or drink of the offerings of idolaters (including in this prohibition non-Jewish wine—*yain nesech*). 112: To desist from all manner of land work in the 'Sabbatical year' (see 326, 327, 328, 329, 330). 113: Not to eat or cook or derive any benefit from a mixture of meat and milk (see 92, 472). 114: Not to kindle fire on the Sabbath. 115: All operations in connection with the *burnt-offering* must be carried out in accordance with the enactments. 116: All operations in connection with the *meal-offering* must be performed according to the enactments. 117: No leaven nor honey may be offered as or with a *fire-offering.* 118: No saltless offering may be offered (see 119). 119: Every *offering* must be salted (see 118). 120: If the Beth-Din or the Great Sanhedrin gave an erroneous ruling (entailing the penalty of *excision*) and the community in consequence acted in wrongfulness, the latter must bring a *sin-offering*. 121: If an individual sinned unwittingly (and was liable to the punishment of *excision*) he must bring a *sin-offering*. 122: One who knows of evidence must testify. 123: One must bring a *guilt-offering* on discovering that guilt had been incurred. 124: Not to sever the head of a *bird-offering*, i.e., either the gullet or the windpipe is nipped (or pinched). 125: The *sin-offering* of a sinner may not be embellished with oil. 126: The sinner's *sin-offering* may not be accompanied with frankincense. 127: One guilty of the misappropriation of sacred property adds *one-fifth* [in actual practice *one-fourth*] to the value of the property when making restitution. 128: An individual must bring a *guilt-offering* for his sin if he be in doubt whether he committed or did not commit sin that entails the penalty of *excision* if committed in wilfulness or requires a *sin-offering* if committed unwantonly. 129: No sacrifice atones for theft, robbery, deprivation, malappropriation and the like; what has been misappropriated must first be restored. 130: An offering must be brought for every conscious sin. 131: The ashes were to be removed regularly from off the Altar. 132: The Altar fire was to be kept alight (see *133*). 133: The Altar fire was not to be allowed to be extinguished (see *132*). 134: The priests could eat of the remainder of the *meal-offerings* (see *135, 136, 137*). 135: Not to prepare or eat the remains of *meal-offerings* with leaven. 136: The High Priest had to offer the *meal-offering* every day (see *134, 135, 137*). 137: Not to eat the *meal-offering* of a priest. 138: A *sin-offering* must be prepared and offered according to the regulations. 139: Not to eat aught of *sin-offerings* brought in the Interior within the Partition Vail. 140: To carry out the laws regarding the *guilt-offering*. 141: To carry out the laws regarding the *sacrifice* of the *peace-offering*. 142: Not to leave over uneaten of the *thanksgiving-offering* to the morrow (see 143, 215). 143: Any remainder of the flesh of a *holy sacrifice* was to be burned when the particular time for the eating thereof had gone by (see *142, 215*). 144: Not to eat of *rejection* (or *abhorred thing*). 145: Not to eat of the flesh of a *holy sacrifice* that had become unclean (see 146). 146: If *holy sacrifices* and the flesh of such became unclean they had to be burned (see *145*). 147: Not to eat of the *forbidden fat*. 148: Not to eat of the blood of cattle or beast or fowl. 149: Priests may not let their hair grow long (some render this that priests were not to enter the Temple with long hair like mourners). 150: No priest to enter the Temple in torn garments. 151: No priest to leave the Temple during the service. 152: No priest the worse for drink to enter the Temple. 153: Only *clean animals, viz., cloven-hooved ruminants*, may be used for food (see 154). 154: Not to use for food *unclean animals, viz.*, those that do not *both* chew the cud *and* have cloven hoofs (see 153). 155: Only *clean fish, viz.*, that have *both fins and scales*, may be used for food (see *156*). 156: Not to eat *unclean fish, viz.*, that do not possess *both* scales *and* fins (see 155). 157: Not to eat *unclean* fowl (see 470). 158: The only winged swarming creatures that may be eaten are those that go on all fours and have jointed legs above their feet wherewith to leap upon the earth (see 159, *163, 471*.) 159: A list of the eight prolific creatures (or swarming things) that are forbidden for food are given in *Leviticus* 11, 29, 30 and in *Tractate Sabbath* 14[1] (see 158, *163, 471*). 160: The laws of foodstuffs that become susceptible to uncleanness on wetting. 161: Carrion is both unclean and renders unclean by contact and by carrying. 162: Not to eat of swarming things that swarm upon the earth (see 158, 159, *163, 164, 165, 471*). 163: Not to eat of swarming things that are begotten in fruits and seeds (see 158, 159, *162, 164, 165, 471*). 164: Not to eat of swarming things that swarm in the water (see *158, 159, 162, 164, 165, 471*). 165: Not to eat of creeping things that exist in unwholesome conditions (see *158, 159, 162, 163, 164, 471*). 166: Laws of uncleanness of the woman who has given birth. 167: No unclean person may eat of the *holy things* before he is cleansed in the ritual bath and has then awaited sundown (and has brought the needful *atonement-offering* where required). 168: A woman after childbirth must bring the required *offering* on completion of the days of her purification. 169: One showing symptoms of leprosy must be examined by the priest to be certified clean or unclean or to be isolated for later examination (see 171). 170: The hair of *scurf* (or *mange*) may not be shaven off. 171: A leper must carry out the laws of leprosy as enjoined (see 169, 172, 173, 174, 176). 172: The laws of leprosy symptoms in garments must be observed (see 169, 171, 173, 174, 176, 177). 173: To carry out the laws of the leper as enjoined (see 169, 171, 174, 176). 174: The leper must shave off all his hair (see 169, 171, 173, 176). 175: The unclean is cleansed by immersion in a ritual bath containing *40 seahs* of valid water. 176: When a leper is declared cured he must bring an *offering* (see 169 *et seq.*). 177: To declare unclean a leprosy infected dwelling (see 172). 178: The law of the *zav* [*one afflicted with an issue*] who has had two fluxes and is unclean and communicates uncleanness (see 179, 182, 183). 179: A *zav* [*one afflicted with an issue*] having experienced three fluxes—brings an offering when he is healed (see 178, 182, 183). 180: The semen of a male is unclean and renders unclean. 181: The menstruant is unclean and renders unclean. 182: A *zavah* [*a woman afflicted with an issue*] is unclean and renders unclean (see 178, 179, 181, 183). 183: A *zavah* [*a woman afflicted with an issue*] brings an *offering* when she recovers from her complaint (see 178, 179, 181, 182). 184: No priest may enter into any place except to carry out the duties of service. 185: The High Priest must perform the whole service on the Day of Atonement in proper sequence as enjoined. 186: Not to offer the *holy sacrifices* outside the Temple. 187: To cover up the blood of beast and fowl after slaughtering. 188: Not to commit incest—not to have any sexual intimacy with near of kin (see 35, 189 *et seq.*). 189: Not to be guilty of homosexuality (or sodomy) with one's father (see 35, 188, 190 *et seq.*, 209). 190: Not to commit incest with one's mother (see 35, 188, 189, 191 *et seq.*). 191: Not to commit incest with one's father's wife. (see 35, 188 *et seq.*, 192 *et seq.*). 192: Not to commit incest with a sister born of his father or of his mother, not even if she be the daughter of a woman outraged by his father or she be the daughter begotten in adultery by his mother (see 35, 188 *et seq.*, 193 *et seq.*). 193: Not to commit incest with the daughter of his son (see 35, 188 *et seq.*, 194 *et seq.*). 194: Not to commit incest with the daughter of his daughter (see 35, 188 *et seq.*, 195 *et seq.*). 195: Not to commit incest with his daughter (see **Note** * to 195 in the first Table; see 35, 188 *et seq.*, 196 *et seq.*). 196: Not to commit incest with the daughter of his father's wife (not his mother; see 35, 188 *et seq.*, 197 *et seq.*). 197: Not to commit incest with his paternal aunt (see 35, 188 *et seq.*, 198 *et seq.*). 198: Not to commit incest with his maternal aunt (see 35, 188 *et seq.*, 199 *et seq.*). 199: Not to practise sodomy (or homosexuality) with his paternal uncle (see 35, 188 *et seq.*, 200 *et seq.*). 200: Not to commit incest with the wife of his paternal uncle (see 35, 188 *et seq.*, 201 *et seq.*). 201: Not to commit incest with his son's wife (not even if she is divorced or a widow; see 35, 188 *et seq.*, 202 *et seq.*). 202: Not to commit incest with his brother's wife (see 35, 188 *et seq.*, 203 *et seq.*). 203: Not to marry a woman and her daughter (see 35, 188 *et seq.*, 204 *et seq.*). 204: Not to wed (*i.e.*, not to commit incest with) a woman and the daughter of her son (born of a former husband; see 35, 188 *et seq.*, 205, 206). 205: Not to commit incest with a woman and the daughter of her daughter (born of a former husband; see 35, 188 *et seq.*, 206). 206: Not to take to wife the sister of his wife (during her lifetime, not even if he had divorced her; see 35, 188 *et seq.*). 207: Not to have sexual connection with a menstruant, not even to have any contact with her. 208: Not to allow one's son(s) to pass through fire (in idolatrous service to Moloch). 209: Not to practise homosexuality (or sodomy, buggery, pederasty; see 189). 210: Not to have unnatural sexual intercourse with an animal (see 211). 211: A woman must not bring any animal upon her for unnatural sexual connection. 212: One must fear one's parents. 213: Not to pay regard to idols —neither by look nor by speech nor by thought. 214: Not to fashion any idol, not even for an idolater. 215: Not to eat the remainder of *holy sacrifices* after the fixed time for their eating (see 142, 143). 216: Not to reap the *field-corner* (see 217). 217: The produce of the *field-corner* must be left for the poor (see 216). 218: Not to gather the ears of corn that fall at reaping (see 219). 219: The ears of corn that fall at reaping must be left for the poor (see 218). 220: Not to glean all the grapes of the vineyard (see 221, 222, 223). 221: To leave of the gleanings (grapes) and of the corner of the vineyard for the poor (see 220, 222). 222: Not to glean the (single) grapes that fall at the gleaning (see 220, 221, 223). 223: To leave the (single) grapes that fall at the gleaning for the poor (see 220, 221, 222). 224: Not to steal money—not even if merely to annoy one's fellow, not even with the intention to restore it, not even if intending to return it fourfold or fivefold; and naught may be bought from a thief. 225: Not to deny possessing someone's money or aught else if one has such. 226: Not to swear falsely when denying the possession of somebody's money. 227: Not to take a false oath (see 37). 228: Not to oppress one's fellow by holding on to his money by force or by deception or in any other wise. 229: Not to take aught without authority by force or by violence or in any other manner. 230: Not to withhold the wage of a hired labourer beyond the time appointed for its payment. 231: Not to curse any living Jewish person even though he be deaf or out of hearing. 232: Not to mislead anyone with evil counsel. 233: Not to corrupt justice (see 79, 81, 234, 235). 234: A judge must not favour an important or influential or wealthy litigant (or any suitor whatsoever; see 79, 81, 235). 235: Justice must be dispensed in righteousness (see 79, 81, 233, 234). 236: Not to be a talebearer (informer, defamer, slanderer). 237: Not to withhold help to one's fellow in danger or difficulty or in monetary straits. 238: Not to bear hatred and enmity towards one's fellow man (see 242). 239: To rebuke a wrongdoer, even many times, irrespective of age or position. 240: Not to shame one's fellow in public—not even when rebuking him for wrongdoing. 241: Not to requite evil for evil. 242: Not to bear a grudge against one's fellow who has wronged him (see *238*). *243*: *To love one's fellow man as oneself.* *244*: Not to interbreed creatures of different species. *245*: Not to sow or plant together two different kinds of seeds (see *548*, *549*.) *246*: Not to eat of the fruit of a new tree in the first three years of its planting (see *247*). *247*: The owner must take the fourth year fruit of a new tree to Jerusalem to be consumed there (see *246*). *248*: Not to be a glutton and a drunkard, not to eat of the flesh of an animal while it still has life in it (see *452*). *249*: Not to practise or put faith in any form of superstition or soothsaying or in supernatural insight (see *250*, *510-515*). *250*: Not to practise or believe in divination (prevision, prediction, astrology, fortune telling) and the like (see *249*, *255*, *256*). *251*: Not to shave the temples (the fore-head and behind the ears; see *252*). *252*: Not to shave the tip of the beard or its sides (see *251*). *253*: Not to tattoo any part of one's body. *254*: To reverence the Sanctuary. *255*: Not to practise or believe in spiritualism, necromancy, conjuration, magic, enchantment, sorcery, witchcraft, wizardry (see *250*, *256*). *256*: Not to believe in or practise the subjects of ghosts, familiar spirits (see *250*, *255*). *257*: To show reverence and respect to the Law and to those versed in it. *258*: Not to deceive in measuring and weighing (see *259*, *602*). *259*: Not to use incorrect weights and measures—not to neglect to adjust them correctly constantly. *260*: Not to curse one's parents. *261*: If one takes a woman and her mother (both being prohibited because of a former relationship to him), all three suffer the penalty of death by burning. *262*: Not to follow the evil practices and customs of idolaters and the like. *263*: A common priest may not be defiled for the dead (see *264*). *264*: A common priest may only defile himself for the dead of his kin (his father, mother, brother, a virgin sister, son, daughter, wife; see *263*). *265*: A priest who is a *tevul yom* (*sc.*, who has immersed in the ritual bath to purify himself from unclean-ness) may not officiate at service in the Temple before sundown. *266*: A High Priest or a common priest may not marry a harlot (prostitute, whore, strumpet; see *267*, *268*, *274*). *267*: A High Priest or a common priest may not marry a woman of impaired stock (see *266*, *268*, *272*). *268*: A High Priest or a common priest may not marry a divorced woman (see *266*, *267*). *269*: To give a priest honour and precedence. *270*: A High Priest may not enter the abode where lies a corpse (see *271*). *271*: A High Priest may not defile himself by contact with or by carrying for even his dead parents (see *270*). *272*: A High Priest must marry only a virgin maiden (see *267*, *273*). *273*: A High Priest may not marry a widow or a woman of impaired stock or a harlot (see *266*, *267*, *268*, *272*). *274*: A High Priest may not have sexual intercourse with a widow (even if he has not betrothed her). *275*: No priest with a permanent blemish (or defect) may officiate at Temple services (see *276*, *277*). *276*: No priest may officiate at Temple services while suffering from a temporary defect (or blemish; see *275*, *277*). *277*: No priest with a blemish (or defect) may enter the Sanctuary (see *275*, *276*). *278*: No priest while unclean may engage in any Temple service. *279*: No unclean priest may eat of *priest's-due*. *280*: A non-priest may not eat of *priest's-due*. *281*: No tenant nor a hired servant of a priest may eat of *priest's-due*. *282*: No uncircumcised priest may eat of *priest's-due* nor of the *holy sacrifices* (see **Note** § to the first Table). *283*: A priest's daughter whose husband is a non-priest may not eat of the *holy things*. *284*: None may eat of *tevel* (*viz.*, produce from which *priest's-due* and *tithes* had not been separated). *285*: No animal with a blemish (or defect) may be offered on the Altar (see *286–292*, *441*, *494*). *286*: An animal *offering* must be free from a blemish (or defect; see *285*, *287–292*). *287*: No animal with a defect (or blemish) may be offered as a *holy sacrifice* (see *285*, *286*, *288-292*). *288*: Not to slaughter for an *offering* any animal found to have a blemish (or defect; see *285*, *286*, *287*, *289-292*). *289*: Not to burn on the Altar aught of an animal that had a blemish or defect (see *285-288*, *290-292*). *290*: Not to sprinkle (or toss) against the Altar the blood of an animal *offering* with a blemish (or defect; see *285-289*, *291*, *292*). *291*: Not to castrate (or emasculate) any living thing (whether man or beast). *292*: Not to offer blemished (or defective) animals brought by heathens (see *285-291*). *293*: An animal *offering* must be at least eight days old. *294*: Not to slaughter an animal and its offspring on the same day. *295*: Not to do aught that might profane the Divine Name. *296*: One must be prepared to suffer martyrdom for his faith. *297*: To rest from work on the first day of Passover (see *298*, *300*, *301*). *298*: Not to perform any work on the first day of Passover (see *297*, *300*, *301*). *299*: To offer the *additional-offering* on each of the seven days of Passover. *300*: To rest from work on the seventh day of Passover (see *297*, *298*, *301*). *301*: Not to engage in any work on the seventh day of Passover (see *297*, *300*, *301*). *302*: To offer on the second day of Passover (the 15th day of Nisan) the *omer meal-offering*. *303*: Not to eat bread made from the new corn before the end of the 16th day of Nisan (see *304*, *305*). *304*: Not to eat parched corn from the new corn before the completion of the 16th day of Nisan (see *303*, *305*). *305*: Not to eat fresh ears of corn of the new corn before the 16th day of Nisan has passed. 306: To count from the second day of Passover (the 15th of Nisan inclusive when the *omer* was brought) day by day, and week by week, 49 days that are seven complete weeks (see 307). 307: To bring on the 50th day (*sc.*, the Festival of Weeks or Pentecost) of the *omer* of the new corn the *two unleavened loaves* with the accompanying *offerings* (as well as the *additional-offering*; see 306, 404). 308: To rest from work on the Festival of Weeks (or Pentecost; see *309*). *309*: Not to perform any manner of work on the Festival of Weeks (see 308). 310: To rest from work on the New Year (see *311*). *311*: Not to engage in any manner of work on the New Year (see 310). 312: To bring an *additional-offering* on the New Year. 313: To observe the Fast of the Day of Atonement on the 10th day of Tishri. 314: To bring an *additional-offering* on the Day of Atonement. *315*: Not to do any work on the Day of Atonement (see *317*). 316: Not to eat or drink on the Day of Atonement. 317: To abstain from all manner of work whatever on the Day of Atonement (see *315*). 318: To desist from any work on the first day of the Festival of Tabernacles see *319, 321, 323*). *319*: Not to engage in any kind of work soever on the first day of the Festival of Tabernacles (see 318, 321, 323). 320: To bring an *additional-offering* on each of the seven days of the Festival of Tabernacles. 321: To rest from work on the Eighth Day of [Solemn] Assembly (the eighth day of the Festival of Tabernacles; see 318, *319, 323*). 322: To offer an *additional-offering* on the Eighth Day of [Solemn] Assembly (the eighth day of the Festival of Tabernacles). 323: Not to do any work on the Eighth day of [Solemn] Assembly (the eighth day of the Festival of Tabernacles). 324: To use at the service on the first day of the Festival of Tabernacles *a palm branch [lulav], a citron [ethrog], two twigs of the willow of the brook [aravoth]*, and *three twigs of myrtle [hadasim]*. 325: To dwell in a booth during the seven days of the Festival of Tabernacles. *326*: Not to work the land—agriculture—during the 'year of release' (the 'seventh year,' the 'Sabbatical year'; see 112, *327-330*). *327*: Not to do any tree work—arboriculture—in the 'seventh year' (see *326, 328, 329, 330*). *328*: Not to harvest the aftergrowth during the 'seventh year' (see *326, 327, 329, 330*). *329*: Not to gather or glean the fruits from trees in the 'seventh year' (see *326, 327, 328, 330*). 330: The Great Sanhedrin was to keep count year by year of seven-year periods to the fiftieth year which is the 'year of Jubilee' (see *331-335*). 331: To sound the *shofar* [horn] on the Day of Atonement of the Jubilee year to proclaim the manumission of slaves, the restoration of land to the former owners and the cessation of work on the land (see *332-335*, 340, 341). 332: To sanctify the year of Jubilee by cessation from work on the land and by the declaration of the ownerless state [*hefker*] of all aftergrowth (see 331, *333, 334, 335*). 333: No work on the land [agriculture] and no work on trees [arboriculture] may be carried out in the year of Jubilee (see 331, 332, *334, 335*). *334*: Not to reap or glean any aftergrowth in the year of Jubilee (see 331, 332, *333, 335*). *335*: Not to glean or gather in the fruits of trees in the year of Jubilee (see *331-334*). 336: The laws of buying and selling. *337*: Not to practise deception in trade (buying and selling). *338*: Not to deceive and mislead with words. *339*: Not to sell land in perpetuity (see 331). 340: All land must be restored to the former owners, without payment or price. 341: The vendor of a house in a walled city may repurchase it within the whole of the second year after the sale, otherwise it remains the property of the vendee in perpetuity (*i.e.*, it does not revert to the former owner in the year of Jubilee). NOTE: A field may be rebought at any time after two years from the date of the sale (see 331, 340). *342*: Not to sell open lands and fields around the cities of the Levites. *343*: Not to lend on usury [interest]. *344*: Not to put a Hebrew bondman to shameful work or to hard oppressive labour or to degrading tasks (see *346*). *345*: Not to sell a Hebrew bondman by auction in the market place but unostentatiously and humanely. *346*: Not to make a Hebrew bondman do unnecessary tasks (see *344*). 347: A Canaanite bondman may be kept for work for ever. *348*: Not to permit a Canaanite in the Holy Land to employ a Hebrew bondman for work who has sold himself to hard labour. *349*: Not to prostrate oneself in worship, not even to God, before any 'figured stone' or idol or the like. 350: The laws of 'valuation' (see 353, 354, 355). *351*: Not to exchange (or substitute) an animal dedicated for an *offering* (see 352). 352: Any exchange (or substitute) for an *offering* is as holy as the *offering* itself (see 351). 353: The laws of the 'valuation' of cattle (see 350). 354: The laws of the 'valuation' of houses which owners dedicated and wish to redeem from the Temple treasury (see 355). 355: The laws of the 'valuation' of fields which having been dedicated the owners desire to redeem from the Temple treasury (see 350, 354). *356*: Not to change the 'name' (*sc.*, the purpose) of an *offering*—an animal dedicated for a particular *offering* may not be used for another *offering*. 357: The laws of devoted things—whether they are for the Eternal or for the Temple or for the priests. *358*: Not to sell fields or real estate or movables that have been dedicated but must be given to the priests (see *359*). *359*: One cannot redeem devoted fields or real estate or movables (see *358*) *360*: To tithe all clean cattle every year (which tithe was consumed in Jerusalem after offering the forbidden fat and the blood on the Altar; see *361*). *361*: Tithe of cattle may not be sold (see *360*).

Numbers

362: The unclean were to be isolated (or quarantined) outside the camp. *363*: No unclean person may enter the Temple grounds from the Nicanor Gate to the Court of the Israelites. *364*: To confess one's sins and to do repentance. *365*: To bring the wife suspected of unfaithfulness to the priest for trial (see *366, 367*). *366*: Not to add *oil* to the *meal-offering* of the wife suspected of unfaithfulness (see *365, 367*). *367*: Not to add *frankincense* to the *meal-offering* of the wife suspected of unfaithfulness (see *366, 367*). *368*: A nazirite may not drink wine or any strong drink (see *369-377*). *369*: A nazirite may not eat fresh grapes (see *368, 370-377*). *370*: A nazirite may not eat dried grapes or raisins (see *368, 369, 371-377*). *371*: A nazirite may not eat grape seeds (see *368, 369, 370, 372-377*). *372*: A nazirite may not eat grape skins (see *368-371, 373-377*). *373*: A nazirite may not shave off even a single hair (see *368-372, 374-377*). *374*: A nazirite must let the hair of his head grow all the days of his naziriteship (see *368-373, 375, 376, 377*). *375*: A nazirite may not enter a shelter where lies a corpse (see *368-374, 376, 377*). *376*: A nazirite may not defile himself for any dead whatsoever (see *368-375, 377*). *377*: When a nazirite has completed his period of naziritism or when he has contracted any uncleanness he shaves off the hair of his head and brings his *offerings* (see *368-376*). *378*: The priests were to recite the *Priestly Blessing* every day. *379*: The priests or Levites were to carry the Ark on their shoulders when necessary. *380*: One who had been unable to prepare the *Passover-offering* on the 14th day of Nisan has to do so on the 14th day of Iyyar (see *5 et seq., 381, 382, 383*). *381*: One preparing the *Passover-offering* on the 14th day of Iyyar must eat of it together with unleavened bread and bitter herbs (see *5 et seq., 380, 382, 383*). *382*: Not to leave aught of the *Passover-offering* to the next morning (of the 15th day of Iyyar; see *5 et seq., 380, 381, 383*). *383*: Not to break a bone of the *Passover-offering* of the 14th day of Iyyar (see *5 et seq., 380, 381, 382*). *384*: To sound the trumpets in the Temple at the *morning-offering* on the Festivals and New Moons. *385*: To separate the *priest's-share of the dough* and give it to the priest. *386*: To make *fringes* [*tsitsiyoth*] at the four corners of a garment. *387*: Not to engage in thoughts or acts leading to apostasy or adultery. *388*: The Temple was to be guarded at night by the priests within and by the Levites without (see *391, 509*). *389*: A Levite may not perform the service of a priest or of another Levite, and a priest may not perform the service of a Levite or of another priest. *390*: No Temple service may be performed by a non-priest. *391*: Not to neglect the watch over the Temple (see *388, 509*). *392*: To redeem a firstborn, born of a Jewish mother (see *18*). *393*: Not to redeem a *clean firstling* (see *22, 23*). *394*: The Levites were to be the Temple gate-keepers and to form the choir at *offerings*. *395*: To separate *first tithe* for the Levites (see *396*). *396*: The Levites were to separate *a tenth of the first tithe* for the priests (this *tenth* was termed *tithe of priest's-due* or *minor priest's-due*; see *395*). *397*: The laws regarding the *red heifer* and its burning [incineration] for the ashes. *398*: The laws of the uncleanness for the dead [the corpse]. *399*: The laws of the *red heifer water-ashes* and the sprinkling thereof. *400*: Laws of inheritance (heritage, heritance). *401*: To offer daily the *two continual offerings*, one in the morning and one before dusk. *402*: To offer on the Sabbath the *additional-offering* in addition to the *two continual offerings* (see *401*). *403*: To offer the *additional-offering* on New Moon as well as the *two daily continual offerings* (see *401*). *404*: To offer the *additional-offering* on Pentecost and also the *two daily continual offerings* (see *401*). *405*: To sound and hear the *shofar* [horn] on the New Year. *406*: The laws of the annulment (abrogation, cancellation) of vows. *407*: Not to fail to fulfil a vow; not to change or modify a vow. *408*: To give the Levites cities to dwell in. *409*: Not to put to death one accused of murder who has not been tried and convicted (see *410*). *410*: To banish to a city of refuge one who slew another unintentionally (see *409, 413, 520, 521*). *411*: Not to admit the evidence of only one witness in a capital crime; and no witness after he has testified may offer further testimony. *412*: Not to accept money from a murderer to redeem him from the death penalty (see *413*). *413*: Not to accept money from a slayer to redeem him from banishment to a city of refuge (see *410, 412, 520 521*).

Deuteronomy

414: Not to make any distinctions between the status of litigants or in the character or extensiveness of disputes in the dispensation of justice. *415*: A judge must not show fear of persons in the dispensation of justice. *416*: Not to covet another's possessions (see *38*). *417*: To know that there is **Only One God the Eternal,** to believe in **His Unity or Oneness,** and that **He alone is the Creator of the whole Universe** (see 25, 26). *418*: To love *God the Eternal*, and to observe His laws. *419*: To study and teach the Law. *420*: To recite the *Shema* daily. *421*: To wear the *Tephillin* on the arm. *422*: To wear the *Tephillin* over the forehead. *423*: To fix a *Mezuzzah* on the doorpost. *424*: Not to provoke the prophet or teacher who righteously corrects the people and instructs them to do what is right. *425*: To rid utterly the Holy Land of the pagans (see *426, 427, 428*). *426*: Not to show pity or compassion in ridding the Holy Land of the pagans (see 425, *427, 428*). *427*: Not to intermarry with pagans (see 425, 426, 428). *428*: Not to derive any benefits whatsoever from pagan (heathen, idolatrous) objects of worship (see 425, *426, 427, 429*). *429*: Not to have in one's possession aught of idols and the like (see 27, *428*). *430*: To thank God the Eternal for what one has eaten—to recite the *Grace atfer Meals.* *431*: To treat the stranger humanely. *432*: To fear God the Eternal and keep from sin. *433*: To pray to God daily. *434*: To associate with those that study the Law. *435*: To swear by the Name of God in truth. *436*: To destroy utterly idolatry and places of idolatrous practices (see *437*). *437*: Not to destroy aught that pertains to Godliness (see 436). *438*: Whosoever donates an *offering* or aught else for Temple use must bring it to the Temple at not later than the next Pilgrim Festival. *439*: Not to offer an *offering* outside the Temple Court (see 440, 487). *440*: All *offerings* must be offered only within the Temple premises (see *439, 487*). *441*: An animal *offering* that has suffered a blemish (or defect) must be redeemed (see *285-290, 494*). *442*: Not to eat of *second tithe of corn* outside Jerusalem (see *443*). *443*: Not to eat of *second tithe of wine* outside Jerusalem (see *444*). *444*: Not to eat of *second tithe of oil* outside Jerusalem (see *442, 443*). *445*: A priest may not eat of a sound *firstling* outside Jerusalem. *446*: Not to eat of the flesh of a *sin-offering* or of a *guilt-offering* outside the Temple hangings (see *447, 448*). *447*: Not to eat of a *burnt-offering* (see *446, 448*). *448*: Not to eat of the flesh of a *thanksgiving-offering* or of a *peace-offering* before the tossing (or sprinkling) of the blood (see *446, 447*). *449*: The priest may not eat of the *firstfruits* before such had been deposited in the Forecourt. *450*: Not to neglect to support the Levite in the Holy Land. *451*: An animal for food to be ritually slaughtered. *452*: Not to eat flesh cut from a living animal (see *248*). *453*: All *offerings* to be offered up in the Temple. *454*: Not to add aught to the Law (see *455*). *455*: Not to diminish aught from the Law (see *454*). *456*: Not to hearken to the idolatrous prophet (see *457-462*). *457*: Not to consent to the enticer to idolatry (see 456, 458-462). *458*: Not to hearken to the enticer to idolatry (see *457, 459-462*). *459*: Not to deliver the enticer to idolatry from death (see *456, 457, 458, 460, 461, 462*). *460*: Not to plead for the life of the enticer to idolatry (see *456-459, 461, 462*). *461*: Not to withhold evidence to convict the enticer to idolatry (see *456-462*). *462*: Not to entice to idolatry (see *456-461*). *463*: To search and examine witnesses thoroughly. *464*: An apostate city must be burned down and its inhabitants slain (see *465, 466*). *465*: Not to rebuild an apostate city (see 464, 466). *466*: Not to derive any benefit from the wealth of an apostate city (see *464, 465*). *467*: Not to cut oneself for the dead (see *468*). *468*: Not to make the head bald for the dead (see *467*). *469*: Not to eat aught abominable; not to eat of *offerings* that have become invalid. *470*: To eat only clean fowl (see *157*). *471*: Not to eat winged swarming things (see 158, 159, *162-165*). *472*: Not to eat carrion; not to eat meat with milk (see *92, 113*). *473*: To separate *second tithe.* *474*: To separate the *poor-man's tithe.* *475*: Not to press for payment of a debt in the 'year of release' [the 'seventh year,' the 'Sabbatical year'; see *476, 477, 480*]. *476*: Repayment of a debt may be demanded from the foreigner in the 'year of release' (see *475*). *477*: To release the debtor from his debt in the 'year of release' (see *475, 476*). *478*: Not to refrain from dispensing kindness and charity (see *479, 481*). *479*: To give charity to the utmost (see *478*). *480*: Not to refrain from lending for fear of loss in the 'year of release' (see *475, 476, 477*). *481*: Not to set free a Hebrew bondman empty handed at the advent of the 'year of release' (see *478, 482*). *482*: To furnish a Hebrew bondman liberally when set free at the advent of the 'year of release' or the 'year of Jubilee' (see *478, 481*). *483*: Not to work with cattle dedicated for *offerings* (see *484*). *484*: Not to shear the wool of cattle dedicated for *offerings* (see *483*). *485*: Not to eat unleavened bread after midday of the 14th day of Nisan (see 9). *486*: Not to leave over to the third day of the flesh of the *Festival offering* [*chagigah*] brought with the *Passover-offering. 487*: Not to offer up the *Passover-offering* on an altar outside the Temple (see 5 *et seq.*, 439, 440). *488*: To rejoice on the *Three Pilgrim Festivals* (Passover, Pentecost or the Festival of Weeks, and Succoth or the Festival of Tabernacles; see *489, 490*). *489*: All males must appear in the Temple on the *Three Pilgrim Festivals* (see *488, 490*). *490*: Not to appear in the

Temple at the *Three Pilgrim Festivals* without a special *burnt-offering* and *peace-offering(s)* (see 488, 489). *491*: Judges (to apply the rules of the Law and to dispense justice) and officers (to carry out the verdicts of the judges) to be appointed in each town. *492*: Not to plant even a single tree in the Temple grounds or near the Altar. *493*: Not to set up a pillar or tall structure (lest it be used for idolatrous practices). *494*: Not to offer up an animal with a blemish (or defect)—whether permanent or temporary (see 285-292, 441). *495*: To obey the behests of the Great Sanhedrin. *496*: Not to digress from the teachings of the Sages. *497*: To appoint only a king that will rule according to the Law (see *498-503*). *498*: Not to appoint a foreigner as king (see 497, 499, 501, 502, 503). *499*: The king may not possess more horses than absolutely necessary (see 497, 498, 501, 502, 503). *500*: Not to settle permanently in Egypt. *501*: A king may not have more than eighteen wives (see 497, 498, 499, 502, 503). *502*: The king may not accumulate gold and silver (see 497, 498, 499, 501, 503). *503*: The king must possess his own Scroll of the Law and have it with him always (see 497, 498, 499, 501, 502). *504*: The priests and Levites—the whole tribe of Levi—cannot have either inheritance or share of spoil (see 505). *505*: Not to apportion any inheritance to the priests and Levites (see 504). *506*: The priest is entitled to the *shoulder*, the *cheeks* and the *maw* of a *sacrifice*. *507*: (Major) *priest's-due* must be separated for the priest. *508*: The *first of the fleece* of the sheep must be given to the priest. *509*: The Levites were to serve on the Temple watches [*mishmaroth*] (see 388, *391*). *510*: Not to let enchanters and the like exist among the people (see 62, 249, 255, 256, 511-515). *511*: Not to allow diviners, soothsayers, sorcerers (magicians, wizards, witches) to exist among the people (see 62, 510, 512-515). *512*: Not to let charmers (enchanters, magicians, wizards, witches, fortune tellers) exist among the people (see 62, 510, 511, 513, 514, 515). *513*: Not to allow spiritualists (diviners, fortune tellers, astrologers) to exist among the people (see 62, 510, 511, 512, 514, 515). *514*: Not to allow conjurors of ghosts and evil spirits to exist among the people (see 62, 510-513, 515). *515*: Not to permit necromancers to exist among the people (see 62, 510-514). *516*: To hearken to and obey the utterances of a true prophet (see *517, 518, 519*). *517*: Not to tolerate the false prophet (see 516, *517*, 519). *518*: Not to let live the false prophet (see 516, *517*, *519*). *519*: Not to fear to slay the false prophet (condemned by the Beth-Din of 71; see 516, *517*, *518*). *520*: To set apart *three cities of refuge* (west of the River Jordan)† and to maintain the roads leading to them in good condition and free from obstacles (see *409-413*, 521). *521*: Not to have pity or compassion for a murderer (see *409-413*, 520). *522*: Not to remove or alter landmarks to rob someone of his land (see *36*). *523*: Not to admit the testimony of one witness only. *524*: The law of the false witness (see *37*). *525*: Not to fear the enemy in war. *526*: To appoint an *anointed priest* to exhort and encourage the army before battle. *527*: To offer terms of peace to the townsfolk of any city to avoid assault. *528*: Not to fail to destroy utterly the seven nations of Canaan. *529*: Not to destroy fruit trees. *530*: The law of *the slain found in the field and the heifer whose neck was to be broken* (see *531*). *531*: Not to plough over or sow the rough valley where they bring *the heifer whose neck is to be broken* (see *530*). *532*: The law of 'the captive woman of goodly form' (see *533, 534*). *533*: Not to sell 'the captive woman of goodly form' after copulating with her (see *532, 534*). *534*: Not to use 'the captive woman of goodly form' as a hand-maid after copulating with her (see *532, 533*). *535*: To hang on the gallows the blasphemer and the idolater (see *536, 537*). *536*: Not to leave hanging a corpse after nightfall (see 535, 537). *537*: The corpse of one executed (and of anyone else) must be buried on the day of death (see 535, *536*). *538*: To restore aught found to its owner (see *539*). *539*: Not to ignore and keep someone's loss (see 538). *540*: Not to fail to help one whose beast falls under its burden (see 80, 541). *541*: To help one unload and load the beast that has fallen down (or to help load the burden that has fallen off). *542*: A woman may not dress in man's garments (see *543*). *543*: A man may not wear the raiment of a woman (see *542*). *544*: A mother bird and its young must not together be taken from the nest (see 545). *545*: The mother bird must be set free before taking its young from the nest (see 544). *546*: One must make a (safety) parapet for his roof. *547*: Not to leave about any obstacles and the like that may cause accidents. *548*: Not to plant diverse kinds in a vineyard (see 245, 549). *549*: Not to derive any benefit from planting diverse kinds (see 245, 548). *550*: Not to yoke together for work diverse kinds of animals (see 244). *551*: Not to wear mingled stuff of wool and linen. *552*: One acquires a wife by either (1) betrothal with money, or (2) a document, or (3) copulation. *553*: If one wrongly accuses his wife of the absence of the 'tokens of virginity' (*viz.*, the absence of the hymen or maidenhead) he is penalised (see *554*). *554*: The wrongfully slandered wife cannot

† As well as three cities of refuge east of the Jordan.

ever be divorced (see 553). 555: If one ravaged an unprotesting betrothed virgin both are slain by stoning (see 556, 557, 558). 556: If one outraged in a field a betrothed virgin, she is not to be punished; only the ravisher is stoned to death (see 555, 557, 558). 557: If one ravished an unbetrothed virgin, he must pay her father an indemnity and he must also marry her (see 555, 565, 558). 558: One cannot ever divorce the wife with whom he had copulated when she was an unbetrothed virgin (see 557). 559: An Israelitess may not be wed to one with crushed or maimed privy parts. 560: A bastard may not marry an Israelitess. 561: An Israelitess must not be wedded to an Ammonite or to a Moabite. 562: Not to seek the well-being of the Ammonites and Moabites. 563: Not to exclude an Edomite from the third generation onward to become a proselyte (see 564). 564: Not to prevent an Egyptian after the second generation onward from becoming a proselyte (see 563). 565: One unclean must not stay in the camp: he may not return before he is cleansed. 566: To prepare a place outside the camp for excreting (see 567). 567: To have at hand a tool for digging up the soil to cover up one's excreta [excretes] (see 566). 568: If a bondman escaped from abroad to the Holy Land he must not be restored to his foreign owner (see 569). 569: Not to reduce to bondage a bondman (viz., he must be set free) who escaped from abroad to the Holy Land (see 568). 570: Not to have sexual connection without both betrothal [marriage] and the marriage contract [kethubah]. 571: Not to offer up on the Altar an offering obtained with the earnings of a harlot (prostitute, whore, strumpet). 572: Interest [usury] on loans may be demanded from heathens (see 66, 67, 68, 573). 573: Not to impose or accept interest [usury] for loans made to Israelites (see 66, 67, 68, 572). 574: Not to delay (longer than the third Pilgrim Festival) the payment of a donation or vow (see 575). 575: To fulfil a vow exactly as vowed (see 574). 576: A hired labourer in the vineyard may eat of the produce (see 577, 578). 577: A hired labourer while harvesting may not keep in his own receptacle more than he can eat (see 576, 578). 578: A hired labourer may not eat of the produce while at work (see 576, 577). 579: A wife must be divorced with a document (a bill of divorcement—get; see 580). 580: One may not remarry his divorced wife if she had been married or betrothed after he had divorced her (see 579). 581: A man does not engage in army service (or in public service) during the first year of his married life (see 582). 582: A couple are free to enjoy their first year of married life without having to perform national or public service (see 581). 583: Not to take in pledge articles necessary for the preparation of food. 584: Not to neglect the symptoms of leprosy (see 169-177). 585: Not to take a pledge by force for any loan (see 586, 587, 591). 586: A creditor may not retain overnight a debtor's pledge who is in need of it—the debtor recovers it nightly and returns it daily (see 585, 587). 587: The creditor must return a pledge at sundown when the debtor needs it (see 585, 586, 591). 588: A hired labourer or workman must receive his wage at the end of his day's work. 589: Not to admit the evidence of one of near kin of the litigant. 590: Not to pervert justice due to the stranger or to the orphan. 591: Not to take a pledge from a woman (see 585, 586, 587). 592: The forgotten sheaf must be left for the stranger, for the orphan, and for the widow (see 593). 593: The owner must not remove the forgotten sheaf for himself (see 592). 594: The maximum number of lashes [stripes] is 39 [technically termed '40 less 1'; see 595]. 595: Not to exceed 40 lashes [stripes; see 594]. 596: Not to muzzle a beast when it is threshing the corn. 597: A yevamah ought not to be married to other than her yavam (see 598, 599). 598: The duty of marrying a yevamah devolves on her yavam (see 597, 599). 599: If a yavam refuses to marry his yevamah she performs the ceremony of chalitzah [levirate separation; see 597, 598]. 600: To rescue a fugitive or one persecuted without regard of any risk to the pursuer's or persecutor's life (see 601). 601: Not to have pity for the pursuer or persecutor (see 600). 602: Not to keep in one's possession defective weights (see 258, 259). 603: To remember the history of the iniquitous unprovoked attack of Amalek on the Hebrews in the Wilderness (see 604, 605). 604: To destroy utterly the Amalekites (603, 605). 605: Not to forget the evil that Amalek sought against the Hebrews (see 603, 604). 606: To recite the 'Portion of the First Fruits' when bringing the first fruits to the Temple (see 607-610). 607: To recite the declaration concerning the clearance of the separated tithes (see 606, 608, 609, 610). 608: To declare that one had not eaten of tithe in mourning (see 606, 607, 609, 610). 609: To declare that one had not eaten of second tithe in uncleanness (see 606, 607, 608, 610). 610: To declare that second tithe money had not been expended except on food and drink (see 606-609). 611: To act according to the Law tempered with tender mercy and lovingkindness. 612: To assemble all Israel on the Festival of Tabernacles. 613: It is the duty of every Jew to possess a Scroll of the Law of his own; see 503.

תַּרְיַג מִצְוֹת, *The 613 Commandments.* It is necessary to emphasize

(1) that there are disagreements regarding the correct positions of some of the 613 *Commandments* in the numerical order, (2) that some authorities give varying complete or partial texts for the bases of some of the *Commandments,* and (3) that some add to or vary the meanings they apply to some of the texts. The Tables present a 'common multiple' or more often 'a common measure' of the various versions, and here follow some additional **Notes.**

26: In other words 'Prohibition of the belief of the existence of any but the **One God'.**   *38:* 'Not to covet another's wife' in particular.   *39:* See רמבם, הלכות ע׳כ, Chapter 3, paragraph 10, 'Not even for mere decoration, and not for worship'. *42:* In other words 'To treat a Hebrew servant according to law'. *43:* 'The master is to perform יעוד (or ייעוד), *betrothal of a Hebrew handmaid',* i.e., either to espouse his Hebrew maid-servant or betroth her to his son with her consent (see קדּושׁין, 18b, 19a).   *44:* Some add: 'It is a master's duty to *designate* (viz., to perform יעוד.—see 43 above) her for himself and she requires no other rite of espousal than *the passing of his purchase-money to her father'.* וְהֶפְדָּהּ means that he must allow her a deduction from the amount of her ransom—if she desires to be released from service—corresponding to the number of years she served him. *45:* לְמָכְרָהּ means that neither the owner nor her father has the right to sell her to another Jewish man (but various authorities give to this different views; see רמבם, הלכות עבדים, Chapter 4, paragraph 10).   *55:* In the *Pentateuchal* text וְשִׁלַּח, *and shall send in,* refers to the damage done by *treading,* and וּבִעֵר, *and shall devastate,* refers to the damage caused by *grazing;* in *Mishnaic* language שָׁלַח comes under the category of רֶגֶל, *foot,* and וּבִעֵר comes under the category of שֵׁן *tooth* (see בָּבָא קַמָּא 1¹).   *67:* Some word this 'Exaction with regard to loans to the poor is prohibited'.   *74:* Some add 'Not to hear one litigant except in the presence of the other'.   *76:* Some append 'Not to decide in capital cases by a majority of one against the accused'.   *77:* According to the רמבם this means 'Having first defended someone in a capital case he may not afterward plead against-him'.   *78:* The חֲכָמִים maintain that the verse speaks of capital cases and deduce from לֹא תִהְיֶה אַחֲרֵי רַבִּים לְרָעוֹת, *thou shalt not follow the multitude to do evil,* that the guilt of an accused must not be decided by a preponderance of one judge, and from אַחֲרֵי רַבִּים לְהַטֹּת, *after a multitude to pervert justice,* that if the judges by a majority of two declare an accused guilty then this is the decision (see סַנְהֶדְרִין 2a). *81:* In general 'A judge must not show more regard for one party than for the other, and he must not be biased or prejudiced against any party'.   *82:* If an accused has been condemned, a retrial takes place if fresh evidence is furnished in his favour.   *86:* Some give this the meaning 'Not to swear by idols'.   *87:* Some add 'Not to lead any Israelite to idolatry'.   *93:* viz., the שִׁבְעָה גוֹיִם; see *Deuteronomy* **7,** 1, *Joshua* **24,** 11.   *98:* It was the duty of the priests to keep the lamps

149

alight.   112: This is the deduction: the literal rendering is *Six days shalt thou work but on the seventh day thou shalt rest* ; but also landwork must cease towards the end of the *6th year*, that is on the advent of the *7th year* (similarly work ceases on the *6th day* of the week before the advent of the *7th day* or *Sabbath*, as this verse is interpreted thus by some חֲכָמִים who maintain it does not refer to the *Sabbatical year*); but the obligatory harvesting of the עוֹמֶר (see *Leviticus* **23, 10**) overrides the *Sabbath* law and the *Sabbatical year* law.   114: Though this transgression is included in the *4th Commandment* of the *Decalogue* it is specifically indicated here that, unlike other forms, it entails the penalty of the *40 stripes* but not the death penalty; others maintain that it is here singled out to indicate that if one were guilty of several acts of transgression on the Sabbath at the same time and under the same circumstances atonement must be made for each act separately (see שַׁבָּת 70a, פְּסָחִים 5b, סַנְהֶדְרִין 35b).   139: This means that naught may be eaten of a *sin-offering*—all is burnt—it is brought into the Interior if its blood had to be tossed (or sprinkled) on the *outer altar*; some read 'into the Interior within the Partition Vail' instead of 'into the Interior'.   153: Some add 'And to search diligently for the marks of *clean beasts*'.   155: Some add 'And to search diligently for the marks of *clean fish*'.   158: Some add 'And to search diligently for the marks of *clean creatures*'. 173: Some add 'The leprosy is cleansed with *cedar wood, and scarlet, and hyssop*' (see *Leviticus* **14, 4**).   265: It is obligatory for a common priest to defile himself for the dead of his kin, and, שֶׁאִם לֹא * רָצָה מְטַמְּאִין אוֹתוֹ וְעַל כָּרְחוֹ, *if he** be not willing to do so he is defiled against his will*, to oblige him to perform the מִצְוָה.   *Perhaps רָצָה, *he were not willing*.   282: The text in *Leviticus* **22, 10** is וְכָל־זָר לֹא־יֹאכַל קֹדֶשׁ, *There shall no layman eat of the holy thing* (see **Note**§ to the first Table of the *negative commandment 17*), *Exodus* **12, 48**, וְכָל־עָרֵל לֹא־יֹאכַל בּוֹ, *and no uncircumcised person shall eat thereof*.   287: Some add 'It is prohibited to inflict a blemish on קָדָשִׁים'. 306: Some add 'From the day—the 16th of Nisan—we begin to *count the omer*'. 349: 'stone', *viz.*, a plain stone or figured stone or stone pillar or statue or the like.   This verse contains two prohibitions, (1) *not to erect a pillar for a meeting place for worship, not even or the worship of God*, and (2) *not to make a floor of stone to prostrate oneself on it, not even before God*; see מְגִלָּה 22b, and רמבם הלכות עבודת כוכבים, 6[8]. 414: According to the רמבם it implies 'Not to appoint as judge one who is not learned in the Law'.   470: Some add 'And to search diligently for the marks of *clean fowls*'.   476: But this exaction, though permitted, is not a מִצְוָה, *i.e.*, one may relinquish any claim for refund from the foreigner in the 'year of release', שְׁנַת הַשְּׁמִטָּה; the *commandment* is contained in the rest of the verse, though not quoted here, וַאֲשֶׁר יִהְיֶה לְךָ אֶת־אָחִיךָ תַּשְׁמֵט יָדֶךָ, *but that which is thine with thy brother thine hand shall remit*.   494: This is to be observed by laymen as well as priests; see זְבָחִים 36ab for *Halachahs* derived from this verse (*Deuteronomy* **17, 1**).   572: It would seem that the order of numbering of 572, 573 ought to be reversed for the *Pentateuchal* text as basis for 572 follows that for *573*. In *Deuteronomy*, **23, 21**, the first part לַנָּכְרִי תַשִּׁיךְ, *Unto a foreigner thou 'mayest' lend upon interest*, addressed to the creditor is precluded from *being a* מִצְוָה because of the meaning '*mayest*', but the following וּלְאָחִיךָ לֹא תַשִּׁיךְ, *but to thy brother thou 'shalt not' lend upon interest*, is distinctly *a negative commandment*. There is great disagreement on this verse among many authorities. See *573*. *573:* Compare *572. Deuteronomy* **23,** 20, לֹא תַשִּׁיךְ, לְאָחִיךָ, *Thou shalt not lend upon interest to thy brother*, is rendered by some *Thou shalt not pay interest to thy brother*, implying as a warning to a borrower not to pay interest to (or not to borrow on interest from) a creditor (see בָּבָא מְצִיעָא 75b). Compare *Leviticus* **25,** 37.

PRAYERS
BENEDICTIONS
HADRAN
AND
CONCLUDING PRAYERS

INTRODUCTION

Many *Mishnayoth* editions give at the end of one or more of the six *Orders* special compositions and compilations under the above headings.

They are given in Volume V (קָדָשִׁ֫ים) with **Notes,** but without any translation, in a form convenient for recital.

These are here presented with the **Notes** revised and (in many cases) extended, and all these paragraphs are accompanied with original translations—the English renderings set *alongside* the paragraphs for easy comparison and the **Notes** arranged *after* each section for easier reference for the student.

Where opportunity offers the recital of the **Hadran** (with the paragraphs following) is coupled with an introductory Rabbinical concluding discourse and is made the occasion of a ritual festive gathering;* and such a procedure is used particularly in the morning of עֶ֫רֶב פֶּ֫סַח (the Eve of Passover) in the synagogue or home to exempt the firstborn present at the ceremony from the תַּעֲנִית בְּכוֹרִים (the *Fast of the Firstborn*).

* This religious joyous celebration is termed a סִיּוּם (literally *Conclusion*).

·155

PRAYERS
BENEDICTIONS
HADRAN
AND
CONCLUDING PRAYERS

בכניסתו לבית המדרש מהו אומר

To be recited on entering the house of study.

May[1] it be Thy will, O Eternal my God, that no offence may occur through me [by an erroneous decision], and that I do not err against a *Halachah*, and may my colleagues rejoice in me that I do not pronounce as clean what is unclean, or what is clean as unclean, or as prohibited what is permitted, or what is prohibited as permitted, and may my colleagues not err against *Halachah* that I may rejoice in them.

יְהִי רָצוֹן מִלְּפָנֶיךָ ה' אֱלֹהַי שֶׁלֹּא יֶאֱרַע דְּבַר תַּקָּלָה עַל יָדִי, וְלֹא אֶכָּשֵׁל בִּדְבַר הֲלָכָה, וְיִשְׂמְחוּ בִּי חֲבֵירַי, שֶׁלֹּא אוֹמֵר עַל טָמֵא טָהוֹר, וְלֹא עַל טָהוֹר טָמֵא, וְלֹא עַל מוּתָּר אָסוּר, וְלֹא עַל אָסוּר מוּתָּר, וְלֹא יִכָּשְׁלוּ חֲבֵרַי בִּדְבַר הֲלָכָה וְאֶשְׂמַח בָּהֶם.

1 See בְּרָכוֹת 28b (compare בְּרָכוֹת 4[2]).

ביציאתו מהו אומר

To be recited when leaving the house of study.

I[2] give thanks to Thee, O Eternal my God, that thou hast appointed my lot to be with[3] those that sit in the house of study and not with those who abide at the corners, for I rise betimes, and they rise betimes—I rise betimes for the study of the Law, but they rise betimes for vanities, I toil and they toil[4]—I toil and receive reward, but they toil and do not receive reward, I run

מוֹדֶה אֲנִי לְפָנֶיךָ ה' אֱלֹהַי, שֶׁשַּׂמְתָּ חֶלְקִי מִיּוֹשְׁבֵי בֵּית הַמִּדְרָשׁ, וְלֹא שַׂמְתָּ חֶלְקִי מִיּוֹשְׁבֵי קְרָנוֹת, שֶׁאֲנִי מַשְׁכִּים, וְהֵם מַשְׁכִּימִים, אֲנִי מַשְׁכִּים לְדִבְרֵי תוֹרָה, וְהֵם מַשְׁכִּימִים לִדְבָרִים בְּטֵלִים, אֲנִי עָמֵל וְהֵם עֲמֵלִים, אֲנִי עָמֵל וּמְקַבֵּל שָׂכָר, וְהֵם עֲמֵלִים וְאֵינָם מְקַבְּלִים

157

and they run—I run to the life of the hereafter, but they run to the pit of destruction, as it is said,[5] *But Thou, O God, wilt bring them down*[6] *into the nethermost pit;   men of blood and deceit shall not live out half their days; but as for me, I will trust in Thee.*

שָׂכָר, אֲנִי רָץ וְהֵם רָצִים, אֲנִי רָץ לְחַיֵּי הָעוֹלָם הַבָּא, וְהֵם רָצִים לִבְאֵר שַׁחַת, שֶׁנֶּאֱמַר, וְאַתָּה אֱלֹהִים תּוֹרִידֵם לִבְאֵר שַׁחַת אַנְשֵׁי דָמִים וּמִרְמָה לֹא יֶחֱצוּ יְמֵיהֶם וַאֲנִי אֶבְטַח בָּךְ·

2 See בְּרָכוֹת 28b. 3 מִיּוֹשְׁבֵי בֵּית הַמִּדְרָשׁ, *viz.*, those who are engaged in study. מִיּוֹשְׁבֵי קְרָנוֹת, *those seated at street corners, traders, idlers.* 4 Some point this word עֹמְלִים [or עוֹמְלִים, the regular *Kal participle* of the verb עָמַל]. 5 *Psalm* 55, 24. 6 Scripture gives תּוֹרִדֵם.

וקודם שיתחיל ללמוד יברך ברכת התורה כמסודר

To be recited before commencing study of the Law.

Blessed[7] art Thou, O Eternal, our God, King of the universe, Who hast hallowed us by Thy commandments, and hast commanded us to occupy ourselves with the words of the Law.   And[8] make pleasant, therefore, we beseech Thee, O Eternal our God, the words of Thy Law in our mouth, and in the mouths[9] of Thy people the house of Israel, so that we with our offspring, and[10] the offspring of our offspring, and the offspring of Thy people the house of Israel, may we all[11] know Thy Name and learn Thy Law for its own sake.[12] Blessed

בָּרוּךְ אַתָּה ה' אֱלֹהֵינוּ מֶלֶךְ הָעוֹלָם אֲשֶׁר קִדְּשָׁנוּ בְּמִצְוֹתָיו וְצִוָּנוּ לַעֲסוֹק בְּדִבְרֵי תוֹרָה· וְהַעֲרֶב נָא ה' אֱלֹהֵינוּ אֶת־דִּבְרֵי תוֹרָתְךָ בְּפִינוּ, וּבְפִיּוֹת עַמְּךָ בֵּית יִשְׂרָאֵל, וְנִהְיֶה אֲנַחְנוּ וְצֶאֱצָאֵינוּ, 10וְצֶאֱצָאֵי צֶאֱצָאֵינוּ, וְצֶאֱצָאֵי עַמְּךָ בֵּית יִשְׂרָאֵל, 11כֻּלָּנוּ יוֹדְעֵי שְׁמֶךָ וְלוֹמְדֵי תוֹרָתְךָ 12לִשְׁמָהּ· בָּרוּךְ אַתָּה ה' הַמְלַמֵּד תּוֹרָה לְעַמּוֹ יִשְׂרָאֵל·

art Thou, O Eternal, Who teachest [the] Law to Thy people Israel.

7 See בְּרָכוֹת 11b. Both paragraphs are given in the Morning Service. 8 Compare the variation of this section further on. From וְהַעֲרֶב begins a separate paragraph in the Prayer Book.   9 The Prayer Book has the *singular* form וּבְפִי *and in the mouth of*, instead of the *plural* form וּבְפִיּוֹת. 10 The phrase וְצֶאֱצָאֵי צֶאֱצָאֵינוּ is omitted in some Prayer Books or bracketed in small type in others. 11 כֻּלָּנוּ

instead of כֻּלָנוּ in some Prayer Books. 12 לִשְׁמָה, or *for no selfish purpose, for no ulterior motive;* this is almost equivalent to the expression לְשֵׁם שָׁמַיִם, *for the glory of God* [literally *for the honour of heaven*]; לִשְׁמָה is placed in brackets in some Prayer Books and is omitted in others.

וְאַחַר כָּךְ יְסַיֵּים בְּבְרָכָה זוּ
The preceding Blessing is then concluded with the following Blessing and Prayer.

Blessed[13] art Thou, O Eternal our God, King of the universe, Who hast chosen us from all nations, and hast given us Thy Law. Blessed art Thou, O Eternal, Giver of the Law.

בָּרוּךְ אַתָּה ה׳ אֱלֹהֵינוּ מֶלֶךְ הָעוֹלָם, אֲשֶׁר בָּחַר בָּנוּ מִכָּל הָעַמִּים, וְנָתַן לָנוּ אֶת־תּוֹרָתוֹ. בָּרוּךְ אַתָּה ה׳ נוֹתֵן הַתּוֹרָה.

13 See בְּרָכוֹת 11b. This Blessing is given in the Morning Service, and it is also the introductory Blessing recited by one called up to a Reading of the Law.

אַחַר בִּרְכַּת הַתּוֹרָה יֹאמַר זֶה
To be recited after the Blessing over the Law.

Lo, I desire to study in such wise that this learning[14] shall lead me to ·[upright] practice and to righteous ways, and to the knowledge of the Law.

הִנְנִי רוֹצֶה לִלְמוֹד כְּדֵי שֶׁיְּבִיאֵנִי תַּלְמוּד זֶה לִידֵי מַעֲשֶׂה, וְלִידֵי מִדּוֹת יְשָׁרוֹת, וְלִידֵי יְדִיעַת הַתּוֹרָה, וַהֲרֵינִי עוֹשֶׂה לְשֵׁם יִחוּד קוּדְשָׁא בְּרִיךְ הוּא וּשְׁכִינְתֵּיהּ.

14 The *definite* form הַתַּלְמוּד (instead of תַּלְמוּד) is given in some texts. A short concluding sentence from the *Zohar* of an exceedingly mystic character dealing with the *Tetragrammaton* is advisedly omitted here, especially as it is in no wise of the nature of a prayer or supplication and further has no direct bearing or essential connection with this beautiful prayer. The part from הֲרֵינִי is left untranslated as it would necessitate comment at great length which would be out of place here particularly on account of its esoteric, acroamatic qualities.

וְיֹאמַר כֵּן שְׁלֹשָׁה פְעָמִים
At the conclusion (סִיוּם) of the study of the Order or Tractate as the case may be (and of the following rabbinical exposition if any) the **Hadran** (הדרן) *is recited three times.*

May[15] our[16] glorification be upon thee, O Order ......,[16] O Tractate ......,[16] and may thy glory be upon us; may our mind be upon thee, O Order ......,[16] O Tractate

הַדְרָן עֲלָךְ סֵדֶר ·· [16] or
מַסֶּכֶת ·· [16] וַהֲדָרָךְ עֲלָן דַּעְתָּן
עֲלָךְ סֵדֶר ·· [16] or מַסֶּכֶת ·· [16]

159

......,[16] and may thy mind be upon us; may we not be forgotten of thee, O *Order* ......,[16] O *Tractate* ......,[16] and mayest thou not be forgotten of us, neither in this world nor in the world to come.

וְדַעְתָּךְ עֲלָן לָא נִתְנְשֵׁי מִינָךְ סֵדֶר ...[16] or מַסֶּכֶת ...[16] וְלָא תִּתְנְשֵׁי מִינָן לָא בְּעָלְמָא הָדֵין וְלָא בְּעָלְמָא דְאָתֵי.

15 Here this word is vocalised הַדְרָן as derived from הָדָר, *glory.* The exact origin of this prayer is not known with certainty. This word is pronounced popularly הַדְרָן, **Hadran,** and is given in modern usage by many the interjectural meaning *Recapitulate !, Revise !, Repeat !;* it has in this form become the accepted title of this section, and in this sense the introductory phrases . . . הַדְרָן עֲלָךְ סֵדֶר . . . מַסֶּכֶת וְהַדְרָךְ עֲלָן may be paraphrastically rendered *It is our obligation to revise thee, O Order . . . O Tractate, thy revision devolves upon us as a duty, O Order . . . O Tractate;* the term הַדְרָן is of *Aramaic (Chaldee)* origin, derived from the *verb* [*Afel conjugation*] אַהֲדַר, *return, restore, lead back, turn around, reply, carry in procession,* **repeat, review**; compare מוֹעֵד קָטָן, 28a, אַהֲדְרִי לְתַלְמוּדָאַי, *that I may revise my studies, and* בְּרָכוֹת 38b, מְהַדַּר (*or* מַהֲדַר) תַּלְמוּדֵיהּ, *recapitulating his studies.* **16** Here is pronounced the title of the particular סֵדֶר (*Order*) or מַסֶּכֶת (*Tractate*) as the case may be.

וְאַחַר כָּךְ יֹאמַר זֶה

The Hadran is followed by the recital of the following four paragraphs.

May it be Thy will, O Eternal our God, and God of our fathers, that Thy Law should be our occupation in this world, and that it should be with us in the world to come. —Chanina bar[17] Pappa,[18] Rami bar Pappa, Nachman bar Pappa, Achai bar Pappa, Abba Mari bar Pappa, Rafram bar Pappa, Rachish bar Pappa, Surchav bar Pappa, Ada bar Pappa, Daro bar Pappa.

יְהִי רָצוֹן מִלְּפָנֶיךָ ה' אֱלֹהֵינוּ וֵאלֹהֵי אֲבוֹתֵינוּ שֶׁתְּהֵא תוֹרָתְךָ אוּמָנוּתֵינוּ בָּעוֹלָם הַזֶּה וּתְהֵא עִמָּנוּ לָעוֹלָם הַבָּא· [17]חֲנִינָא [17]בַּר [18]פַּפָּא רָמִי בַּר פַּפָּא נַחְמָן בַּר פַּפָּא אַחַאי בַּר פַּפָּא אַבָּא מָרִי בַּר פַּפָּא רַפְרַם בַּר פַּפָּא רָכִישׁ בַּר פַּפָּא סוּרְחָב בַּר פַּפָּא אָדָא בַּר פַּפָּא דָרוֹ בַּר פַּפָּא·

17 בַּר = בֶּן, *son of.* **18** פַּפָּא; popular pronunciation פָּאפָּא. The significance of the reference to the ten sons of Rav Pappa is very obscure, and all the explanations given so far for their inclusion are far from satisfactory.

Make[19] pleasant, we beseech Thee, O Eternal our God, the words of Thy Law in our mouth and in the mouth of Thy people the house of

[19]הַעֲרֶב נָא ה' אֱלֹהֵינוּ אֶת־דִּבְרֵי תוֹרָתְךָ בְּפִינוּ וּבְפִי עַמְּךָ בֵּית יִשְׂרָאֵל וְנִהְיֶה כֻּלָּנוּ אֲנַחְנוּ

160

Israel, so that all of us, we and our offspring and the offspring of Thy people the house of Israel, yea we all,[20] may know Thy Name and learn Thy Law. Thy[21] commandments[22] make me wiser than mine enemies, for they are ever with me. Let[23] my heart be undivided in Thy statutes, in order that I may not be put to shame. I[24] will never forget Thy precepts[25] for with them Thou hast quickened me. Blessed[26] art Thou, O Eternal, teach me Thy statutes. Amen![27]
Amen! Amen! For ever and evermore.

וְצֶאֱצָאֵינוּ וְצֶאֱצָאֵי עַמְּךָ בֵּית יִשְׂרָאֵל ·כֻּלָּנוּ יוֹדְעֵי שְׁמֶךָ וְלוֹמְדֵי תוֹרָתֶךָ· ·מֵאוֹיְבַי תְּחַכְּמֵנִי ·מִצְוֹתֶךָ כִּי לְעוֹלָם הִיא לִי· ·יְהִי לִבִּי תָמִים בְּחֻקֶּיךָ לְמַעַן לֹא אֵבוֹשׁ· ·לְעוֹלָם לֹא אֶשְׁכַּח ·פִּקּוּדֶיךָ כִּי בָם חִיִּיתָנִי· ·בָּרוּךְ אַתָּה ה' לַמְּדֵנִי חֻקֶּיךָ· ·אָמֵן אָמֵן אָמֵן סֶלָה וָעֶד·

19 In some texts this paragraph and the preceding one form one paragraph. 20 כּוּלָנוּ instead of כֻּלָּנוּ in some texts. 21 See *Psalm* 119, 98. Scripture gives מֵאֹיְבַי. 22 The Scripture gives מִצְוֹתֶךָ. 23 See *Psalm* 119, 80. 24 See *Psalm* 119, 93. 25 Some Scriptural texts give פִּקֻּדֶיךָ. 26 See *Psalm* 119, 12. 27 Or *May it be so!* or *Be it so!* or *It is true.*

We[28] give thanks unto Thee, for Thou art the Eternal Our God and the God of our fathers, the God of all flesh, Our Creator and the Creator of all things in the beginning. Blessings and thanksgivings be to Thy great and holy Name, for Thou hast maintained us in life and hast sustained us; so mayest Thou continue to maintain us in life and to sustain us. And mayest Thou assemble our exiles to Thy holy courts to observe Thy statutes, and to do Thy will,[29] and to serve Thee with a perfect heart; for we[30] give thanks unto Thee. Blessed be the God to Whom thanksgivings are due.

·מוֹדִים אֲנַחְנוּ לָךְ שָׁאַתָּה הוּא ה' אֱלֹהֵינוּ וֵאלֹהֵי אֲבוֹתֵינוּ אֱלֹהֵי כָּל־ בָּשָׂר, יוֹצְרֵנוּ יוֹצֵר בְּרֵאשִׁית· בְּרָכוֹת וְהוֹדָאוֹת לְשִׁמְךָ הַגָּדוֹל וְהַקָּדוֹשׁ עַל שֶׁהֶחֱיִיתָנוּ וְקִיַּמְתָּנוּ; כֵּן תְּחַיֵּינוּ וּתְקַיְּמֵנוּ· וְתֶאֱסוֹף גָּלֻיּוֹתֵינוּ לְחַצְרוֹת קָדְשֶׁךָ לִשְׁמֹר חֻקֶּיךָ וְלַעֲשׂוֹת ·רְצוֹנֶךָ וּלְעָבְדְּךָ בְּלֵבָב שָׁלֵם; עַל ·שֶׁאֲנַחְנוּ מוֹדִים לָךְ· בָּרוּךְ אֵל הַהוֹדָאוֹת·

28 This is known as מוֹדִים דְּרַבָּנָן, and is recited in an undertone when the Reader or Cantor (חַזָּן or שְׁלִיחַ צִבּוּר, בַּעַל תְּפִלָּה) recites the *18th Benediction* (מוֹדִים) of the

161

סֵדֶר עֲבוֹדַת יִשְׂרָאֵל‎, עֲמִידָה‎. It is an abstract of several Rabbinical prayers (see *Baer*, Page 100). This paragraph is not indicated in some editions of the **Hadran**. 29 רְצוֹנְךָ‎† in some texts. 30 שֶׁאָנוּ‎ instead of שֶׁאֲנַחְנוּ‎ in some texts.

May it be Thy will, O Eternal my God and God of my fathers, that in like manner as Thou hast aided me to conclude *Order* ......[16] *Tractate* ......[16] even so mayest Thou aid me to begin [the study of] other *Tractates** and books, and to conclude them, to learn and to teach, to observe and to do and to fulfil all the words of the study of Thy Law in love, and may the merit of all the *Tannaim*§ and *Amoraim*† and scholars† stand in my behalf and my seed that the Law shall not depart from my mouth and from the mouth of my seed and the seed of my seed for ever. And may it be fulfilled in me: *When*[31] *thou walkest it shall lead thee, when thou liest down it shall watch over thee, and when thou awakest it shall talk with thee; For*[32] *by me thy days shall be multiplied, and the years of thy life shall be increased; Length*[33] *of days is in her right hand, riches and honour are in her left hand; The*[34] *Eternal will give strength unto His people, the Eternal will bless His people with peace.*

יְהִי רָצוֹן מִלְּפָנֶיךָ ה' אֱלֹהַי וֵאלֹהֵי אֲבוֹתַי כְּשֵׁם שֶׁעֲזַרְתַּנִי לְסַיֵּים סֵדֶר ··· [16] מַסֶּכֶת ··· [16] כֵּן תַּעַזְרֵנִי לְהַתְחִיל *מַסֶּכְתּוֹת וּסְפָרִים אֲחֵרִים וּלְסַיְּימָם, לִלְמוֹד וּלְלַמֵּד, לִשְׁמוֹר וְלַעֲשׂוֹת וּלְקַיֵּים אֶת־כָּל־דִּבְרֵי תַלְמוּד תּוֹרָתְךָ בְּאַהֲבָה, וּזְכוּת כָּל־§הַתַּנָּאִים †וַאֲמוֹרָאִים וְתַלְמִידֵי חֲכָמִים יַעֲמוֹד לִי וּלְזַרְעִי שֶׁלֹּא תָמוּשׁ הַתּוֹרָה מִפִּי וּמִפִּי זַרְעִי וְזֶרַע זַרְעִי עַד עוֹלָם· וְתִתְקַיֵּים בִּי, יי[31]בְּהִתְהַלֶּכְךָ תַּנְחֶה אוֹתָךְ בְּשָׁכְבְּךָ תִּשְׁמוֹר עָלֶיךָ וַהֲקִיצוֹתָ הִיא תְשִׂיחֶךָ; יי[32]כִּי בִי יִרְבּוּ יָמֶיךָ וְיוֹסִיפוּ לְךָ שְׁנוֹת חַיִּים; [33]אוֹרֶךְ יָמִים בִּימִינָהּ עוֹשֶׁר וְכָבוֹד בִּשְׂמֹאלָהּ; יי[34] עוֹז לְעַמּוֹ יִתֵּן ה' יְבָרֵךְ אֶת־ עַמּוֹ בַשָּׁלוֹם·

31 See *Proverbs* 6, 22. **32** See *Proverbs* 9, 11. **33** See *Proverbs* 3, 17. **34** See *Psalm* **29**, 11.

וְאִם הֵם עֲשָׂרָה [מִנְיָן] יֹאמַר זֶה

The following composite Kaddish (קדיש) is recited when there is present a Minyan (מנין—not less than ten adult males).

Aggrandised[35] and hallowed be His great Name[36] in the world which He[37] in future will renew,[38] and [wherein] He will revive[39] the dead

יי[35]יִתְגַּדַּל וְיִתְקַדַּשׁ [36]שְׁמֵיהּ רַבָּא בְּעָלְמָא [37]דְּהוּא עָתִיד [38]לְאִתְחַדָּתָא יי[39]וּלְאַחֲיָא מֵתַיָּא, וּלְאַסָּקָא

162

and bring (them)[40] to eternal life; and He will rebuild the city of Jerusalem, and He will beautify His Temple[41] in the midst thereof, and He will eradicate[42] idolatrous worship from the earth, and He will reestablish[43] the heavenly[44] worship to its former state; and the Holy One, *blessed be He*,[45] will establish His reign in His kingdom[46] and in His glory,[47] during your life[48] and during your days, and during the life of all the house of Israel, speedily and at a near time, and say ye, *Amen*,[49] *let His great Name*[50] *be blessed for ever and to all eternity.* Blessed, and praised, and glorified, and exalted, and extolled, and honoured,[51] and aggrandised and lauded[52] be the Name[53] of the Holy One,[54] *Blessed be He*;[55] though He be high[56] above all the benedictions and hymns, praises and consolations, that are uttered[57] in the world; and say ye, *Amen.*[58]

יִתְהוֹן) לְחַיֵּי עָלְמָא ; וּלְמִבְנֵא⁴⁰
קַרְתָּא דִירוּשְׁלֵם וּלְשַׁכְלֵל⁴¹
הֵיכָלֵיהּ בְּגַוַּהּ, ⁴²וּלְמֶעְקַר פּוּלְחָנָא
נוּכְרָאָה מֵאַרְעָא, ⁴³וּלְאַתָבָא
פּוּלְחָנָא ⁴⁴דִשְׁמַיָּא לְאַתְרֵיהּ ;
וְיַמְלִיךְ ⁴⁵קוּדְשָׁא ⁴⁵בְּרִיךְ הוּא
⁴⁶בְּמַלְכוּתֵיהּ ⁴⁷וִיקָרֵיהּ ⁴⁸בְּחַיֵּיכוֹן
וּבְיוֹמֵיכוֹן וּבְחַיֵּי דְכָל בֵּית יִשְׂרָאֵל
בַּעֲגָלָא וּבִזְמַן קָרִיב, וְאִמְרוּ ⁴⁹אָמֵן
⁵⁰יְהֵא שְׁמֵיהּ רַבָּא מְבָרַךְ לְעָלַם
וּלְעָלְמֵי עָלְמַיָּא· יִתְבָּרַךְ וְיִשְׁתַּבַּח
וְיִתְפָּאַר וְיִתְרוֹמַם וְיִתְנַשֵּׂא ⁵¹וְיִתְהַדָּר
וְיִתְעַלֶּה ⁵²וְיִתְהַלָּל ⁵³שְׁמֵיהּ
⁵⁴דְּקוּדְשָׁא ⁵⁵בְּרִיךְ הוּא ; ⁵⁶לְעֵילָא
מִן־כָּל־בִּרְכָתָא וְשִׁירָתָא תֻּשְׁבְּחָתָא
וְנֶחֱמָתָא ⁵⁷דַּאֲמִירָן בְּעָלְמָא ;
וְאִמְרוּ ⁵⁸אָמֵן·

35 The first section (יִתְגַּדַּל to וִיקָרֵיהּ) forms the introductory portion of the mourner's קַדִּישׁ [*Sanctification*] recited at the cemetery after a burial. This part is in *Aramaic* (*Chaldee*). **36** שְׁמֵהּ instead of שְׁמֵיהּ is given in some texts. After שְׁמֵיהּ רַבָּא the congregants respond with אָמֵן. **37** Some texts have דִּי הוּא instead of דְּהוּא. **38** Some vowelise this לְאִתְחַדְתָּא. Some render it *in the world that will be created anew*. **39** Some vowelise this וּלְאַחֲיָא. In some texts וּלְאַחֲיָאָה. **40** יִתְהוֹן is omitted in some texts. יָתְהוֹן in some texts. **41** הֵיכְלֵהּ and הֵיכְלֵהּ instead of הֵיכָלֵיהּ, and also דִּי־יְרוּשְׁלֵם instead of דִירוּשְׁלֵם and בְּנֵהּ instead of בְּגַוַּהּ are given in some texts. Some render this *and He will establish His Temple*. **42** Some vowellise this וּלְמֶעְקַר פָּלְחָנָא and נֻכְרָאָה in some texts. **43** Some vowelise this וּלְאַתָבָא. **44** Some texts give דִּי־שְׁמַיָּא instead of דִשְׁמַיָּא. In some texts לְאַתְרֵהּ, וְיַמְלַךְ קֻדְשָׁא, and (further on) דִּי־כָל־בֵּית instead of respectively לְאַתְרֵיהּ, וְיַמְלִיךְ קוּדְשָׁה and דְּכָל בֵּית. **45** The congregants respond with בְּרִיךְ הוּא in an undertone. Some render this *and may the Holy One, blessed be He, reign in His sovereignty and His glory.* **46** בְּמַלְכוּתֵהּ instead of בְּמַלְכוּתֵיהּ is given in some texts. **47** Some texts give וִיקָרֵהּ instead of וִיקָרֵיהּ. **48** From בְּחַיֵּיכוֹן to בְּעָלְמָא וְאִמְרוּ אָמֵן is part of every form of קַדִּישׁ. **49** The congregants respond with אָמֵן, then recite יְהֵא שְׁמֵיהּ רַבָּא מְבָרַךְ

163

לְעָלַם וּלְעָלְמֵי עָלְמַיָּא with the Reader. **50** Some texts have שְׁמַהּ instead of שְׁמֵיהּ.
51 Some vocalise this וְיִתְהַדָּר. **52** Some vocalise this וְיִתְהַלָּל. **53** שְׁמַהּ instead of
שְׁמֵיהּ is given in some texts. **54** דִּי־קֻדְשָׁא instead of דְּקוּדְשָׁא is given in some texts.
55 The congregants recite בְּרִיךְ הוּא. **56** During the עֲשֶׂרֶת יְמֵי תְּשׁוּבָה (the *Ten
Days of Penitence*) the formula is לְעֵילָא וּלְעֵילָּא, *though He be supremely high above.*
In some texts לְעֵלָּה and וּלְעֵלָּה. **57** In some texts דִּי־אֲמִירָן is given instead of
דַּאֲמִירָן. **58** The congregants respond with אָמֵן.

Unto[59] Israel, and unto the Rabbis, and unto their disciples, and unto all the disciples of their disciples, and unto all who[60] occupy themselves[61] with [the study of] the Law, in this[62] place or in any other place, may there be unto[63] them and unto you abundant peace, grace, and lovingkindness, and tender mercy, and long life, and ample sustenance,[64] and salvation from the Father Who is in heaven[65] and on earth,[66] and say ye, *Amen.*[67]

May there be abundant peace from heaven, and a happy life for us and for all Israel, and say ye, *Amen.*[68]

He Who maketh peace in His high places, may He in His tender mercy make peace for us and for all Israel, and say ye, *Amen.*[69]

[49]עַל יִשְׂרָאֵל וְעַל רַבָּנָן וְעַל
תַּלְמִידֵיהוֹן וְעַל כָּל־תַּלְמִידֵי
תַלְמִידֵיהוֹן וְעַל כָּל ־ [50]מַאן
[51]דְּעָסְקִין בְּאוֹרַיְתָא דִּי בְאַתְרָא
[52]הָדֵין וְדִי בְכָל אֲתַר וַאֲתַר יְהֵא
[53]לְהוֹן וּלְכוֹן שְׁלָמָא רַבָּא חִנָּא
וְחִסְדָּא וְרַחֲמִין וְחַיִּין אֲרִיכִין [54]וּמְזוֹנֵי
רְוִיחֵי וּפֻרְקָנָא מִן־קֳדָם אֲבוּהוֹן
[55]דְּשְׁמַיָּא [56]וְאַרְעָא, וְאִמְרוּ [57]אָמֵן.

יְהֵא שְׁלָמָא רַבָּא מִן־שְׁמַיָּא וְחַיִּים
וְטוֹבִים עָלֵינוּ וְעַל כָּל־יִשְׂרָאֵל,
וְאִמְרוּ [58]אָמֵן.

עוֹשֶׂה שָׁלוֹם בִּמְרוֹמָיו הוּא [1]בְּרַחֲמָיו
יַעֲשֶׂה שָׁלוֹם עָלֵינוּ וְעַל כָּל־
יִשְׂרָאֵל, וְאִמְרוּ [59]אָמֵן.

59 This part to the end is part of the קַדִּישׁ known as the קַדִּישׁ דְּרַבָּנָן (the *Rabbinic Kaddish*), and is recited during the Morning Service (1) after . . . רַבִּי יִשְׁמָעֵאל (following . . . אַיֵּהוּ מְקוֹמָן), and (2) after . . . אָמַר רַבִּי אֶלְעָזָר (following the אָמַר רַבִּי אֶלְעָזָר אֵין כֵּאלֹהֵינוּ etc.) and (3) in the Friday Evening Service after . . . (following the . . . בַּמֶּה מַדְלִיקִין), (4) at the conclusion of a *Rabbinical sermon,* and (5) at the conclusion of a *Rabbinical study or lesson.* This section is in Aramaic (*Chaldee*), **60** מָן instead of מַאן is given in some texts. **61** In some texts דִּי־עָסְקִין is given instead of דְּעָסְקִין. **62** Instead of הָדֵין some texts have הָדָן. **63** In some texts לָנָא וּלְהוֹן, *unto us and unto them,* is given instead of לְהוֹן וּלְכוֹן, *unto them and unto you.* **64** The *singular* וּמְזוֹנָא רְוִיחָא is given in some texts instead of the *plural* וּמְזוֹנֵי רְוִיחֵי.

65 Some texts have דִּי־בִשְׁמַיָּא instead of דִשְׁמַיָּא. **66** וְאַרְעָא is omitted in some texts. **67** The congregants respond with אָמֵן (and then, as indicated in some texts, continue in an undertone to recite יְהִי שֵׁם ה' מְבֹרָךְ מֵעַתָּה וְעַד עוֹלָם, *Let the Name of the Eternal be blessed from this time forth and for evermore—Psalm* **113**, 2). **68** The congregants respond with אָמֵן (and as indicated in some texts recite in an undertone עֶזְרִי מֵעִם ה' עֹשֵׂה שָׁמַיִם וָאָרֶץ, *My help is from the Eternal, Who made heaven and earth—Psalm* **121**, 2). The words יְהֵא שְׁלָמָא רַבָּא מִן־שְׁמַיָּא are *Aramaic (Chaldee).* **69** The congregants respond with אָמֵן.

∗ מַסֶּכְתּוֹת: this *plural* form [*singular* מַסֶּכֶת, *Tractate, Treatise, Thesis*] clearly suggests or includes the term סֵדֶר, *Order*, which is made up of מַסֶּכְתּוֹת.

§ תַּנָּא (*plural* תַּנָּאִים), תַּנָּאֵי (*plural* תַּנָּאִין), teacher, especially *an authority quoted in* מִשְׁנָה *and* בְּרַיְיתָא, in contradistinction to אֲמוֹרָה (see next **Note** †, and also Volume I, זְרָעִים, GENERAL INTRODUCTION).

† אֲמוֹרָה (*plural* אֲמוֹרָאִים, אֲמוֹרִין), *interpreter, lecturer, speaker*, particularly (also called מְתוּרְגְּמָן in this sense) *an expounder in lengthy popular discourses, briefly and in soft voice, the exposition of a Tanna* (see the preceding **Note** §); in a particular sense the *Amoraim* were the Talmudic authorities who lived after the final compilation of the *Mishnah* and whose discussions on the views of the *Tannaim* or authors of the *Mishnah* and *Boraitha* are recorded in the גְּמָרָא.

‡ תַּלְמִיד חָכָם, literally *a wise disciple* (or *scholar*), *a disciple of a sage*; frequently in the *plural*—תַּלְמִידֵי חַכָמִים—referring to *a number of scholars* as opposed to a single authority.

‖ רַבָּן (*plural* רַבָּנִין, רַבָּנִין, רַבָּנִים), (1) *chief, teacher*, (2) *Rabban*, a title of scholars, (3) especially in the *plural* (corresponding to the חֲכָמִים, *Sages*, of the *Mishnah*), referring to *a number of scholar* as opposed to a single authority.

¶ The words טוֹבִים and בְּרַחֲמָיו [בְּרַחֲמָיו in some texts] are omitted in the קַדִּישׁ יָתוֹם [*Mourner's Kaddish*] and in the קַדִּישׁ תִּתְקַבֵּל [*Reader's Kaddish*] or קַדִּישׁ שָׁלֵם [*Complete Kaddish*]. Some texts give יַעֲשֶׂה בְרַחֲמָיו instead of בְּרַחֲמָיו יַעֲשֶׂה.

The קַדִּישׁ תִּתְקַבֵּל (also termed קַדִּישׁ שָׁלֵם תִּתְקַבֵּל) is so called because of the last word in the extra paragraph (inserted before the יְהֵא שְׁלָמָא רַבָּא paragraph), viz., תִּתְקַבֵּל צְלוֹתְהוֹן וּבָעוּתְהוֹן דִּי־כָל־יִשְׂרָאֵל (or דְּכָל יִשְׂרָאֵל) קָדָם אֲבוּהוֹן דִּי־בִשְׁמַיָּא וְאִמְרוּ אָמֵן, *May the prayers and supplications of all Israel be accepted by their Father Who is in heaven, and say ye Amen*; when the Reader recites this the congregation says softly: קַבֵּל בְּרַחֲמִים וּבְרָצוֹן אֶת תְּפִלָּתֵנוּ, *Accept our prayer in tender mercy and in favour*, and responds with אָמֵן when the Reader recites וְאִמְרוּ אָמֵן.